THE OFFICIAL GUIDE TO

American Attitudes

THE OFFICIAL GUIDE TO

American Attitudes

Who
thinks what
about
the issues
that
shape
our lives.

by Susan Mitchell

New Strategist Publications, Inc.
Ithaca, New York

New Strategist Publications, Inc.
P.O. Box 242, Ithaca, New York 14851
607 / 273-0913

Susan Mitchell, 1958—
The Official Guide to American Attitudes

ISBN 0-885070-02-0

Printed in the United States of America

for my son, Sam
and "my girls," Elizabeth and Catherine

Table of Contents

Everyone has an opinion about "public arena" issues—gun control, sex education, the death penalty, taxes, and so on. These opinions can be well-informed or seriously misinformed. Often, they are inflamed by the media or politicians.

For many years, the environment has been one of the chief worries of Americans, along with crime, the economy, and health care. But while Americans want to protect the environment, the record is decidedly mixed on their personal efforts to save the planet.

On racial issues, we are a nation divided—not just by race, but by sex, age, and educational attainment as well. And while people's attitudes about most of the racial issues examined here have changed substantially over the last two decades, gaps between groups remain.

Although most Americans are religious, we are a religiously diverse nation. While there is consensus on the big questions—Do you believe in God? Is there life after death?—on most other questions there is difference of opinion and practice.

While Americans are sometimes divided in their opinions about work and money, they are surprisingly optimistic about their financial situation despite corporate downsizing, a sluggish economy, and an uncertain future.

Tables

Chapter 4. Religion

Chapter 5. Work and Money

Chapter 6. Marriage and Family

Introduction

Change has been a constant in the United States for over 200 years, but the pace has accelerated since the middle of this century. New technologies have radically altered the way we live and work. The traditional household of the 1950s, made up of a stay-at-home mom, working dad, and children, has fractured into dual-income families, single-parents, and single-person households. We are more racially and ethnically diverse than ever.

It is no surprise, then, that over the last 20 years Americans have changed their minds about many issues. The biggest changes are found on issues relating to race and the roles of women. Twenty years ago, far more Americans believed in separate societies for blacks and whites and traditional roles for men and women. Since then, men and women, blacks and whites, old and young, the most and the least educated have changed their minds about race and women's roles.

Racial tension is still very real in the 1990s, but the most overtly racist attitudes and forms of discrimination are greatly diminished. Far fewer Americans favor laws that exclude blacks from white neighborhoods or prevent people of different races from marrying. The idea that blacks have less innate ability than whites has lost credibility with Americans.

Likewise, women's inroads into politics and business are accepted matter-of-factly by most Americans. Compared to 20 years ago, far fewer Americans insist that women should stick to homemaking and leave politics and breadwinning up to men.

Most Americans are still religious, but there is more religious diversity than there was 20 years ago. Especially among the young, a growing share of people say they are Catholic or have no religion. Americans are less confident of religious leaders and less "fundamentalist" in their interpretation of the Bible.

In the public arena, Americans are more conservative, more concerned about crime, and have a decidedly more negative view of the nation's leaders—especially elected officials—than was the case in 1974. They are more pessimistic about the lot of the average person, but they are less likely to view government alone as the answer to our problems.

Most Americans say they are pretty happy, but two decades ago, they were more likely to say they were very happy. People are now less likely to believe other people are trustworthy, helpful, or fair.

There has not been much change in the percentage saying they are satisfied with their financial situation. People are slightly more likely to view hard work, rather than a combination of luck and hard work, as the key to success. Americans are still most likely to consider a sense of accomplishment the most important job characteristic, but the proportion citing a high income has increased slightly. If younger generations are any indicator, high incomes will become more important in the future.

Sexual mores have changed since the 1970s. The increased acceptance of cohabitation, premarital sex, and homosexuality continue the liberalization of attitudes that began in the "free love" era of the 1960s. But attitudes toward adultery and pornography have become more conservative.

Americans are less likely to say their marriages are very happy. But they get as much satisfaction from family life as they did 20 years ago. They are less likely to feel large families are ideal—two children are now considered the perfect number by a majority of Americans.

Men and Women

Men and women generally agree on the major issues but diverge—sometimes sharply—on issues that involve them personally, such as women's roles. Women are far more likely to view pornography as detrimental to society and to believe it should be entirely illegal. Men are more accepting of premarital sex and cohabiting couples.

The sexes are about equally likely to favor sex education in the schools. Both men and women believe their taxes are too high and worry that the courts let criminals off too easily. They don't differ much in their political leanings or their political party affiliation. Both sexes support fair housing laws, would vote for a black presidential candidate, and are concerned that allowing more immigrants into the U.S. will hurt the country.

Conventional wisdom holds that women are more liberal than men. On some questions women are more likely to take a point of view that would be considered "liberal." They are less supportive of the death penalty and more supportive of gun control, for example. They want government to play a more active role in health care and helping the poor than men do.

Men and women are about equally likely to view hard work rather than luck as the key to success. They both believe in the upward mobility of generations, saying they are better off than their parents were and that their kids will be better off than they are.

Similar percentages of men and women say they have very happy marriages, but that divorce is sometimes the best solution for unhappy couples—even if children are involved. Men and women have come a long way in their opinions about women's roles, and there's no disagreement about women's abilities and rights in the political and business arenas. But women are more likely to believe women can combine motherhood and career successfully; men are more likely to say a traditional division of labor—male breadwinner, female homemaker—is the best arrangement. Women are more supportive of maternity leave for working women and child care benefits for dual-income families.

Women are more religious than men. They are more likely to believe without a doubt in the existence of God, to believe in an afterlife, to pray and attend religious services regularly, and to take the Bible literally. Women are more likely than men to believe in astrology, but less likely to believe in evolution.

Women get more satisfaction from family life and friendships than men do. But, surprisingly, they are more likely than men to think it's acceptable to go it alone. They are less likely than men to think not having children means an empty life, or that single parents cannot do as good a job raising children as two parents.

Blacks and Whites

The different experiences of blacks and whites over hundreds of years have clearly left their mark on attitudes. Blacks and whites hold different opinions about many issues relating to race, and the differences do not stop there. They disagree on many pocketbook issues as well.

It should surprise no one that blacks and whites see most race issues differently. Blacks are more likely to support busing, fair housing laws, and a black presidential candidate than whites, for example.

Both blacks and whites are concerned about the consequences of more immigrants coming to the U.S. But blacks are more supportive than whites of bilingual ballots and education. Blacks are more likely to be liberal Democrats and to view the government's role in health care and helping the poor as an active one. Whites are more likely to support the death penalty, but both races feel the courts aren't harsh enough with criminals.

Blacks are more traditionally religious than whites. They are more likely than whites to be Protestant, while whites are more likely than blacks to be Catholic. Blacks are more likely to have an unwavering belief in God and to interpret the Bible literally. They are also more active in religious practice.

Both blacks and whites say children are a joy rather than a burden to parents. In general, whites are more positive toward marriage. Blacks are more likely to say a bad marriage is not preferable to no marriage and they do not think unhappy couples—especially childless ones—should remain married.

Blacks and whites hold similar views regarding women's roles. Both races support women's participation in business and politics. But white households are more likely to divide chores along traditional sex lines, while black households are more egalitarian.

On average, blacks have lower incomes than whites and this is reflected in opinions on a number of issues. They are less likely than whites to be "green" on pocketbook environmental issues: They are less willing to pay higher taxes or prices or accept a lower standard of living to protect the environment. They are more likely to feel the situation of the average person is getting worse. They are more likely than whites to say they are unhappy with their personal financial situation and less likely to say it has improved over the last few years. High income is the most important job characteristic for blacks, while for whites it is a feeling of accomplishment.

Life is generally less difficult for whites than for blacks. This is reflected in the fact that whites are more likely to say they are very happy, to get great satisfaction from their friendships and the place they live, to find life exciting, and to say they are in good health. Blacks have much less faith in humanity than do whites—they are far more likely than whites to say people take advantage of others, are not trustworthy, and are selfish.

The Generations

The generation gap is alive and well. Times have changed, attitudes have changed, but the generations do not see eye to eye. And they never will. On many issues, each ten-year age group is increasingly likely to agree or disagree. On other issues, there is a distinct line at age 50 or 60, with a wide difference of opinion separating baby boomers and Generation Xers from older generations. Younger generations are more comfortable with much of the ongoing social change than are older generations. Even when older generations have changed their point of view, a generation gap often remains.

People of different ages are in general agreement about the role of government in helping the poor and issues relating to crime. But younger generations are more likely to say they are liberal and politically independent.

The enormous changes in attitudes about race over the last 20 years are apparent in the differences of opinion between young and old. On many race issues, older generations hold more traditional views. They are more likely to say "blacks shouldn't push where they aren't wanted," to oppose fair housing laws, and to support laws against interracial marriage. Younger generations, themselves more racially diverse, are more comfortable with the idea of a black president and allowing multilingual education and election ballots.

The women's movement influenced younger generations' opinions about many women's issues. Baby boomers and younger adults are less likely than older people to believe men and women should stick to traditional roles at home, at work, or in politics. They practice what they preach, as well. Younger people, especially those under age 30, are more likely to share household chores while older generations still practice a traditional division of labor. Young adults are also more likely to support maternal and child-care benefits for workers.

The young have a more positive view of working mothers and single parents. They are less likely than older people to think not marrying or not having children makes life less meaningful. And they are raising their children with different values. They are more likely to view independent thinking as the most important trait to instill in children; older generations are more likely than the young to feel it's most important for children to learn obedience.

There are also generation gaps in religious attitudes. The young are more likely to have doubts about the existence of God. They are more diverse in their religious preferences and more likely to have no religion. Older generations are more traditionally religious, praying and attending religious services more frequently than the young. Older Americans are more likely to believe in a literal interpretation of the Bible.

Older generations continue to be appalled by many of the changes in sexual mores, while the young are more accepting of homosexuality, premarital sex, pornography, and sex education in the schools.

When it comes to work and money, attitudes are linked to stage of life. The young are least satisfied with their personal finances, but are most likely to say their financial situation is improving. Older Americans are most satisfied with their personal finances, but least likely to say their finances are improving.

The Role of Education

Education influences attitudes on many issues, such as the environment, but its role is less clear in other areas. The relationship between age and education (younger people are better educated) or income and education (the well-educated have higher incomes) make it difficult to ascertain whether education, age, or socioeconomic status is the most important determinant of attitudes.

Education strongly influences opinions about women's roles. Those with lower levels of education (who are also more likely to be older) are more likely to favor traditional sex roles.

People with higher levels of education generally have higher incomes, and this undoubtedly influences their outlook on questions about work and money. The well-educated are more satisfied with their financial situation than the less-educated and less likely to consider a high income as the most important job characteristic. People with college degrees are less likely to believe the average person's situation is getting worse. But the highly educated also hold generally negative opinions about the leaders of the nation's major institutions, including elected officials.

There is a strong relationship between education and environmental issues. People with college degrees are more likely to say they would pay more and accept a lower standard of living to protect the environment. (Here, the higher incomes of the well-educated probably influence attitudes.) The college-educated are also more likely to favor environmental regulation.

Higher educational levels are also linked to attitudes about racial issues. The college-educated are more supportive of fair housing laws, more likely to vote for a black president, and more likely to view a lack of education as the cause of the socioeconomic differences between blacks and whites. Those with less education are more likely to support laws against interracial marriage, more likely to believe "blacks shouldn't push where they are not wanted," and more likely to want to reduce immigration levels.

There are also differences in religious outlook and practice by educational level. Those with lower levels of education are more likely to say they have no doubts about God, to interpret the Bible literally, and to have a great deal of confidence in religious leaders.

Those with less education are more conservative about sexual mores. They are more likely to condemn premarital and homosexual sex. They are also more concerned about pornography and more likely to believe it should be illegal to distribute pornography to people of any age.

Education makes a big difference in personal outlook. Those with higher levels of education are more likely to be very happy, to have excellent health, and to find life exciting. They are more likely to think others are trustworthy, fair, and helpful.

Regardless of education, most Americans say they have very happy marriages, but those with lower levels of education are more likely to get great satisfaction from their family life and to consider children life's greatest joy.

About the Data

The findings presented in this book, from the General Social Survey (GSS), are a snapshot of the continually changing attitudes and opinions of Americans. The GSS provides an invaluable road map to American thought, but it is important to remember that the mental landscape can at times be foggy. Many factors can influence the results of opinion surveys, such as question wording. Polls that ask if "homosexuality" is acceptable, for example, yield higher positive responses than the more specific General Social Survey question about "sexual relations between two adults of the same sex." The explicit mention of sexual activity in the GSS makes people more uncomfortable—and less likely to respond positively—than the less explicit term "homosexuality."

Some attitudes and behaviors are notoriously hard to measure, such as those surrounding race or sexuality. Respondents may give answers they consider socially acceptable, rather than an honest response. It is hard to know, for example, if everyone who answers yes to the abstract question "would you vote for a black presidential candidate?" would actually do so in the voting booth.

Nonetheless, a well-designed and -executed survey, such as the General Social Survey, minimizes these problems. And by looking at broad categories of Americans, it is possible to get a feeling for where we come together—or stand apart—as a nation. The longitudinal nature of many of the survey questions offers us an especially valuable look at how attitudes have changed over the past two decades and, by looking at the attitudes of younger age groups, what the future holds.

The General Social Survey is taken by the National Opinion Research Center (NORC) of the University of Chicago. NORC is the oldest non-profit, university-affiliated national survey research facility in the nation. It has conducted the GSS every year from 1972 through 1994, except for 1979, 1981, and 1992. NORC is now conducting the GSS every two years, with the next one scheduled for 1996. Each survey uses an independently drawn sample of non-institutionalized English-speaking persons aged 18 or older living in the United States. The questions that appear above each table in this book are worded exactly or almost exactly as they appear on the survey. Some have been edited for space considerations. GSS researchers have changed the wording of some questions over the years, such as the substitution of "black" for "Negro," but these changes do not affect the continuity of the results.

The questions presented in this book are drawn from the hundreds included in the 1994 General Social Survey. Whenever possible, responses to the same question in the 1974 and 1984 surveys are also shown to reveal attitudinal change over the past 20 years. Not every question from the 1994 survey was asked in the 1974 or 1984 surveys, however. In those cases, responses from the closes available year are substituted.

For more information about the General Social Survey, contact the National Opinion Research Center, University of Chicago, 1155 East 60th Street, Chicago, IL, 60637; telephone (312) 753-7500. GSS data are also distributed by the Roper Center for Public Opinion Research, University of Connecticut—Storrs, P.O. Box 440, Storrs, CT, 06268; telephone (203) 486-4440.

CHAPTER

1

The Public Arena

Everyone has an opinion about "public arena" issues—gun control, sex education, the death penalty, taxes, and so on. These opinions can be well-informed or seriously misinformed. Often, they are inflamed by the media or politicians. Three of the issues examined in this chapter are thought of as controversial, for example, although public opinion about them is remarkably united.

Solid majorities of Americans say they:

- Are extremely or very proud to be an American (84 percent);

- Favor sex education in the public schools (85 percent);

- Would require people to obtain a police permit before buying a gun (78 percent).

Despite this unity, the politicians continue to argue the merits of these issues. They have gotten the message about crime, however. The public:

- Feels the courts do not deal harshly enough with criminals (85 percent);

- Favors the death penalty for people convicted of murder (74 percent).

Solid majorities of Americans also:

- Favor continuing membership in the United Nations (82 percent);

- Believe public officials don't really care about the average person (74 percent);

- Have only some confidence in the leaders of the nation's major institutions.

There is less agreement on other issues. Much smaller majorities say they:

- Would like to see doctors given the right to end the life of someone with an incurable disease at the request of the patient and family (68 percent);

- Believe the situation of the average person is getting worse (67 percent);

- Believe their federal taxes are too high (62 percent);

- Feel Americans are divided about the most important values (55 percent);

- Think the government classifies too many documents as "secret" (54 percent).

In several areas, Americans are so divided there is no majority opinion.

- A plurality of Americans (43 percent) believe that improving the lives of the poor should be a responsibility shared by government and the poor. But 26 percent feel it is primarily the government's role, while 28 percent believe it is up to the individual.

- A plurality of Americans (46 percent) say the government should be primarily responsible for making sure people can pay for health care. Thirty-one percent feel the responsibility lies with government and the individual.

- Americans are nearly evenly split on whether they think of themselves as Democrat (36 percent), independent (33 percent), or Republican (28 percent).

- They are also divided among liberals (26 percent), moderates (35 percent), and conservatives (35 percent).

Little Argument Between the Sexes

On most of the public arena questions, men and women are near agreement. Similar percentages say they:

- Favor sex education in the public schools (85 percent of women and 84 percent of men);

- Are very or extremely proud to be an American (84 percent of women and 85 percent of men);

- Feel they pay too much federal tax (61 percent of women and 64 percent of men). Substantial minorities of both sexes feel the tax level is about right, however (34 percent of women and 32 percent of men);

- Feel the courts are not harsh enough on criminals (86 percent of women and 83 percent of men);

- Think of themselves as Democrats (38 percent of women and 33 percent of men), Republicans (28 percent of women and 29 percent of men), or independent (32 percent of women and 35 percent of men);

- Are liberal (26 percent of women and men), moderate (36 percent of women, 34 percent of men), or conservative (33 and 38 percent, respectively).

- Favor continued United Nations membership (81 percent of women and 83 percent of men);

- Don't believe public officials care much about the average person (75 percent of women and 71 percent of men);

- Feel the average person's situation is getting worse (69 percent of women and 65 percent of men);

- Believe Americans are divided about our most important values (56 percent of women and 54 percent of men);

- Think the government keeps too many documents secret (55 percent of women and men).

- Have only some confidence in the leaders of the nation's major institutions.

There are a few areas where men and women disagree, sometimes substantially.

- Men are slightly more likely than women to approve of the death penalty (79 percent of men and 71 percent of women).

- Women are slightly more likely than men to think the government should make sure its citizens can pay for health care (49 percent of women compared with 42 percent of men). Men would rather leave it up to the individual (26 percent of men compared with 15 percent of women).

- Men are more likely to approve of allowing a doctor to terminate the life of an incurably ill person at his or her request (72 percent of men and 64 percent of women).

- Men and women favor different solutions to the problem of improving living standards of the poor. Nearly half of women (47 percent) compared with 39 percent of men believe the answer lies in the combined efforts of government and individuals. While 35 percent of men say it's up to the individual, only 21 percent of women agree, a gap of 14 percentage points.

- There is also a 14 percentage point gap between men and women on the issue of gun control. An overwhelming 84 percent of women favor gun control compared with 70 percent of men.

Less Agreement Between Blacks and Whites

Public issues may not provoke much of a battle between the sexes, but black and white opinions remain far apart on many topics. There are some areas of agreement, however.

- Black and white Americans are in general agreement on sex education in the public schools (favored by 86 percent of blacks and 84 percent of whites).

- Both races strongly believe the courts are not harsh enough on criminals (80 percent of blacks and 85 percent of whites).

- Both blacks and whites feel public officials don't genuinely care about the problems of average people (76 percent of blacks and 73 percent of whites).

- Blacks and whites agree the government keeps too many documents secret (58 percent of blacks and 53 percent of whites).

Several issues are likely to provoke debates at a town meeting, however.

- Blacks are less likely to say they are "very" or "extremely" proud to be an American (75 percent compared with 87 percent of whites).

- Blacks are more likely than whites to favor gun control (84 percent compared with 77 percent).

- Blacks are also more likely to feel they pay too much in taxes (69 percent of blacks and 61 percent of whites).

- Whites are more likely than blacks to say the U.S. should continue to belong to the United Nations (84 percent of whites compared with 71 percent of blacks).

- Similar proportions of blacks and whites (38 and 35 percent respectively) say they are moderate in their political leanings, but they diverge when it comes to liberalism or conservatism. About one-third of blacks, but only about one-quarter of whites are liberal. In contrast, 38 percent of whites, but only 23 percent of blacks say they are conservative.

- The races are divided in their political identification. Blacks are more than twice as likely as whites to think of themselves as Democrats (68 percent versus 31 percent). Only 6 percent of blacks, but 32 percent of whites say they are Republicans. Whites are more likely than blacks to be independent (34 percent versus 23 percent).

- The races are divided in their opinions about who should help the poor. About half of blacks feel this is a government responsibility compared with only 23 percent of whites. Whites are most likely to say it is a combined responsibility (45 percent), a position taken by one-third of blacks. Thirty-one percent of whites, but only 13 percent of blacks, say it is the individual's responsibility to take care of him or herself.

- Blacks and whites are also poles apart on the death penalty. A bare majority (51 percent) of blacks say they support the death penalty compared with 78 percent of whites.

- There is a wide gap in opinion over whether doctors should be allowed to end the life of the incurably ill. Only 50 percent of blacks, but fully 70 percent of whites, support this.

- Eighty percent of blacks, compared with not quite two-thirds of whites, say they believe "the lot of the average man is getting worse."

- Black Americans are far more likely than whites to feel it is government's responsibility to make sure people can pay for health care (73 percent of blacks compared with 42 percent of whites).

- Blacks are more likely to believe the nation is divided when it comes to important values (74 percent of blacks compared with 51 percent of whites).

- Blacks and whites differ in their level of confidence in the leaders of most of the nation's major institutions.

Generations Are Divided on Many Issues

On many of the public arena issues there is marked divergence in attitudes by age. But there are also areas of agreement.

- There is virtually no difference of opinion on the death penalty. About three-quarters of all age groups support the death penalty.

- All Americans show strong support for requiring a permit to purchase a gun (ranging from 75 to 81 percent). While the level of support varies by age group, there is no trend in the variation (i.e., higher or lower support by age).

- Young adults are slightly less likely to believe the courts are not harsh enough on criminals. Among people in their 20s, 79 percent say this, while 84 to 87 percent of other age groups hold this belief.

- There is general agreement that things are getting worse for the average American (ranging from 63 to 70 percent).

- Younger generations are more likely to think the government should help the poor, but the differences are small (30 percent of people under age 30 say this, compared with 21 percent of those aged 70 or older).

- Between 81 and 85 percent of people under age 70 agree that the U.S. should remain in the United Nations. Less support is found only among the oldest Americans (73 percent of those aged 70 or older).

- People under age 30 are more likely than older Americans to think helping people pay for health care is primarily a government responsibility (52 percent of people under age 40 compared with 40 to 44 percent of older people).

- Almost all agree that the government keeps too many documents secret (ranging from 54 to 58 percent). People aged 70 or older stand apart, with only 40 percent agreeing. Eighteen percent of the oldest age group say they don't know.

- There is also no clear age-related trend in the proportion of people who feel public officials don't really care about the average person's problems (ranging from 69 to 77 percent).

It would be surprising if the generations agreed on everything, and in fact they don't.

- Those most likely to become incurably ill are least in favor of allowing doctors to practice euthanasia—in other words, support declines with age. About three-quarters of people under age 40, but only 53 percent of those aged 70 or older, support euthanasia for the incurably ill.

- Sex education is a divisive issue for people of different ages. Support falls with age, ranging from a high of 94 percent among people in their 20s to a low of 64 percent among people aged 70 or older.

- The oldest Americans (aged 60 or older) are more likely to identify with the Democratic party (43 percent compared with only 29 percent of people under age 30). Younger generations are more inclined to see themselves as independent. The proportion of people who consider themselves Republicans shows less variation by age.

- Liberalism also shows a distinct generational pattern, with younger age groups more likely to consider themselves liberal (28 to 30 percent of people under age 60 compared with 16 to 18 percent of those aged 60 or older). There is less age variation among moderates and conservatives.

- People aged 50 or older are more likely to say they are very or extremely proud to be an American (90 to 92 percent compared with 81 to 83 percent of people aged 30 to 49 and 79 percent of those under age 30).

- The proportion of people who believe they pay too much in federal taxes rises from 57 percent of people in their 20s to a peak of 72 percent among people in their 50s. Income also rises with age and peaks when people are in their 40s and 50s. Around retirement age, the proportion who feel taxes are too high falls off sharply, with only 54 percent of people in their 60s and 39 percent of those aged 70 or older saying they pay too much.

- Younger people are more likely to believe the nation is divided (ranging from 64 percent of people under age 30 to 47 percent of those aged 60 or older).

- The generations disagree somewhat in the levels of confidence they have in the leaders of the nation's major institutions.

Disagreement Between the Most- and Least-Educated

On several issues, the least-educated Americans stand apart from the rest of the public. One reason for this is that those without a high school diploma tend to be older than those with higher levels of education. The different opinions of the least-educated show up on a variety of issues. Most Americans say they:

- Strongly support sex education in the public schools (ranging from 87 to 90 percent). But only 71 percent of people without a high school diploma agree;

- Are very or extremely proud to be an American (ranging from 80 to 88 percent);

- Believe taxes are too high (ranging from 62 to 64 percent), but only a small majority of those without a high school diploma (53 percent) agree;

- Believe Americans are divided on the most important values (52 to 57 percent).

A plurality agree that:

- The government should be primarily responsible for making sure Americans can pay for health care (43 to 49 percent).

On some issues, it is the most highly-educated Americans who stand apart. Most people:

- Feel the courts are not harsh enough on criminals (from 84 to 86 percent), but a smaller proportion (74 percent) of people with graduate degrees agree;

- Favor the death penalty (69 to 77 percent). But only 64 percent of people with graduate degrees support it.

On some issues, the differences by education are striking, but there is no clear pattern of more or less agreement with increasing education.

- A plurality of people of all educational backgrounds believe that helping the poor is a combined responsibility of the government and those in need, but people without a high school diploma and those with bachelor's degrees square off when it comes to the government's role. Fully 34 percent of those without a high school diploma believe the government should do everything possible to help the poor, compared with only 18 percent of those with bachelor's degrees.

- These two groups also stand apart when it comes to political party identification. Fully 43 percent of people who did not complete high school identify themselves as Democrats compared with 30 percent of those with bachelor's degrees. Conversely, 21 percent of people who did not graduate from high school and 38 percent of people with bachelor's degrees consider themselves Republicans.

- Graduate degree holders are most likely to say they are liberal (39 percent compared with 23 to 28 percent of the other educational groups), while people with bachelor's degrees are most likely to say they are conservative (46 percent compared with 32 to 34 percent of others).

- Those with the most education are less likely than others to feel the government keeps too many documents secret (45 percent of those with graduate degrees, compared with 50 to 56 percent of people with less education).

- People with different educational backgrounds differ in how much confidence they have in the leaders of the nation's major institutions.

Support for other public arena issues does increase or decrease steadily with education.

- People who have not completed college are least supportive of requiring a permit to purchase a gun (76 to 78 percent). Support rises to 81 to 84 percent among college graduates.

- People without a high school diploma are least supportive (59 percent), and those with graduate degrees are most supportive (76 percent), of allowing doctors to end the lives of the incurably ill at the patient's request.

- People with a high school diploma or less education are more likely than those with college degrees to believe things are getting worse for the average person (around 70 percent compared with 55 to 59 percent of college graduates). They are also more likely to have lower incomes, which may influence their opinion on this issue.

- College graduates are more likely than those with less education to support continued United Nations membership for the United States (89 to 93 percent compared with 83 percent of high school graduates and only 61 percent of those who did not complete high school).

- Over three-quarters of people with a high school diploma or less education believe public officials don't really care about the average person's problems. But only 64 percent of people with bachelor's degrees and 53 percent of those with graduate degrees agree.

United or Divided?

Americans debate and disagree, but does this really mean the nation is divided? Do we agree on the most important values? Unfortunately, over half of Americans believe the nation is divided. Only 39 percent say we are in agreement on the important things.

Women and men are equally likely to say we are divided (56 percent of women and 54 percent of men) as are people with different levels of education (from 52 to 57 percent).

Blacks are far more likely than whites to see fundamental divisions in society. Three-quarters of blacks, compared with 51 percent of whites, say the nation is divided.

Younger Americans have a dimmer view than their elders. Sixty-four percent of people under age 30 say we are a nation divided, as do 54 to 56 percent of people aged 30 to 59. In contrast, a 47 percent minority of people aged 60 or older say we are divided. Half of people in their 60s say Americans are united about the most important values.

United or Divided? 1994

"Some say that Americans are united and in agreement about the most important values. Others think that Americans are greatly divided when it comes to the most important values. What is your view?"

(percent responding by sex, race, age, and education, 1994)

	united	divided	don't know
Total	39%	55%	5%
Women	39	56	5
Men	40	54	5
Black	23	74	3
White	43	51	5
Aged 18 to 29	32	64	4
Aged 30 to 39	37	56	6
Aged 40 to 49	41	55	3
Aged 50 to 59	42	54	4
Aged 60 to 69	50	47	3
Aged 70 or older	41	47	10
Not a high school graduate	40	52	8
High school graduate	39	57	4
Bachelor's degree	42	54	4
Graduate degree	36	56	7

Note: Percents may not add to 100 because no answer is not included.
Source: General Social Survey, National Opinion Research Center, University of Chicago

American Pride

Fully 84 percent of adults are very or extremely proud to be American. Nearly half (46 percent) are extremely proud.

Similar proportions of men and women say they are proud to be Americans. This is also true of people with different educational backgrounds, although people with bachelor's degrees are slightly less likely than those with other levels of education to say they are "extremely proud" (37 percent of people with bachelor's degrees compared with 44 to 49 of people with other levels of educational attainment).

Blacks are considerably less likely than whites to say they are extremely proud to be American (35 percent compared with 49 percent of whites). Blacks are more likely to say they are only "somewhat proud."

The proportion of people saying they are "extremely proud" to be an American rises with age. Only 36 to 37 percent of people aged 18 to 39 and 49 percent of those in their 40s say this, compared with 54 to 58 percent of people aged 50 or older.

American Pride, 1994

"How proud are you to be an American?"

(percent responding by sex, race, age, and education, 1994)

	extremely proud	very proud	somewhat proud	not very proud
Total	46%	38%	13%	1%
Women	44	40	13	1
Men	49	36	12	2
Black	35	40	22	2
White	49	38	11	1
Aged 18 to 29	37	42	16	4
Aged 30 to 39	36	45	17	1
Aged 40 to 49	49	34	15	1
Aged 50 to 59	54	36	8	1
Aged 60 to 69	58	34	7	0
Aged 70 or older	58	33	5	1
Not a high school graduate	49	39	11	1
High school graduate	49	37	12	1
Bachelor's degree	37	43	18	1
Graduate degree	44	38	10	5

Note: Percents may not add to 100 because "don't know" and no answer are not included.
Source: General Social Survey, National Opinion Research Center, University of Chicago

The U.S. and the U.N.

The occasional "U.S. out of the U.N." bumper sticker to the contrary, the vast majority of Americans (82 percent) believe the United States should continue its membership in the United Nations. Support for this position has even grown slightly since 1975.

Women and men are about equally likely to say the nation should stay in the U.N. Men are much more likely to say this in 1994 than they were in 1975.

Support for remaining in the U.N. has grown among whites since 1975, but among blacks, it has remained the same. There is now a substantial gap in opinions between the races. Whites are considerably more likely to favor remaining in the U.N. (84 percent compared to 71 percent of blacks).

There is general agreement among Americans under age 70 that the U.S. should retain its U.N. membership (ranging from 81 to 85 percent). A smaller percentage of people aged 70 or older agree (73 percent). Opinions by generation have not changed much since 1975 when people were almost 20 years younger. The overall percentage of Americans favoring U.N. membership has increased because older generations (who were much less supportive) have died.

Support for retaining U.N. membership is highest among the college educated (from 89 to 93 percent). High school graduates are slightly less in favor (83 percent), while people who did not complete high school are the least supportive (61 percent). This is the only segment that is less likely to favor continued U.N. membership in 1994 than it was in 1975.

The U.S. and the U.N., 1994

"Do you think our government should continue to belong to the United Nations or should we pull out now?"

(percent responding by sex, race, age, and education, 1994)

	stay in	pull out	don't know
Total	82%	13%	5%
Women	81	12	6
Men	83	13	3
Black	71	21	8
White	84	12	5
Aged 18 to 29	84	10	5
Aged 30 to 39	85	10	4
Aged 40 to 49	82	14	3
Aged 50 to 59	81	14	6
Aged 60 to 69	85	15	0
Aged 70 or older	73	16	11
Not a high school graduate	61	23	16
High school graduate	83	13	4
Bachelor's degree	93	7	0
Graduate degree	89	9	0

Note: Percents may not add to 100 because no answer is not included.
Source: General Social Survey, National Opinion Research Center, University of Chicago

The U.S. and the U.N., 1975 to 1994

"Do you think our government should continue to belong to the United Nations or should we pull out now?"

(percent responding by sex, race, age, and education, 1975-94)

	stay in			pull out		
	1994	1985	1975	1994	1985	1975
Total	82%	77%	75%	13%	17%	18%
Women	81	77	77	12	15	14
Men	83	78	73	13	20	23
Black	71	71	72	21	17	23
White	84	78	76	12	18	17
Aged 18 to 29	84	85	84	10	12	11
Aged 30 to 39	85	87	82	10	10	15
Aged 40 to 49	82	80	81	14	16	15
Aged 50 to 59	81	68	75	14	27	17
Aged 60 to 69	85	69	57	15	23	33
Aged 70 or older	73	63	54	16	25	29
Not a high school graduate	61	66	68	23	22	21
High school graduate	83	79	78	13	18	17
Bachelor's degree	93	88	84	7	11	14
Graduate degree	89	84	82	9	12	16

Note: Percents may not add to 100 because "don't know" and no answer are not included.
Source: General Social Survey, National Opinion Research Center, University of Chicago

Political Party Identification

The Democrats win the Presidency. The Republicans win Congress. Nobody wins the loyalty of the American electorate. Since 1974, the proportion of people identifying themselves as Democrats has declined, while the Republican proportion has grown. The proportion who are independent has remained at roughly the same level since 1974.

Overall in 1994, 36 percent of people said they usually think of themselves as Democrats, 28 percent as Republicans, and 33 percent as independents. While men and women agree on this question, there are substantial differences by race, age, and educational attainment.

The strongest support for the Democrats is found among blacks. Thirty-nine percent say they are strong Democrats. Except for blacks, few Americans say they are strong Democrats or strong Republicans, explaining why voters are increasingly likely to cross party lines when voting for individual candidates.

The post-Watergate generation (aged 18 to 29) is independent minded (39 percent). Only 28 to 29 percent of young adults identify themselves as Republican or Democrat. But with each older age group, the percentage who identify themselves as Democrats rises, peaking at 43 percent among people aged 60 or older.

Tracking ten-year age groups over time, there has been a small shift from independent to Republican. Fortysomething boomers, for example, are less likely to think of themselves as independents and more likely to identify themselves as Republican than they once were.

Republican identification increases with education. People with at least a bachelor's degree are more likely to identify themselves as Republicans than they were in 1974.

Political Party Identification, 1994

"Generally speaking, do you usually think of yourself as a Republican, Democrat, independent, or what?"

(percent responding by sex, race, age, and education, 1994)

	Democrat	independent	Republican
Total	36%	33%	28%
Women	38	32	28
Men	33	35	29
Black	68	23	6
White	31	34	32
Aged 18 to 29	29	39	28
Aged 30 to 39	35	34	29
Aged 40 to 49	34	38	25
Aged 50 to 59	36	30	30
Aged 60 to 69	43	30	27
Aged 70 or older	43	23	31
Not a high school graduate	43	32	21
High school graduate	35	35	27
Bachelor's degree	30	28	38
Graduate degree	34	34	30

Note: Percents may not add to 100 because "other" and no answer are not included.
Source: General Social Survey, National Opinion Research Center, University of Chicago

Strength of Party Identification, 1994

"Generally speaking, do you usually think of yourself as a Republican, Democrat, independent, or what? If Republican or Democrat: Would you call yourself a strong Republican/ Democrat or not a very strong Republican/Democrat? If independent, do you think of yourself as closer to the Republican or Democratic party?"

(percent responding by sex, race, age, and education, 1994)

| | Democrat | | Independent | | | Republican | |
	strong	not very strong	lean Democrat	neither	lean Republican	strong	not very strong
Total	14%	22%	11%	12%	9%	11%	17%
Women	15	23	11	13	8	10	18
Men	13	19	12	12	11	12	17
Black	39	29	12	9	2	2	4
White	10	21	11	12	11	12	20
Aged 18 to 29	8	21	13	15	11	8	20
Aged 30 to 39	12	23	12	13	9	11	17
Aged 40 to 49	13	21	13	14	10	9	16
Aged 50 to 59	16	21	11	9	10	14	16
Aged 60 to 69	20	22	11	10	9	10	17
Aged 70 or older	22	21	7	10	6	13	17
Not a high school graduate	22	22	10	16	7	8	13
High school graduate	12	23	12	13	10	11	17
Bachelor's degree	11	19	9	8	12	15	24
Graduate degree	18	16	15	10	10	12	18

Note: Percents may not add to 100 because "other" and no answer are not included.
Source: General Social Survey, National Opinion Research Center, University of Chicago

Political Party Identification, 1974 to 1994

"Generally speaking, do you usually think of yourself as a Republican, Democrat, independent, or what?"

(percent responding by sex, race, age, and education, 1974-94)

	Democrat			Independent			Republican		
	1994	1984	1974	1994	1984	1974	1994	1984	1974
Total	36%	37%	42%	33%	37%	31%	28%	25%	22%
Women	38	38	43	32	34	29	28	25	23
Men	33	34	41	35	40	33	29	24	21
Black	68	65	62	23	26	20	6	7	10
White	31	32	39	34	38	32	32	27	24
Aged 18 to 29	29	30	35	39	46	44	28	22	15
Aged 30 to 39	35	37	41	34	39	34	29	21	19
Aged 40 to 49	34	36	46	38	41	30	25	22	19
Aged 50 to 59	36	45	45	30	30	26	30	24	27
Aged 60 to 69	43	42	45	30	27	22	27	30	27
Aged 70 or older	43	39	45	23	23	13	31	36	36
Not a high school graduate	43	48	51	32	35	23	21	15	19
High school grad.	35	33	40	35	37	33	27	27	22
Bachelor's degree	30	26	25	28	36	46	38	36	27
Graduate degree	34	39	36	34	34	40	30	25	22

Note: Percents may not add to 100 because "other" and no answer are not included.
Source: General Social Survey, National Opinion Research Center, University of Chicago

Political Leanings

Americans today are more likely to say they are conservative than they were two decades ago. Some of this shift is the result of changing attitudes within the nation's largest generation, the baby boom.

Women and men are about equally likely to say they are liberal, moderate, or conservative. But wide gaps are apparent by race, age, and education. About one-third of blacks, compared with one-quarter of whites, say they are liberal. In general, liberalism declines (and conservatism increases) with age.

The oldest boomers were the radicals of the 1960s. In 1974, 42 percent of them (then in their 20s) described themselves as liberals; only 16 percent said they were conservative. By 1994, with the oldest boomers in their 40s, fully 40 percent identified themselves as conservatives. The liberal percentage was down to 29 percent.

Liberals have a stronger constituency among the better-educated. Only 23 percent of those without a high school diploma call themselves liberals, versus 39 percent of people with graduate degrees. In contrast, there appears to be no strong relationship between educational level and conservatism.

Political Leanings, 1994

"We hear a lot of talk these days about liberals and conservatives. On a seven-point scale from extremely liberal to extremely conservative, where would you place yourself?"

(percent responding by sex, race, age, and education, 1994)

	extremely liberal	liberal	slightly liberal	moderate, middle of the road	slightly conserv-ative	conserv-ative	extremely conserv-ative
Total	2%	11%	13%	35%	16%	16%	3%
Women	2	11	13	36	15	15	3
Men	3	11	12	34	17	17	4
Black	4	15	15	38	11	9	3
White	2	10	12	35	17	18	3
Aged 18 to 29	4	14	13	35	14	15	3
Aged 30 to 39	2	11	14	38	16	13	3
Aged 40 to 49	3	11	15	30	19	18	3
Aged 50 to 59	2	12	14	35	14	14	6
Aged 60 to 69	1	6	9	38	18	22	2
Aged 70 or older	1	10	7	37	13	19	4
Not a high school graduate	3	10	10	34	11	16	4
High school graduate	2	10	13	40	15	15	3
Bachelor's degree	1	12	15	25	24	19	3
Graduate degree	5	19	16	24	14	16	4

Note: Percents may not add to 100 because "don't know" and no answer are not included.
Source: General Social Survey, National Opinion Research Center, University of Chicago

Political Leanings, 1974 to 1994

"We hear a lot of talk these days about liberals and
conservatives. On a seven-point scale from extremely
liberal to extremely conservative, where
would you place yourself?"

(percent responding by sex, race, age, and education, 1974-94)

	liberal (slightly to extremely)			moderate			conservative (slightly to extremely)		
	1994	1984	1974	1994	1984	1974	1994	1984	1974
Total	26%	23%	29%	35%	38%	38%	35%	34%	28%
Women	26	24	28	36	40	40	33	31	26
Men	26	22	30	34	35	36	38	40	30
Black	34	29	38	38	38	32	23	24	19
White	24	23	28	35	39	39	38	36	29
Aged 18 to 29	30	26	42	35	41	39	32	29	16
Aged 30 to 39	28	30	30	38	39	35	32	29	29
Aged 40 to 49	29	22	23	30	38	36	40	37	38
Aged 50 to 59	28	14	20	35	35	42	34	45	33
Aged 60 to 69	16	25	21	38	32	42	43	39	31
Aged 70 or older	18	11	26	37	40	35	35	38	29
Not a high school graduate	23	23	27	34	38	40	32	29	25
High school grad.	25	20	27	40	42	41	33	36	28
Bachelor's degree	28	32	41	25	26	23	46	41	36
Graduate degree	39	37	43	24	25	22	34	38	34

Note: Percents may not add to 100 because "don't know" and no answer are not included.
Source: General Social Survey, National Opinion Research Center, University of Chicago

Confidence in Leaders

The confidence of Americans in their leaders is eroding. While most people say they have "some" confidence in the leaders of the nation's major institutions, a minority have a "great deal" of confidence. More than a third of Americans have "hardly any" confidence in the leaders of the press, organized labor, the executive branch of the federal government, and Congress.

Men and women both have low levels of confidence in the leaders of the nation's major institutions. Men are more likely than women to have a great deal of confidence in the scientific community, the military, and the Supreme Court. Women have more confidence in the leaders of organized labor and Congress.

Whites are more likely than blacks to say they have a great deal of confidence in the scientific community, the military, the Supreme Court, and major companies. Blacks are more likely to have a great deal of confidence in education, organized labor, and Congress.

The youngest and the oldest are most likely to have a great deal of confidence in various institutions. There is one institution that shows a striking generational pattern, however: Fully 48 percent of people under age 30 say they have a great deal of confidence in the scientific community, a proportion that drops steadily to 28 percent among people aged 60 or older.

People with college degrees are more likely than those with less education to have a great deal of confidence in the scientific community and the Supreme Court. They are less likely to have a great deal of confidence in the military or education.

Confidence in Leaders, 1994

"As far as the people running the following
institutions are concerned, would you say you have
a great deal of confidence, only some confidence,
or hardly any confidence at all in them?"

(percent responding by sex, race, age, and education, 1994)

	medicine			scientific community			the military		
	great deal	only some	hardly any	great deal	only some	hardly any	great deal	only some	hardly any
Total	41%	48%	10%	38%	49%	7%	37%	48%	12%
Women	40	49	10	35	50	7	32	51	13
Men	43	47	9	42	48	7	43	45	11
Black	45	45	8	26	51	15	28	53	16
White	41	48	10	40	49	6	38	48	12
Aged 18 to 29	52	43	6	48	42	7	43	41	14
Aged 30 to 39	43	47	9	41	49	6	33	52	14
Aged 40 to 49	36	54	9	39	52	6	31	50	16
Aged 50 to 59	38	50	11	37	49	10	38	52	7
Aged 60 to 69	35	48	16	28	56	9	36	53	8
Aged 70 or older	41	42	12	28	49	6	45	40	8
Not a high school graduate	42	42	13	26	46	12	42	37	13
High school grad.	40	48	11	36	51	8	38	49	12
Bachelor's degree	44	50	6	51	45	2	34	54	12
Graduate degree	45	50	4	54	43	1	30	51	16

(continued)

(continued from previous page)

	Supreme Court			major companies			education		
	great deal	only some	hardly any	great deal	only some	hardly any	great deal	only some	hardly any
Total	30%	50%	16%	25%	61%	10%	25%	56%	17%
Women	27	51	17	23	63	10	24	57	18
Men	34	48	16	28	59	10	26	56	16
Black	24	53	18	17	59	20	37	49	13
White	30	50	17	26	62	8	23	58	18
Aged 18 to 29	37	50	12	26	65	9	30	54	16
Aged 30 to 39	30	52	16	25	63	10	19	64	16
Aged 40 to 49	30	52	16	23	67	9	20	60	19
Aged 50 to 59	28	51	17	30	58	10	27	54	18
Aged 60 to 69	29	48	18	26	60	10	28	51	19
Aged 70 or older	24	42	23	25	49	14	32	44	17
Not a h.s. graduate	26	44	20	19	57	15	34	47	15
High school grad.	27	53	18	25	63	10	24	58	17
Bachelor's degree	36	51	12	33	58	8	20	60	20
Graduate degree	52	36	9	26	66	6	24	58	18

	financial institutions			federal government			the press		
	great deal	only some	hardly any	great deal	only some	hardly any	great deal	only some	hardly any
Total	18%	61%	20%	11%	51%	35%	10%	49%	39%
Women	17	62	19	11	52	34	9	50	38
Men	18	59	22	11	51	36	10	48	40
Black	19	47	32	15	56	25	11	41	43
White	18	63	19	10	51	37	9	50	39
Aged 18 to 29	22	61	16	11	56	32	12	44	42
Aged 30 to 39	15	64	21	10	52	37	11	53	35
Aged 40 to 49	14	61	24	8	57	34	7	51	41
Aged 50 to 59	16	60	24	11	50	37	9	45	45
Aged 60 to 69	18	62	19	16	45	39	9	54	36
Aged 70 or older	26	53	14	17	43	31	10	47	36
Not a h. s. graduate	23	52	20	16	45	32	16	45	33
High school grad.	18	60	21	10	50	38	9	49	40
Bachelor's degree	15	67	18	9	57	34	6	53	40
Graduate degree	16	68	14	17	60	21	8	51	40

(continued)

(continued from previous page)

	organized labor			Congress		
	great deal	only some	hardly any	great deal	only some	hardly any
Total	10%	52%	32%	8%	50%	39%
Women	9	56	28	7	53	36
Men	11	48	38	9	46	43
Black	18	53	22	16	48	31
White	9	52	34	6	50	41
Aged 18 to 29	14	60	21	9	54	34
Aged 30 to 39	8	55	32	6	51	42
Aged 40 to 49	6	53	39	7	48	43
Aged 50 to 59	8	50	37	8	49	41
Aged 60 to 69	14	44	36	10	47	39
Aged 70 or older	13	41	30	8	50	33
Not a high school graduate	17	43	27	13	45	32
High school graduate	10	54	32	7	51	40
Bachelor's degree	4	53	39	4	50	45
Graduate degree	4	51	40	6	52	39

Note: Percents may not add to 100 because "don't know" and no answer are not included.
Source: General Social Survey, National Opinion Research Center, University of Chicago

Confidence in Banks

Twenty years ago, one-third of Americans had a great deal of confidence in the leaders of banks and financial institutions. In 1994, only 18 percent had a great deal of confidence. A solid majority (61 percent) have only some confidence, and a sizable minority (20 percent) have hardly any confidence in financial institutions.

Women and men are about equally likely to have a great deal, only some, or hardly any confidence in banks and financial institutions. This is similar to 1974, except in that year, men were more likely to say they had hardly any confidence in financial institutions.

Blacks are far more likely than whites to say they have hardly any confidence in the leaders of financial institutions (32 percent compared with 19 percent of whites). In 1974, blacks and whites were essentially in agreement.

People under age 30 or aged 70 or older are more likely than the middle-aged to have a great deal of confidence in banks. Conversely, the middle group is most likely to have hardly any confidence in the leaders of financial institutions.

People who did not complete high school are more likely than those with at least a high school diploma to have a great deal of confidence in financial leaders. This was also true in 1974.

Confidence in Banks and Financial Institutions, 1975 to 1994

"As far as the people running banks and financial institutions are concerned, would you say you have a great deal of confidence, only some confidence, or hardly any confidence at all in them?"

(percent responding by sex, race, age, and education, 1975-94)

	a great deal			only some			hardly any		
	1994	*1984*	*1975*	*1994*	*1984*	*1975*	*1994*	*1984*	*1975*
Total	18%	31%	32%	61%	54%	54%	20%	11%	11%
Women	17	33	33	62	53	56	19	9	8
Men	18	29	31	59	55	51	22	13	15
Black	19	25	28	47	50	56	32	15	12
White	18	32	32	63	55	54	19	10	11
Aged 18 to 29	22	34	22	61	54	62	16	10	15
Aged 30 to 39	15	27	25	64	54	61	21	17	13
Aged 40 to 49	14	23	28	61	62	61	24	9	9
Aged 50 to 59	16	25	35	60	60	49	24	13	11
Aged 60 to 69	18	34	50	62	57	36	19	5	9
Aged 70 or older	26	49	49	53	34	40	14	7	5
Not a high school graduate	23	30	36	52	48	50	20	11	9
High school grad.	18	32	30	60	55	56	21	11	12
Bachelor's degree	15	33	32	67	58	56	18	6	11
Graduate degree	16	34	24	68	50	58	14	15	14

Note: Percents may not add to 100 because "don't know" and no answer are not included.
Source: General Social Survey, National Opinion Research Center, University of Chicago

Confidence in Education

Americans are only half as likely in 1994 as they were in 1974 to say they have a great deal of confidence in the nation's educational leaders. Twenty years ago, about half of Americans had a great deal of confidence in them. By 1994 only one-quarter did. A majority (56 percent) have only some confidence in educational leaders.

Women and men are in agreement on this issue, as they were in 1974. But other groups disagree.

Blacks are more likely than whites to say they have a great deal of confidence in education, as was the case in 1974 as well. Only 23 percent of whites have a great deal of confidence compared to 37 percent of blacks.

Parents of school-age children are least likely to have a great deal of confidence in education. While 27 to 32 percent of other age groups have a great deal of confidence, only 19 to 20 percent of people aged 30 to 49 agree.

By education, those who did not complete high school are most likely to say they have a great deal of confidence in educational leaders (34 percent compared with 20 to 24 percent of people with a high school diploma or college degree.)

Confidence in Education, 1974 to 1994

"As far as the people running education are concerned, would you say you have a great deal of confidence, only some confidence, or hardly any confidence at all in them?"

(percent responding by sex, race, age, and education, 1974-94)

	a great deal			only some			hardly any		
	1994	1984	1974	1994	1984	1974	1994	1984	1974
Total	25%	28%	49%	56%	58%	41%	17%	11%	8%
Women	24	29	49	57	56	41	18	11	8
Men	26	27	49	56	61	42	16	10	8
Black	37	30	65	49	57	28	13	6	6
White	23	27	47	58	59	43	18	11	8
Aged 18 to 29	30	33	48	54	55	44	16	10	7
Aged 30 to 39	19	20	49	64	66	41	16	11	10
Aged 40 to 49	20	24	45	60	62	47	19	9	8
Aged 50 to 59	27	32	46	54	56	45	18	12	9
Aged 60 to 69	28	33	54	51	54	32	19	10	11
Aged 70 or older	32	30	58	44	49	32	17	11	3
Not a high school graduate	34	30	55	47	47	33	15	15	9
High school grad.	24	28	48	58	61	44	17	9	7
Bachelor's degree	20	29	38	60	61	53	20	8	9
Graduate degree	24	23	43	58	68	51	18	7	6

Note: Percents may not add to 100 because "don't know" and no answer are not included.
Source: General Social Survey, National Opinion Research Center, University of Chicago

Confidence in Major Companies

A majority of Americans (61 percent) say they have only some confidence in the leaders of big business. Just one-quarter have a great deal of confidence. There has been a shift since 1974 away from both extremes ("a great deal" and "hardly any") toward the middle ground.

There is little difference in the opinions of men and women. In 1974, men were more likely than women to say they had a great deal of confidence in big business leaders. There is also little difference in the opinions of people by age, although in 1974 people under age 40 were less likely than their elders to say they had a great deal of confidence in big business.

Blacks, however, are far more likely than whites to say they have hardly any confidence in the nation's major companies (20 percent of blacks compared with 8 percent of whites). Whites are more likely to have a great deal of confidence (26 percent compared with 17 percent of blacks).

People who did not complete high school are more likely than those with more education to say they have hardly any confidence in business leaders.

Confidence in Major Companies, 1974 to 1994

"As far as the people running major companies are concerned, would you say you have a great deal of confidence, only some confidence, or hardly any confidence at all in them?"

(percent responding by sex, race, age, and education, 1974-94)

	a great deal			only some			hardly any		
	1994	1984	1974	1994	1984	1974	1994	1984	1974
Total	25%	30%	31%	61%	57%	51%	10%	9%	15%
Women	23	27	28	63	60	54	10	8	14
Men	28	35	36	59	53	47	10	10	16
Black	17	12	15	59	71	64	20	12	17
White	26	34	33	62	55	49	8	8	14
Aged 18 to 29	26	30	26	65	63	55	9	5	18
Aged 30 to 39	25	28	26	63	62	52	10	7	19
Aged 40 to 49	23	29	35	67	58	53	9	9	11
Aged 50 to 59	30	34	39	58	50	48	10	13	8
Aged 60 to 69	26	35	36	60	53	44	10	8	16
Aged 70 or older	25	29	34	49	43	45	14	15	11
Not a high school graduate	19	21	30	57	55	48	15	16	16
High school grad.	25	32	30	63	60	53	10	6	14
Bachelor's degree	33	40	35	58	54	50	8	3	13
Graduate degree	26	40	44	66	50	41	6	7	14

Note: Percents may not add to 100 because "don't know" and no answer are not included.
Source: General Social Survey, National Opinion Research Center, University of Chicago

Confidence in the Executive Branch of Government

A bare majority of Americans have only some confidence in the executive branch of the federal government, presided over by the president. Fully 35 percent have hardly any confidence. But this is an improvement since the 1974 survey, taken during the Watergate investigation. In that year, 42 percent of Americans said they had hardly any confidence in the executive branch.

Men and women are about equally likely to say they have only some confidence in the executive branch. Whites are slightly more likely than blacks to say they have hardly any confidence in the executive branch of government (37 percent of whites compared with 25 percent of blacks).

In 1974, older Americans were more likely than younger people to have a great deal of faith in the executive branch of government. In 1994, this is still true, but the differences are not as great. People under age 60 are more likely to say they have only some confidence (50 to 57 percent compared with 43 to 45 percent of people aged 60 or older).

People with graduate degrees are less likely than those with less education to say they have hardly any confidence in the executive branch (21 percent compared with 32 to 34 percent of those with a bachelor's degree or less). In 1974, the reverse was true. In that year, the proportion of people saying they had hardly any confidence rose with education.

Confidence in the Executive Branch of Government, 1974 to 1994

"As far as the people running the executive branch of the federal government are concerned, would you say you have a great deal of confidence, only some confidence, or hardly any confidence at all in them?"

(percent responding by sex, race, age, and education, 1974-94)

	a great deal			only some			hardly any		
	1994	*1984*	*1974*	*1994*	*1984*	*1974*	*1994*	*1984*	*1974*
Total	11%	19%	14%	51%	50%	43%	35%	28%	42%
Women	11	17	12	52	50	46	34	28	40
Men	11	21	15	51	49	39	36	28	44
Black	15	12	12	56	51	45	25	30	41
White	10	19	14	51	50	42	37	28	42
Aged 18 to 29	11	21	9	56	49	45	32	28	45
Aged 30 to 39	10	15	8	52	51	44	37	32	46
Aged 40 to 49	8	18	15	57	50	40	34	28	43
Aged 50 to 59	11	15	18	50	49	39	37	33	40
Aged 60 to 69	16	22	19	45	56	43	39	19	36
Aged 70 or older	17	21	20	43	44	40	31	24	32
Not a high school graduate	16	18	16	45	46	41	32	29	40
High school grad.	10	16	13	50	52	44	38	30	41
Bachelor's degree	9	30	10	57	48	43	34	20	45
Graduate degree	17	25	14	60	52	37	21	20	48

Note: Percents may not add to 100 because "don't know" and no answer are not included.
Source: General Social Survey, National Opinion Research Center, University of Chicago

Confidence in Organized Labor

Americans are increasingly wary of organized labor. While the proportion of Americans saying they have "only some" confidence in the leaders of organized labor has not changed since 1974, the percentage saying they have "hardly any" confidence rose from one-quarter in 1974 to one-third by 1994.

Men were more likely than women to have a great deal of confidence in organized labor in 1974. In 1994, men were more likely than women to say they had hardly any confidence in the union bosses.

Whites are more likely than blacks to say they have hardly any confidence in union leaders (34 percent of whites compared with 22 percent of blacks). Blacks are more likely to say they have a great deal of confidence in union leaders, although the percentage is small.

By age, a majority of people under age 60 have only some confidence in organized labor. Those with the most confidence are Americans aged 60 or older and those under 30.

People who did not complete high school are considerably more likely than those with more education to say they have a great deal of confidence in union leaders (17 percent compared with 10 percent of high school graduates and 4 percent of those with college degrees). The proportion saying they have hardly any confidence rises with education (from 27 percent of people who did not complete high school to about 40 percent of those with college degrees).

Confidence in Organized Labor, 1974 to 1994

"As far as the people running organized labor are concerned, would you say you have a great deal of confidence, only some confidence, or hardly any confidence at all in them?"

(percent responding by sex, race, age, and education, 1974-94)

	a great deal			only some			hardly any		
	1994	1984	1974	1994	1984	1974	1994	1984	1974
Total	10%	9%	18%	52%	52%	53%	32%	36%	25%
Women	9	9	14	56	55	57	28	32	25
Men	11	9	23	48	48	50	38	41	26
Black	18	12	25	53	66	56	22	17	17
White	9	8	17	52	50	53	34	38	27
Aged 18 to 29	14	15	18	60	55	60	21	28	20
Aged 30 to 39	8	7	14	55	54	55	32	36	31
Aged 40 to 49	6	5	15	53	55	54	39	37	29
Aged 50 to 59	8	6	19	50	49	54	37	43	24
Aged 60 to 69	14	7	23	44	52	44	36	38	30
Aged 70 or older	13	9	24	41	40	44	30	41	22
Not a high school graduate	17	13	25	43	52	50	27	27	20
High school grad.	10	9	18	54	52	54	32	37	26
Bachelor's degree	4	5	4	53	49	58	39	44	36
Graduate degree	4	2	7	51	49	53	40	46	38

Note: Percents may not add to 100 because "don't know" and no answer are not included.
Source: General Social Survey, National Opinion Research Center, University of Chicago

Confidence in the Press

The press has a higher "negative rating" than any of the other institutions examined here, except for Congress. Fully 39 percent of Americans say they have hardly any confidence in the leaders of the press; only 10 percent have a great deal of confidence. This is a much more negative view than the public had in 1974.

Men and women are in agreement on this question, as they were in 1974. But blacks and whites see things differently, with whites more likely to say they have only some confidence in the press (50 percent of whites compared with 41 percent of blacks).

Opinions vary by age. People aged 40 to 59 and those under age 30 are more likely than other age groups to say they have hardly any confidence in leaders of the press (41 to 45 percent compared with 35 to 36 percent of other age groups). In 1974, people under age 40 were least likely to say this.

There is only minor variation in opinions about the press by education. People who did not complete high school are more likely than others to report that they have a great deal of confidence in the press. This was also true in 1974.

Confidence in the Press, 1974 to 1994

"As far as the people running the press are concerned, would you say you have a great deal of confidence, only some confidence, or hardly any confidence at all in them?"

(percent responding by sex, race, age, and education, 1974-94)

	a great deal			only some			hardly any		
	1994	1984	1974	1994	1984	1974	1994	1984	1974
Total	10%	17%	26%	49%	59%	55%	39%	21%	18%
Women	9	14	24	50	59	57	38	23	17
Men	10	21	28	48	58	53	40	19	18
Black	11	13	30	41	66	57	43	15	13
White	9	18	25	50	57	55	39	22	18
Aged 18 to 29	12	23	31	44	59	57	42	16	12
Aged 30 to 39	11	18	24	53	58	59	35	23	16
Aged 40 to 49	7	14	22	51	60	58	41	24	19
Aged 50 to 59	9	13	23	45	60	55	45	24	22
Aged 60 to 69	9	15	24	54	59	51	36	22	23
Aged 70 or older	10	13	30	47	55	47	36	22	18
Not a high school graduate	16	18	30	45	57	50	33	18	18
High school grad.	9	18	24	49	57	58	40	23	18
Bachelor's degree	6	13	23	53	66	63	40	20	14
Graduate degree	8	19	25	51	55	56	40	24	18

Note: Percents may not add to 100 because "don't know" and no answer are not included.
Source: General Social Survey, National Opinion Research Center, University of Chicago

Confidence in Medicine

The medical community enjoys more public confidence than any other major institution. This is not saying a lot, however. Only 41 percent of Americans say they have a great deal of confidence in the leaders of the medical community. In 1974, a 60 percent majority had a great deal of confidence in the medical community. The decline in confidence is evident in every demographic segment.

Similar proportions of men and women, blacks and whites, say they have a great deal, only some, or hardly any confidence in the medical community. There is also little difference by education. The less-educated, however, are more likely than those with college educations to say they have hardly any confidence in medicine (11 to 13 percent compared with 4 to 6 percent of people with college degrees).

People under age 30 are more likely than their elders to have a great deal of confidence in the medical community (52 percent compared with 35 to 43 percent). People in their 60s are those most likely to say they have hardly any confidence in the medical community.

Confidence in Medicine, 1974 to 1994

"As far as the people running medicine are concerned, would you say you have a great deal of confidence, only some confidence, or hardly any confidence at all in them?"

(percent responding by sex, race, age, and education, 1974-94)

	a great deal			only some			hardly any		
	1994	*1984*	*1974*	*1994*	*1984*	*1974*	*1994*	*1984*	*1974*
Total	41%	51%	60%	48%	41%	34%	10%	6%	4%
Women	40	48	61	49	43	33	10	7	4
Men	43	54	59	47	39	35	9	5	5
Black	45	40	58	45	51	38	8	6	3
White	41	52	61	48	40	33	10	6	5
Aged 18 to 29	52	59	71	43	36	26	6	4	3
Aged 30 to 39	43	50	62	47	43	32	9	6	4
Aged 40 to 49	36	51	59	54	45	38	9	2	3
Aged 50 to 59	38	44	55	50	48	40	11	8	3
Aged 60 to 69	35	51	52	48	38	35	16	8	11
Aged 70 or older	41	40	52	42	42	37	12	12	6
Not a high school graduate	42	46	57	42	41	35	13	8	5
High school grad.	40	53	63	48	40	33	11	5	3
Bachelor's degree	44	57	58	50	39	36	6	3	7
Graduate degree	45	38	60	50	51	32	4	9	7

Note: Percents may not add to 100 because "don't know" and no answer are not included.
Source: General Social Survey, National Opinion Research Center, University of Chicago

Confidence in the Supreme Court

Half of Americans say they have only some confidence in the Supreme Court. Thirty percent say they have a great deal of confidence in the court, while 16 percent have hardly any. These numbers are essentially unchanged from 1974.

Men are slightly more likely than women, and whites more likely than blacks, to say they have a great deal of confidence in the nation's highest court. These patterns were also true in 1974.

Younger Americans have greater confidence in the Supreme Court than their elders do. Among people under age 30, 37 percent have a great deal of confidence in the High Court, but only 28 to 30 percent of those aged 30 to 69 agree. People aged 70 or older are as likely to say they have hardly any confidence (23 percent) as they are to say they have a great deal (24 percent). In 1974, there was more agreement by age.

The college-educated are more likely than those with less education to say they have a great deal of confidence in the Supreme Court. Conversely, people who did not complete college are more likely to say they have hardly any confidence. Ten percent of people aged 70 or older, and 10 percent of those who did not complete high school (groups with considerable overlap) say they "don't know."

Confidence in the Supreme Court, 1974 to 1994

"As far as the people running the Supreme Court
are concerned, would you say you have a great deal
of confidence, only some confidence, or hardly
any confidence at all in them?"

(percent responding by sex, race, age, and education, 1974-94)

	a great deal			only some			hardly any		
	1994	*1984*	*1974*	*1994*	*1984*	*1974*	*1994*	*1984*	*1974*
Total	30%	34%	33%	50%	49%	48%	16%	12%	14%
Women	27	29	29	51	54	52	17	11	12
Men	34	40	38	48	42	43	16	14	17
Black	24	22	26	53	55	53	18	11	16
White	30	35	34	50	48	47	17	12	14
Aged 18 to 29	37	44	36	50	40	51	12	12	11
Aged 30 to 39	30	28	32	52	57	50	16	12	15
Aged 40 to 49	30	31	36	52	50	49	16	11	13
Aged 50 to 59	28	32	32	51	52	45	17	11	19
Aged 60 to 69	29	32	30	48	55	44	18	8	18
Aged 70 or older	24	28	29	42	41	44	23	18	13
Not a high school graduate	26	25	30	44	47	43	20	17	18
High school grad.	27	34	32	53	51	51	18	12	13
Bachelor's degree	36	46	42	51	43	48	12	8	9
Graduate degree	52	43	48	36	45	40	9	5	10

Note: Percents may not add to 100 because "don't know" and no answer are not included.
Source: General Social Survey, National Opinion Research Center, University of Chicago

Confidence in the Military

Although confidence in the leaders of many institutions has declined considerably, the military is holding its own. Americans are about as likely in 1994 as they were in 1974 to say they have a great deal of confidence in the nation's military leaders. But only 37 percent say so, while a plurality of 48 percent say they have "only some" confidence.

Men are more likely than women and whites are more likely than blacks to say they have a great deal of confidence in military leaders. The proportion of women and blacks who have a great deal of confidence has declined since 1974.

Among different age groups, the youngest and oldest stand apart. Forty-three percent of people under age 30 and 45 percent of those aged 70 or older have great deal of confidence in military leaders compared with 33 to 38 percent of those aged 30 to 69. People aged 18 to 29 in 1994 were more likely than people that age in 1974 to say they have a great deal of confidence in the military. Within other age groups, the proportion who have a great deal of confidence in the military has remained the same or declined.

Confidence in military leaders declines with education. While 42 percent of people who did not complete high school say they have a great deal of confidence, the proportion drops to 30 percent among people with graduate degrees. College graduates were far more likely to have a great deal of confidence in military leaders in 1994 than they were in 1974, when the Vietnam War was ending.

Confidence in the Military, 1974 to 1994

"As far as the people running the military are concerned, would you say you have a great deal of confidence, only some confidence, or hardly any confidence at all in them?"

(percent responding by sex, race, age, and education, 1974-94)

	a great deal			only some			hardly any		
	1994	1984	1974	1994	1984	1974	1994	1984	1974
Total	37%	35%	40%	48%	48%	44%	12%	13%	13%
Women	32	34	39	51	49	45	13	11	13
Men	43	36	41	45	46	43	11	15	14
Black	28	36	36	53	39	50	16	15	13
White	38	34	40	48	50	44	12	13	14
Aged 18 to 29	43	38	37	41	51	44	14	9	19
Aged 30 to 39	33	30	37	52	48	43	14	20	18
Aged 40 to 49	31	32	40	50	48	46	16	13	12
Aged 50 to 59	38	32	43	52	50	46	7	14	7
Aged 60 to 69	36	38	39	53	50	46	8	9	10
Aged 70 or older	45	41	45	40	36	39	8	8	8
Not a high school graduate	42	42	47	37	37	40	13	11	8
High school grad.	38	36	40	49	51	44	12	11	14
Bachelor's degree	34	23	19	54	59	57	12	16	24
Graduate degree	30	23	18	51	53	52	16	18	29

Note: Percents may not add to 100 because "don't know" and no answer are not included.
Source: General Social Survey, National Opinion Research Center, University of Chicago

Confidence in Congress

The public has little confidence in Congressional leaders. About two out of five Americans have hardly any confidence in Congress, half have only some, and only 8 percent have a great deal of confidence in Congress. People were more likely in 1994 than in 1974 to have little confidence in Congressional leaders. This is true of all demographic segments.

Men are more fed up than women. While 43 percent of men have hardly any confidence in Congress, fewer women agree (36 percent).

Whites are more likely than blacks to say they have hardly any confidence in Congress (41 percent of whites compared with 31 percent of blacks). A higher percentage of blacks than whites say they have a great deal of confidence.

Americans aged 70 or older and those under age 30 are less likely than others to say they have hardly any confidence in Congress (33 percent of the oldest and 34 percent of the youngest compared with 39 to 43 percent of others).

In 1974, confidence in Congress rose with education. By 1994 the opposite was the case, with confidence falling with increasing levels of education.

Confidence in Congress, 1974 to 1994

"As far as the people running Congress are concerned, would you say you have a great deal of confidence, only some confidence, or hardly any confidence at all in them?"

(percent responding by sex, race, age, and education, 1974-94)

	a great deal			only some			hardly any		
	1994	1984	1974	1994	1984	1974	1994	1984	1974
Total	8%	13%	17%	50%	62%	59%	39%	21%	21%
Women	7	13	15	53	65	60	36	19	20
Men	9	14	19	46	58	57	43	24	22
Black	16	10	12	48	68	60	31	16	23
White	6	13	18	50	61	59	41	22	21
Aged 18 to 29	9	19	15	54	60	66	34	18	17
Aged 30 to 39	6	10	17	51	63	56	42	25	24
Aged 40 to 49	7	13	20	48	64	59	43	22	19
Aged 50 to 59	8	8	17	49	64	56	41	24	23
Aged 60 to 69	10	12	17	47	66	56	39	20	23
Aged 70 or older	8	13	18	50	58	55	33	19	20
Not a high school graduate	13	14	16	45	55	56	32	25	23
High school grad.	7	14	17	51	64	59	40	20	22
Bachelor's degree	4	13	17	50	64	73	45	20	9
Graduate degree	6	12	25	52	69	58	39	17	16

Note: Percents may not add to 100 because "don't know" and no answer are not included.
Source: General Social Survey, National Opinion Research Center, University of Chicago

Confidence in Science

Confidence in the scientific community has slipped since 1974. In that year, 45 percent of Americans said they had a great deal of confidence in the scientific community. In 1994, the proportion was down to 38 percent.

Men are more likely than women to say they have a great deal of confidence in the scientific community. This was true in 1974 as well.

There is an enormous difference between blacks and whites on this issue. While 40 percent of whites say they have a great deal of confidence, only 26 percent of blacks agree. Fifteen percent of blacks say they have hardly any confidence. This is a smaller gap than in 1974, however.

Younger people are more likely to have a great deal of confidence in the scientific community (48 percent of people under age 30 dropping to 28 percent of those aged 60 or older). This was also true in 1974, but in that year the gap was smaller.

Not surprisingly, people with college degrees (many of whom are themselves working in the sciences) are much more likely than people with less education to say they have a great deal of confidence in the scientific community. Fully 51 to 54 percent of the college-educated, compared with 36 percent of high school graduates and 26 percent of those who did not complete high school, have a great deal of confidence in the leaders of the scientific community.

Confidence in Science, 1974 to 1994

"As far as the people running the scientific community are concerned, would you say you have a great deal of confidence, only some confidence, or hardly any confidence at all in them?"

(percent responding by sex, race, age, and education, 1974-94)

	a great deal			only some			hardly any		
	1994	1984	1974	1994	1984	1974	1994	1984	1974
Total	38%	45%	45%	49%	42%	38%	7%	5%	7%
Women	35	39	41	50	46	41	7	7	6
Men	42	54	49	48	37	34	7	4	7
Black	26	25	21	51	54	45	15	8	17
White	40	48	48	49	41	37	6	5	5
Aged 18 to 29	48	53	53	42	36	38	7	7	6
Aged 30 to 39	41	50	46	49	45	39	6	4	6
Aged 40 to 49	39	42	41	52	43	45	6	3	9
Aged 50 to 59	37	43	45	49	46	33	10	4	9
Aged 60 to 69	28	40	40	56	47	38	9	3	6
Aged 70 or older	28	29	38	49	41	31	6	11	7
Not a high school graduate	26	27	32	46	46	39	12	10	12
High school grad.	36	47	49	51	45	39	8	5	5
Bachelor's degree	51	65	61	45	32	35	2	1	1
Graduate degree	54	62	64	43	31	29	1	2	3

Note: Percents may not add to 100 because "don't know" and no answer are not included.
Source: General Social Survey, National Opinion Research Center, University of Chicago

Gun Control

Despite the inability of politicians to pass significant gun-control legislation, Americans are overwhelmingly supportive of gun control. Over three-quarters say they believe a police permit should be required before an individual is allowed to purchase a gun. Support is highest among blacks, women, and the college educated.

The largest disagreements on this issue are by sex and race. Women are far more supportive of gun control than are men, while blacks are more supportive than whites. The rift between men and women has been evident since 1974, but the gap between blacks and whites is a recent development. In 1974, the same percentages of both races favored gun control. But while white support is at the same level as in 1974, support among blacks has grown.

This is one issue without a generation gap. Strong majorities of all age groups support requiring a police permit to purchase a gun. And while the level of support rises with greater educational attainment, the gap between those least supportive (high school graduates) and most supportive (graduate degree holders) is only 8 percentage points.

Gun Control, 1994

"Would you favor or oppose a law which would require a person to obtain a police permit before he or she could buy a gun?"

(percent responding by sex, race, age, and education, 1994)

	favor	oppose
Total	78%	20%
Women	84	14
Men	70	29
Black	84	13
White	77	22
Aged 18 to 29	78	20
Aged 30 to 39	78	20
Aged 40 to 49	75	24
Aged 50 to 59	78	20
Aged 60 to 69	76	21
Aged 70 or older	81	16
Not a high school graduate	78	19
High school graduate	76	22
Bachelor's degree	81	18
Graduate degree	84	15

Note: Percents may not add to 100 because "don't know" and no answer are not included.
Source: General Social Survey, National Opinion Research Center, University of Chicago

Gun Control, 1974 to 1994

"Would you favor or oppose a law which would require a person to obtain a police permit before he or she could buy a gun?"

(percent responding by sex, race, age, and education, 1974-94)

	favor			oppose		
	1994	*1984*	*1974*	*1994*	*1984*	*1974*
Total	78%	69%	75%	20%	28%	23%
Women	84	75	83	14	21	15
Men	70	61	66	29	38	33
Black	84	76	75	13	19	22
White	77	68	75	22	30	24
Aged 18 to 29	78	68	76	20	29	23
Aged 30 to 39	78	71	77	20	27	22
Aged 40 to 49	75	68	74	24	31	26
Aged 50 to 59	78	63	70	20	34	29
Aged 60 to 69	76	73	74	21	24	21
Aged 70 or older	81	71	81	16	23	18
Not a high school graduate	78	71	73	19	25	25
High school graduate	76	66	76	22	30	23
Bachelor's degree	81	70	77	18	30	22
Graduate degree	84	86	71	15	13	29

Note: Percents may not add to 100 because "don't know" and no answer are not included.
Source: General Social Survey, National Opinion Research Center, University of Chicago

The Courts

There are few topics that concern Americans more than crime. So it is not surprising that the great majority believe the courts should get tougher with criminals.

This is not a recent development, however. In 1974, fully 77 percent of Americans felt the courts were not harsh enough on criminals. Tougher laws and sentencing have not satisfied Americans, though; in 1994 an even higher 85 percent said the courts aren't tough enough.

Some demographic segments are less likely to agree that the courts should get tougher. While 85 percent of all Americans say the courts aren't tough enough, a smaller 74 percent of graduate degree holders agree. Likewise, smaller percentages of young adults and blacks say the courts are not harsh enough.

It is important to note, however, that substantial percentages of respondents volunteered that the courts are "about right" in their handling of criminals. If the question included "almost right" as a standard response choice, the percentage saying the courts are not harsh enough might be lower.

The Courts, 1994

"In general, do you think the courts in this area deal too harshly or not harshly enough with criminals?"

(percent responding by sex, race, age, and education, 1994)

	too harshly	not harshly enough	about right*
Total	3%	85%	8%
Women	2	86	7
Men	3	83	9
Black	6	80	8
White	2	85	8
Aged 18 to 29	4	79	10
Aged 30 to 39	2	87	7
Aged 40 to 49	2	85	8
Aged 50 to 59	3	85	8
Aged 60 to 69	2	84	8
Aged 70 or older	1	87	6
Not a high school graduate	4	85	6
High school graduate	3	86	6
Bachelor's degree	1	84	9
Graduate degree	2	74	17

* Volunteered response.
Note: Percents may not add to 100 because "don't know" and no answer are not included.
Source: General Social Survey, National Opinion Research Center, University of Chicago

The Courts, 1974 to 1994

"In general, do you think the courts in this area deal too harshly or not harshly enough with criminals?"

(percent responding by sex, race, age, and education, 1974-94)

	too harshly			not harshly enough			about right*		
	1994	*1984*	*1974*	*1994*	*1984*	*1974*	*1994*	*1984*	*1974*
Total	3%	3%	6%	85%	81%	77%	8%	11%	10%
Women	2	2	5	86	81	77	7	11	10
Men	3	5	6	83	79	78	9	12	9
Black	6	6	10	80	68	70	8	17	7
White	2	3	5	85	82	78	8	10	10
Aged 18 to 29	4	6	8	79	76	68	10	13	13
Aged 30 to 39	2	3	8	87	81	76	7	10	6
Aged 40 to 49	2	1	5	85	83	78	8	12	9
Aged 50 to 59	3	2	1	85	83	82	8	12	11
Aged 60 to 69	2	2	7	84	85	81	8	8	10
Aged 70 or older	1	0	2	87	79	87	6	13	6
Not a high school graduate	4	4	7	85	79	80	6	13	9
High school grad.	3	3	4	86	82	76	6	10	9
Bachelor's degree	1	2	7	84	84	77	9	10	10
Graduate degree	2	3	8	74	72	70	17	18	11

* *Volunteered response.*
Note: Percents may not add to 100 because "don't know" and no answer are not included.
Source: General Social Survey, National Opinion Research Center, University of Chicago

Death Penalty

A majority of Americans favor the death penalty for persons convicted of murder. Support was greater in 1994 (74 percent) in than it was in 1974 (63 percent).

There is some variation in the level of support for the death penalty among most demographic groups. Men were more likely than women to support the death penalty in 1994, as was the case in 1974. Seventy-nine percent of men, compared with 71 percent of women, favor executions.

The lowest level of support for the death penalty is found among blacks (51 percent). There is a 27 percentage point gap in the proportion of black and white Americans who support the death penalty. Although large, this gap is slightly smaller than in 1974.

There is a 13 percentage point gap in support for the death penalty between graduate degree holders and people whose education stopped with a high school diploma. In 1974, there was closer agreement by education.

Substantial percentages of people say they "don't know" whether they favor or oppose the death penalty, reflecting the difficulty Americans have reconciling their concerns about crime with ethical and moral beliefs. Blacks and the elderly are most likely to say they don't know whether they favor or oppose the death penalty.

Death Penalty, 1994

"Do you favor or oppose the death penalty for persons convicted of murder?"

(percent responding by sex, race, age, and education, 1994)

	favor	oppose	don't know
Total	74%	19%	6%
Women	71	22	8
Men	79	17	4
Black	51	39	10
White	78	16	5
Aged 18 to 29	73	21	6
Aged 30 to 39	75	20	5
Aged 40 to 49	75	21	4
Aged 50 to 59	74	20	6
Aged 60 to 69	75	16	9
Aged 70 or older	73	16	9
Not a high school graduate	69	23	8
High school graduate	77	16	6
Bachelor's degree	71	23	6
Graduate degree	64	29	6

Note: Percents may not add to 100 because no answer is not included.
Source: General Social Survey, National Opinion Research Center, University of Chicago

Death Penalty, 1974 to 1994

"Do you favor or oppose the death penalty for persons convicted of murder?"

(percent responding by sex, race, age, and education, 1974-94)

	favor			oppose		
	1994	*1984*	*1974*	*1994*	*1984*	*1974*
Total	74%	69%	63%	19%	24%	32%
Women	71	64	58	22	28	34
Men	79	76	68	17	20	29
Black	51	42	36	39	46	55
White	78	73	66	16	21	29
Aged 18 to 29	73	73	57	21	21	40
Aged 30 to 39	75	69	63	20	25	31
Aged 40 to 49	75	69	66	21	24	31
Aged 50 to 59	74	70	65	20	26	26
Aged 60 to 69	75	67	66	16	24	28
Aged 70 or older	73	60	65	16	30	30
Not a high school graduate	69	60	64	23	31	30
High school graduate	77	72	64	16	22	31
Bachelor's degree	71	75	58	23	19	38
Graduate degree	64	66	56	29	30	38

Note: Percents may not add to 100 because "don't know" and no answer are not included.
Source: General Social Survey, National Opinion Research Center, University of Chicago

Euthanasia

Support for allowing the incurably ill to hasten the end of their lives has grown considerably over the last few decades, especially within certain demographic segments. A majority of Americans (68 percent) now say they favor giving the incurably ill the option of having a doctor end their lives.

Blacks and the elderly are split on the issue, however. Only about half of each group favors euthanasia. These proportions are considerably higher than they were in 1977, however.

Despite growing percentages of the public who favor euthanasia, there is a significant proportion of people within each demographic segment that is against this practice. Men are more in favor of euthanasia than women, whites more than blacks, the young more than the old. Those without a high school diploma are far less likely to support euthanasia than are people with graduate degrees.

Euthanasia, 1994

"When a person has a disease that cannot be cured, do you think doctors should be allowed by law to end the patient's life by some painless means if the patient and his family request it?"

(percent responding by sex, race, age, and education, 1994)

	yes	*no*
Total	68%	27%
Women	64	30
Men	72	23
Black	50	45
White	70	24
Aged 18 to 29	74	23
Aged 30 to 39	74	21
Aged 40 to 49	70	26
Aged 50 to 59	61	33
Aged 60 to 69	63	32
Aged 70 or older	53	35
Not a high school graduate	59	35
High school graduate	69	26
Bachelor's degree	66	28
Graduate degree	76	18

Note: Percents may not add to 100 because "don't know" and no answer are not included.
Source: General Social Survey, National Opinion Research Center, University of Chicago

Euthanasia, 1977 to 1994

"When a person has a disease that cannot be cured, do you think doctors should be allowed by law to end the patient's life by some painless means if the patient and his family request it?"

(percent responding by sex, race, age, and education, 1977-94)

	yes			no		
	1994	*1985*	*1977*	*1994*	*1985*	*1977*
Total	68%	64%	59%	27%	33%	36%
Women	64	60	55	30	37	39
Men	72	69	65	23	29	32
Black	50	43	36	45	52	57
White	70	66	62	24	32	33
Aged 18 to 29	74	73	70	23	25	26
Aged 30 to 39	74	74	60	21	24	37
Aged 40 to 49	70	63	57	26	34	40
Aged 50 to 59	61	55	58	33	41	37
Aged 60 to 69	63	52	55	32	45	40
Aged 70 or older	53	52	45	35	44	43
Not a high school graduate	59	50	52	35	47	40
High school graduate	69	70	62	26	28	34
Bachelor's degree	66	66	61	28	33	34
Graduate degree	76	62	74	18	31	24

Note: Percents may not add to 100 because "don't know" and no answer are not included.
Source: General Social Survey, National Opinion Research Center, University of Chicago

Sex Education

For a topic that ignites enormous controversy, Americans are remarkably united: 85 percent favor sex education in the public schools. And, unlike so many of the "hot button" issues confronting the nation today, men and women, blacks and whites are in agreement.

This is not to say there are no dissenters. By age and education, there are differences of opinion on whether schools are a proper arena for teaching young people about sex. The proportion who support sex education falls off substantially among older people. Over 90 percent of people in their 20s and 30s support sex education, as do well over 80 percent of those in their 40s and 50s. But support drops to 75 percent among people in their 60s and to only 64 percent among people aged 70 or older. But support was higher in almost all age groups in 1994 than it was in 1974.

People without a high school diploma (many of whom are older) are also less likely to support sex education, with only 71 percent saying they favor it. In contrast, 90 percent of people with graduate degrees say they are in favor. Interestingly, although support for sex education is very high among the college-educated, it is slightly lower than it was in 1994.

Sex Education, 1994

"Would you be for or against sex education in the public schools?"

(percent responding by sex, race, age, and education, 1994)

	for	against
Total	85%	12%
Women	85	12
Men	84	12
Black	86	12
White	84	12
Aged 18 to 29	94	5
Aged 30 to 39	92	6
Aged 40 to 49	86	12
Aged 50 to 59	84	12
Aged 60 to 69	75	20
Aged 70 or older	64	28
Not a high school graduate	71	22
High school graduate	87	11
Bachelor's degree	87	11
Graduate degree	90	5

Note: Percents may not add to 100 because "don't know" and no answer are not included.
Source: General Social Survey, National Opinion Research Center, University of Chicago

Sex Education, 1974 to 1994

"Would you be for or against sex education in the public schools?"

(percent responding by sex, race, age, and education, 1974-94)

	favor			oppose		
	1994	1985	1974	1994	1985	1974
Total	85%	82%	79%	12%	15%	17%
Women	85	81	80	12	16	16
Men	84	83	78	12	15	19
Black	86	80	79	12	17	18
White	84	82	79	12	15	17
Aged 18 to 29	94	92	89	5	7	9
Aged 30 to 39	92	90	86	6	9	11
Aged 40 to 49	86	89	86	12	8	10
Aged 50 to 59	84	72	75	12	23	19
Aged 60 to 69	75	75	63	20	22	29
Aged 70 or older	64	60	54	28	34	40
Not a high school graduate	71	66	64	22	29	30
High school graduate	87	86	85	11	12	12
Bachelor's degree	87	93	94	11	6	6
Graduate degree	90	90	95	5	10	6

Note: Percents may not add to 100 because "don't know" and no answer are not included.
Source: General Social Survey, National Opinion Research Center, University of Chicago

Is the Government too Secretive?

For decades, the United States government used the Cold War to justify keeping many documents secret. Now that the Cold War is over is so much secrecy still appropriate? A majority (54 percent) of Americans say no.

There is no real disagreement on this question between men and women or blacks and whites. Except for the oldest Americans, people of different ages are also in agreement. Only 40 percent of people aged 70 or older say the government classifies too many documents as "secret," compared with 54 to 58 percent of younger people.

There is some variation by education, but it is slight. From 45 to 56 percent of all educational groups think there is too much secrecy.

Substantial numbers of Americans don't know if the government is too secretive or not. This is especially true of older people, those who did not complete high school (two groups with considerable overlap), and blacks.

Is the Government too Secretive? 1994

"Given the world situation, the government protects too many documents by classifying them as 'Secret' or 'Top Secret.' Do you agree or disagree?"

(percent responding by sex, race, age, and education, 1994)

	agree strongly	agree	neither agree nor disagree	disagree	disagree strongly	don't know	agree, total	disagree, total
Total	13%	41%	17%	18%	4%	6%	54%	22%
Women	12	42	18	15	3	9	54	18
Men	15	40	15	21	6	3	55	27
Black	18	40	14	13	3	12	58	16
White	12	41	17	19	5	6	53	24
Aged 18 to 29	10	44	16	21	4	4	54	25
Aged 30 to 39	14	44	16	17	5	4	58	22
Aged 40 to 49	15	43	18	18	4	2	58	22
Aged 50 to 59	16	38	19	16	5	6	54	21
Aged 60 to 69	13	43	11	15	5	12	56	20
Aged 70 or older	12	28	18	18	4	18	40	22
Not a high school graduate	16	34	14	18	4	15	50	22
High school grad.	12	44	17	16	5	5	56	21
Bachelor's degree	15	38	18	21	4	4	53	25
Graduate degree	9	36	22	22	5	4	45	27

Note: Percents may not add to 100 because no answer is not included.
Source: General Social Survey, National Opinion Research Center, University of Chicago

Taxes

Most Americans say they pay too much in federal taxes, but this is not a recent development. Since 1976, the first year this question was included in the General Social Survey, a majority of Americans have said their taxes are too high. A substantial minority (one-third) believes the tax level is about right.

There is no real gender gap on this question, but there are differences by age. Among people aged 70 or older, almost half say their tax level is about right. Only a small proportion (39 percent) of the oldest age group feel taxes are too high. Those most likely to say their taxes are too high are people in their peak earning years (aged 50 to 59). Baby boomers (aged 30 to 49) and blacks are also more likely than average to feel they pay too much federal tax.

Over the past two decades, a consistent majority within each demographic segment has said federal taxes are too high. No one is willing to say their tax bill is too low.

Taxes, 1994

"Do you consider the amount of federal income tax which you have to pay as too high, about right, or too low?"

(percent responding by sex, race, age, and education, 1994)

	too high	about right
Total	62%	33%
Women	61	34
Men	64	32
Black	69	23
White	61	35
Aged 18 to 29	57	38
Aged 30 to 39	69	28
Aged 40 to 49	69	27
Aged 50 to 59	72	25
Aged 60 to 69	54	43
Aged 70 or older	39	48
Not a high school graduate	53	36
High school graduate	64	32
Bachelor's degree	64	33
Graduate degree	62	33

Note: Percents may not add to 100 because "too low," pays none, "don't know," and no answer are not included.
Source: General Social Survey, National Opinion Research Center, University of Chicago

Taxes, 1976 to 1994

"Do you consider the amount of federal income tax which you have to pay as too high, about right, or too low?"

(percent responding by sex, race, age, and education, 1976-94)

	too high			about right		
	1994	*1984*	*1976*	*1994*	*1984*	*1976*
Total	62%	63%	58%	33%	32%	33%
Women	61	66	57	34	28	31
Men	64	58	59	32	38	34
Black	69	71	64	23	20	22
White	61	61	57	35	34	34
Aged 18 to 29	57	61	58	38	34	34
Aged 30 to 39	69	70	63	28	28	33
Aged 40 to 49	69	66	62	27	32	32
Aged 50 to 59	72	66	69	25	32	28
Aged 60 to 69	54	61	52	43	33	36
Aged 70 or older	39	43	41	48	36	31
Not a high school graduate	53	58	56	36	32	27
High school graduate	64	65	59	32	31	35
Bachelor's degree	64	60	59	33	36	38
Graduate degree	62	58	57	33	41	43

Note: Percents may not add to 100 because "too low," pays none, "don't know," and no answer are not included.
Source: General Social Survey, National Opinion Research Center, University of Chicago

Are Things Getting Worse?

Americans are "in a funk," as President Clinton once said. In 1994, two-thirds believed that the "lot of the average man was getting worse, not better."

Roughly equal proportions of men and women say things are getting worse. People of different ages are also more or less in agreement on this issue.

But blacks and whites diverge widely on this topic, as do people with different levels of education. Fully 80 percent of blacks say things are getting worse compared with about two-thirds of whites. College graduates are considerably more optimistic than are those with less education. While 55 to 59 percent of people with a college degree say things are getting worse, at least 70 percent of people with less education hold this view. Among all demographic segments, college graduates are most likely to disagree with this sentiment (over 40 percent). This is not surprising, since college graduates are one of the few demographic segments whose incomes have been rising over the past several years.

Are Things Getting Worse? 1994

"In spite of what some people say, the lot of the
average man is getting worse, not better."

(percent responding by sex, race, age, and education, 1994)

	agree	disagree
Total	67%	30%
Women	69	28
Men	65	33
Black	80	18
White	65	32
Aged 18 to 29	70	27
Aged 30 to 39	68	31
Aged 40 to 49	63	35
Aged 50 to 59	70	28
Aged 60 to 69	70	26
Aged 70 or older	64	29
Not a high school graduate	71	23
High school graduate	70	27
Bachelor's degree	59	40
Graduate degree	55	43

Note: Percents may not add to 100 because "don't know" and no answer are not included.
Source: General Social Survey, National Opinion Research Center, University of Chicago

Are Things Getting Worse? 1974 to 1994

"In spite of what some people say, the lot of the average man is getting worse, not better."

(percent responding by sex, race, age, and education, 1974-94)

	agree			disagree		
	1994	1984	1974	1994	1984	1974
Total	67%	54%	59%	30%	43%	38%
Women	69	57	60	28	40	36
Men	65	50	58	33	47	40
Black	80	77	75	18	23	23
White	65	51	57	32	46	40
Aged 18 to 29	70	54	60	27	45	38
Aged 30 to 39	68	55	65	31	43	33
Aged 40 to 49	63	54	58	35	42	40
Aged 50 to 59	70	64	53	28	35	43
Aged 60 to 69	70	52	57	26	43	38
Aged 70 or older	64	49	61	29	46	32
Not a high school graduate	71	66	71	23	30	26
High school graduate	70	54	58	27	44	39
Bachelor's degree	59	42	40	40	58	55
Graduate degree	55	32	30	43	67	69

Note: Percents may not add to 100 because "don't know" and no answer are not included.
Source: General Social Survey, National Opinion Research Center, University of Chicago

Do Public Officials Really Care?

Public officials need to work on their public image. Fully three-quarters of Americans say "most public officials are not really interested in the problems of the average man." This is up 10 percentage points since 1974.

Men and women are about equally likely to feel public officials don't really care (75 percent of women and 71 percent of men). Women's opinions of public officials have deteriorated more than men's since 1974, however.

Blacks and whites are essentially in agreement on this issue (76 percent of blacks and 73 percent of whites). In 1974, blacks were considerably more likely to say this, but the percentage of whites has grown to match black sentiment since then.

There is not much difference of opinion on this issue by age, nor was there in 1974. In 1994, between 69 and 77 percent of people of different ages said public officials don't really care about the average person.

Public officials have a better image among people with higher levels of education. While 76 to 78 percent of people who went no further than high school say officials don't care about the average person, the figure drops to 64 percent among people with bachelor's degrees and to 53 percent among those with graduate degrees. A similar pattern was apparent in 1974.

Do Public Officials Really Care? 1994

"Most public officials are not really interested in the problems of the average man."

(percent responding by sex, race, age, and education, 1994)

	agree	disagree
Total	74%	24%
Women	75	22
Men	71	26
Black	76	21
White	73	24
Aged 18 to 29	69	30
Aged 30 to 39	77	22
Aged 40 to 49	71	26
Aged 50 to 59	76	23
Aged 60 to 69	77	21
Aged 70 or older	74	17
Not a high school graduate	76	18
High school graduate	78	20
Bachelor's degree	64	35
Graduate degree	53	43

Note: Percents may not add to 100 because "don't know" and no answer are not included.
Source: General Social Survey, National Opinion Research Center, University of Chicago

Do Public Officials Really Care? 1974 to 1994

"Most public officials are not really interested in the problems of the average man."

(percent responding by sex, race, age, and education, 1974-94)

	agree			disagree		
	1994	*1984*	*1974*	*1994*	*1984*	*1974*
Total	74%	68%	64%	24%	29%	33%
Women	75	68	62	22	29	34
Men	71	68	66	26	30	32
Black	76	80	78	21	16	20
White	73	66	62	24	31	35
Aged 18 to 29	69	62	61	30	35	36
Aged 30 to 39	77	66	67	22	31	31
Aged 40 to 49	71	69	64	26	28	34
Aged 50 to 59	76	74	64	23	24	35
Aged 60 to 69	77	75	65	21	21	31
Aged 70 or older	74	69	65	17	29	31
Not a high school graduate	76	79	73	18	18	23
High school graduate	78	69	63	20	28	35
Bachelor's degree	64	47	50	35	50	48
Graduate degree	53	44	37	43	55	63

Note: Percents may not add to 100 because "don't know" and no answer are not included.
Source: General Social Survey, National Opinion Research Center, University of Chicago

Who Should Help the Poor?

Conservative politicians have been trying to get the federal government out of the welfare business. But while Americans are less likely today than they were in 1975 to believe government is the answer, they haven't yet embraced an "every man for himself" philosophy.

A plurality (43 percent) of Americans believe responsibility for improving the lot of the poor lies with both government and the individual. Roughly equal numbers believe government should do everything possible to help the poor (26 percent), or that it is up to the individual to take care of himself (28 percent).

Americans in 1994 were less likely to look to government alone to help the poor than they were in 1974. Slightly more believe it is up to the poor to improve their situations, but most of the shift has been in the increasing percentage of people who say it should be a combined effort of government and the individual.

The largest difference of opinion is by race. One-third of blacks feel strongly that the government should do everything possible to improve the standard of living of the poor. This compares with only 10 percent of whites.

By age, the opinions of older boomers (aged 40 to 49) have decidedly shifted over the past two decades. In 1975, 44 percent believed it was the government's responsibility to help the poor. Only 24 percent hold this opinion today. While a plurality of 46 percent look to both government and the individual, 28 percent now say it is up to the individual alone. In 1974, only 17 percent of these boomers (then aged 18 to 29) felt this way.

Who Should Help the Poor? 1994

"Some people think that the government in Washington should do everything possible to improve the standard of living of all poor Americans; they are at point 1. Other people think it is not the government's responsibility, and that each person should take care of himself; they are at point 5. Where would you place yourself on this scale?"

(percent responding by sex, race, age, and education, 1994)

	government (strongly agree)		agree with both		take care of self (strongly agree)
	1	2	3	4	5
Total	13%	13%	43%	16%	12%
Women	14	14	47	12	9
Men	11	12	39	21	14
Black	32	17	33	7	6
White	10	13	45	18	13
Aged 18 to 29	15	15	45	17	7
Aged 30 to 39	12	16	41	19	8
Aged 40 to 49	11	13	46	16	12
Aged 50 to 59	13	13	38	20	13
Aged 60 to 69	15	9	47	11	13
Aged 70 or older	12	9	44	8	22
Not a high school graduate	23	11	43	7	10
High school graduate	12	13	43	16	13
Bachelor's degree	5	13	44	23	14
Graduate degree	9	18	45	22	5

Note: Percents may not add to 100 because "don't know" and no answer are not included.
Source: General Social Survey, National Opinion Research Center, University of Chicago

Who Should Help the Poor? 1975 to 1994

"Some people think that the government in Washington should do everything possible to improve the standard of living of all poor Americans; they are at point 1. Other people think it is not the government's responsibility, and that each person should take care of himself; they are at point 5. Where would you place yourself on this scale?"

(percent responding by sex, race, age, and education, 1975-94)

	government (1 & 2)			agree with both (3)			take care of self (4 & 5)		
	1994	1984	1975	1994	1984	1975	1994	1984	1975
Total	26%	28%	39%	43%	45%	35%	28%	23%	23%
Women	28	28	41	47	48	37	21	18	20
Men	23	27	37	39	40	33	35	31	28
Black	49	49	68	33	40	23	13	6	7
White	23	24	36	45	46	36	31	26	25
Aged 18 to 29	30	31	44	45	46	36	24	20	17
Aged 30 to 39	28	29	39	41	45	34	27	21	24
Aged 40 to 49	24	27	34	46	40	37	28	30	27
Aged 50 to 59	26	28	37	38	45	37	33	24	24
Aged 60 to 69	24	21	42	47	50	29	24	26	27
Aged 70 or older	21	27	34	44	44	34	30	20	28
Not a high school graduate	34	41	49	43	38	31	17	14	15
High school grad.	25	23	34	43	48	37	29	25	28
Bachelor's degree	18	21	30	44	44	36	37	33	34
Graduate degree	27	23	28	45	50	48	27	26	24

Note: Percents may not add to 100 because "don't know" and no answer are not included.
Source: General Social Survey, National Opinion Research Center, University of Chicago

Whose Responsibility Is Health Care?

Americans are not ready to see the government pull out of health care. A plurality of Americans (46 percent) say the government should be primarily responsible for making sure people can pay their health care bills. About one-third believe it is the combined responsibility of government and the individual. Only 20 percent believe the government has no role in this.

Women are slightly more likely than men to say the government should be primarily responsible (49 percent compared with 42 percent of men). Fully 26 percent of men believe it is primarily an individual's problem compared with only 15 percent of women. In 1975, men and women were in closer agreement.

Blacks overwhelmingly believe that making sure people can pay their health care bills is a government responsibility (73 percent compared with only 42 percent of whites). Only 5 percent of blacks, but 22 percent of whites, say it should be left to the individual.

Older Americans are less likely than younger people to believe the government should be primarily responsible for making sure people can pay for health care. Over half of people under age 40 (52 percent) take this position compared with 40 to 44 percent of people aged 40 or older. It is interesting to note that only 40 percent of people aged 60 or older (who are almost universally covered by the government's largest health care program, Medicare) say the government should make sure people can pay for health care. Support for this position was lower among this age group in 1994 than it was in 1975.

There is not much difference of opinion by education, with one exception. People with bachelor's degrees are more likely to say it is the individual's responsibility, and less likely to say it should be shared by government and individuals. The college-educated were more likely in 1994 than in 1974 to say it should be left up to the individual.

Whose Responsibility Is Health Care? 1994

"In general, some people think that it is the responsibility of the government in Washington too see to it that people have help in paying for doctors and hospital bills. Others think that these matters are not the responsibility of the federal government and that people should take care of these things themselves. Where would you place yourself on a scale of 1 to 5, or haven't you made up your mind on this?"

(percent responding by sex, race, age, and education, 1994)

	govern- ment 1	2	agree with both 3	4	take care of self 5
Total	25%	21%	31%	11%	9%
Women	26	23	33	8	7
Men	23	19	28	14	12
Black	50	23	19	2	3
White	21	21	33	12	10
Aged 18 to 29	27	25	28	12	7
Aged 30 to 39	26	26	28	11	7
Aged 40 to 49	24	20	30	14	9
Aged 50 to 59	24	17	36	10	10
Aged 60 to 69	25	15	35	9	10
Aged 70 or older	23	17	34	6	15
Not a high school graduate	31	17	32	4	10
High school graduate	26	20	32	11	9
Bachelor's degree	16	27	26	17	11
Graduate degree	21	28	32	15	3

Note: Percents may not add to 100 because "don't know" and no answer are not included.
Source: General Social Survey, National Opinion Research Center, University of Chicago

Whose Responsibility Is Health Care? 1975 to 1994

"In general, some people think that it is the responsibility of the government in Washington to see to it that people have help in paying for doctors and hospital bills. Others think that these matters are not the responsibility of the federal government and that people should take care of these things themselves. Where would you place yourself on a scale of 1 to 5, or haven't you made up your mind on this?"

(percent responding by sex, race, age, and education, 1975-94)

	government (1 and 2)			agree with both (3)			take care of self (4 and 5)		
	1994	**1984**	**1975**	**1994**	**1984**	**1975**	**1994**	**1984**	**1975**
Total	46%	43%	48%	31%	34%	28%	20%	19%	21%
Women	49	42	46	33	35	30	15	18	21
Men	42	45	51	28	32	26	26	21	21
Black	73	54	69	19	34	22	5	9	7
White	42	41	46	33	33	29	22	21	23
Aged 18 to 29	52	51	56	28	30	25	19	15	16
Aged 30 to 39	52	46	52	28	29	25	18	20	22
Aged 40 to 49	44	42	39	30	32	34	23	24	23
Aged 50 to 59	41	39	39	36	36	33	20	24	26
Aged 60 to 69	40	33	48	35	44	28	19	18	23
Aged 70 or older	40	32	51	34	42	29	21	19	16
Not a high school graduate	48	51	53	32	31	28	14	13	15
High school grad.	46	39	44	32	36	29	20	21	25
Bachelor's degree	43	37	47	26	27	29	28	30	24
Graduate degree	49	50	52	32	32	20	18	16	24

Note: Percents may not add to 100 because "don't know" and no answer are not included.
Source: General Social Survey, National Opinion Research Center, University of Chicago

CHAPTER

2

The Environment

For many years, the environment has been one of the chief worries of Americans, along with crime, the economy, and health care. But while Americans want to protect the environment, the record is decidedly mixed on their personal efforts to save the planet.

Majorities of Americans say:

- Legislation is necessary to insure that businesses protect the environment (76 percent);

- People themselves should also be regulated to insure that they protect the environment (57 percent);

- Science alone cannot solve environmental problems (54 percent);

- If human lives are at stake, the use of animals in medical testing is acceptable (63 percent).

There is less agreement on how much people are willing to sacrifice for the environment. Pluralities say they:

- Would pay much higher prices to protect the environment (45 percent);

- Would not pay higher taxes (43 percent);

- Are "not very" or "not at all" willing to accept a lower standard of living to protect the environment (43 percent).

Personal efforts on behalf of the environment are mixed.

- A large majority recycle at least some of the time (87 percent).

- Well over half (61 percent) choose organic foods sometimes.

- But only 37 percent cut back on driving even occasionally for environmental reasons.

- Even fewer (30 percent) make any effort to avoid eating meat for environmental or moral reasons.

Men and Women Agree About Protecting the Earth

Women are slightly more concerned about protecting the environment than men, though on most questions the sexes are in strong agreement. Similar percentages say they:

- Do not believe science will find a painless solution to environmental problems (54 percent of men and 53 percent of women);

- Would be willing to pay higher prices to protect the environment (45 percent of both men and women);

- Aren't ready to accept a lower standard of living in order to protect the environment (44 percent of men and 43 percent of women);

- Would rather not pay higher taxes, even to protect the environment (44 percent of men and 41 percent of women);

- Prefer to see the environment protected by laws rather than simply the good intentions of ordinary citizens (58 percent of men and 55 percent of women);

- Would not leave it up to businesses to decide what's best for the environment (79 percent of men and 73 percent of women);

- Recycle at least sometimes (88 percent of men and 86 percent of women);

- Don't think "save the planet" when going somewhere (67 percent of men and 61 percent of women say they never cut back on driving for the good of the environment).

There are a few areas where the sexes disagree:

- Women are more likely to buy organic produce (65 percent of women, but only 56 percent of men do so at least occasionally);

- While 36 percent of women sometimes avoid eating meat for moral or environmental reasons, this is true for only 23 percent of men;

- While 71 percent of men agree that it is OK to use animals to test potentially life-saving medicine, only 57 percent of women agree.

Blacks and Whites Differ on "Pocketbook" Issues

Blacks and whites agree that environmental regulation is necessary for business and the general public. But there is less agreement on the way to do this.

- A majority of whites (57 percent) and about half of blacks (48 percent) believe "the government should pass laws to make ordinary people protect the environment." Blacks are more likely than whites, however, to say they "can't choose" (27 versus 19 percent).

- A slightly larger percentage of whites (79 percent) than blacks (73 percent) feel the government should pass laws to insure that businesses are good environmental stewards.

- Black Americans are only slightly more confident than whites that science can solve environmental problems (18 percent of whites, compared with 24 percent of blacks).

- Similar percentages of blacks and whites say it is OK to use animals in medical testing that might save human lives (61 percent of blacks and 64 percent of whites).

Black Americans, on average, have lower incomes than whites. So it is not surprising that there are differences of opinion on pocketbook issues. Blacks are:

- Considerably less willing to "pay much higher prices" to protect the environment (37 percent of blacks compared with 47 percent of whites say they are "very" or "fairly" willing);

- Less likely to say they are willing to pay higher taxes (24 percent of blacks and 35 percent of whites);

- Somewhat less likely to accept a lower standard of living in exchange for a better environment (24 percent of blacks and 32 percent of whites).

There are some differences between blacks and whites in behavior as well as attitudes. Whites are "greener" when it comes to driving less and recycling, but blacks score higher on meatless and organic diets.

- Thirty-eight percent of whites and 25 percent of blacks cut back on driving for environmental reasons at least some of the time.

- A substantial 65 percent of whites, but only 43 percent of blacks, say they always or often recycle. However, the gap is smaller when those who recycle at least some of the time are included: 88 percent of whites and 80 percent of blacks.

- Blacks are somewhat more likely than whites to seek out organic produce (66 percent of blacks buy organic at least some of the time, compared with 59 percent of whites).

- Thirty-seven percent of blacks and 27 percent of whites say they at least sometimes "refuse to eat meat for moral or environmental reasons."

Trends by Generation Not Apparent

Generational trends are less evident on environmental issues than on many others. The age groups tend to agree on most environmental questions, although one or two age groups stand apart from the crowd on some issues.

- A plurality of all age groups (41 to 46 percent) are not willing to accept a lower standard of living to benefit the environment.

- Similarly, pluralities of Americans aged 30 or older (42 to 48 percent) would not be willing to pay much higher taxes to protect the environment. But only 36 percent of 18-to-29-year-olds are not willing to pay much higher taxes to protect the environment.

- People under age 30 are slightly less likely to recycle at least some of the time (83 percent), compared with older Americans (87 to 91 percent).

- Most age groups are in rough agreement on the likelihood of science saving the environment. People in their 40s are the most pessimistic, with only 12 percent believing "science will solve our environmental problems with little change to our way of life."

- Opposition to using animals in medical testing shows some generational trend. Twenty-one percent of people under age 30 are opposed, compared with 17 to 19 percent of people aged 30 to 59 and 14 to 15 percent of those aged 60 or older.

- There is some generational difference of opinion on whether or not laws are necessary to protect the environment. Younger generations are more likely to favor regulation of businesses, especially people in their 30s.

- Younger generations are also more likely to favor laws to "make ordinary people protect the environment" (56 to 60 percent of people under age 60, compared with 48 percent of those aged 70 or older).

- Those most willing to pay higher prices to protect the environment are Americans under age 40 and those in their 60s (47 to 50 percent). Only 41 to 43 percent of other age groups agree.

- The middle-aged are most likely to buy organic produce at least some of the time. Sixty-four to 67 percent of people aged 40 to 69 say they sometimes buy organic, compared with 57 to 58 percent of people under age 40 or aged 70 or older.

- The youngest and oldest Americans are most likely to say they never skip eating meat for environmental reasons—72 to 73 percent of people under age 30 or aged 70 or older, compared with 64 to 69 percent of other age groups.

- Least likely to cut back on driving for environmental reasons are Americans aged 70 or older. Most likely are people in their 40s and those in their 60s (42 to 43 percent say they do so at least sometimes).

Higher Education Makes a Greener Citizen

There is a strong relationship between education and environmental attitudes and behavior. Those with at least a bachelor's degree are most likely to:

- Accept a lower standard of living for the good of the environment (38 to 39 percent of people with at least a bachelor's degree, compared with 25 to 29 percent of those without a college degree);

- Be willing to pay higher taxes (41 to 48 percent of college graduates, versus 28 to 30 percent of those without a college degree);

- Be willing to pay higher prices (54 to 55 percent of college graduates compared with 41 to 42 percent of those without a degree);

- Think it's OK to use animals in medical testing (three-quarters of college graduates, 61 percent of high school graduates, and 54 percent of those without a high school diploma);

- At least occasionally cut back on their driving for environmental reasons (50 percent of graduate degree holders, 43 percent of those with a bachelor's degree, and 33 to 35 percent of those with a high school diploma or less);

- Recycle at least sometimes (94 percent of those with a college degree, versus 76 to 88 percent of those with less education);

- Skip meat occasionally for moral or environmental reasons (41 percent of people with graduate degrees, compared with 23 to 31 percent of others);

- Favor environmental regulation of businesses (84 to 85 percent of college graduates, 77 percent of high school graduates, and 57 percent of people who did not graduate from high school);

- Favor environmental regulation of the public (from 76 percent of graduate degree holders to only 41 percent of those without a high school diploma);

- Believe science will not be able to solve environmental problems (ranging from 70 percent of graduate degree holders to 42 percent of those without a high school diploma).

Higher Prices to Protect the Environment

A substantial percentage of Americans say they are willing to pay higher prices to protect the environment. A plurality of 45 percent would pay more; only 26 percent say they are not very or not at all willing to pay more.

Men and women are in agreement on this issue, but there are large differences by race, age, and education. Only 37 percent of blacks, compared with 47 percent of whites, would be willing to pay more for the environment's sake. The youngest adults (aged 18 to 29) are considerably more likely than the oldest (aged 70 or older) to say they would accept higher prices. The largest gap is between college graduates and those without college degrees. Over half of college graduates, but only 40 to 41 percent of people with a high school diploma or less, are willing to pay higher prices.

Those most likely to say they are not willing to pay higher prices—blacks, the elderly, and people who have not completed college—also have the lowest incomes. Their unwillingness to pay may reflect financial worries more than a lack of concern for the environment.

Higher Prices to Protect the Environment, 1994

"How willing would you be to pay much higher prices in order to protect the environment?"

(percent responding by sex, race, age, and education, 1994)

	very willing	fairly willing	neither	not very willing	not at all	very or fairly willing	not very or not at all willing
Total	8%	37%	24%	17%	9%	45%	26%
Women	9	36	24	17	9	45	26
Men	8	37	24	18	10	45	28
Black	5	32	22	19	15	37	34
White	9	38	24	17	8	47	25
Aged 18 to 29	9	41	24	18	7	50	25
Aged 30 to 39	7	40	27	14	9	47	23
Aged 40 to 49	9	34	27	19	8	43	27
Aged 50 to 59	10	33	23	18	12	43	30
Aged 60 to 69	11	36	20	17	12	47	29
Aged 70 or older	8	33	16	18	11	41	29
Not a high school graduate	8	32	21	16	14	40	30
High school graduate	6	35	24	18	11	41	29
Bachelor's degree	12	43	23	16	3	55	19
Graduate degree	16	38	28	13	4	54	17

Note: Percents may not add to 100 because "can't choose" and no answer are not included.
Source: General Social Survey, National Opinion Research Center, University of Chicago
University of Chicago

Higher Taxes to Protect the Environment

Since most Americans feel their tax bill is already too high, it isn't surprising that only one-third would pay higher taxes to protect the environment. There are some standouts—most notably, those with the highest level of education.

By sex and age, Americans are more or less in agreement on this question, with the exception of people aged 70 or older. The oldest age group is slightly less likely than average to favor higher taxes to protect the environment. There is greater divergence of opinion between blacks and whites, with whites 11 percentage points more likely than blacks to say they would be willing to add to their tax bill for the sake of the environment.

The biggest difference is by education. Nearly half (48 percent) of people with graduate degrees would be willing to pay additional taxes for environmental protection, compared with only 28 percent of people without a high school diploma.

Higher Taxes to Protect the Environment, 1994

"How willing would you be to pay much higher taxes in order to protect the environment? "

(percent responding by sex, race, age, and eudcation, 1994)

	very willing	fairly willing	neither	not very willing	not at all willing	very or fairly willing	not very or not at all willing
Total	6%	28%	21%	26%	17%	34%	43%
Women	5	29	20	26	15	34	41
Men	6	26	21	26	18	32	44
Black	4	20	21	27	22	24	49
White	6	29	20	26	16	35	42
Aged 18 to 29	6	30	26	26	10	36	36
Aged 30 to 39	5	28	23	26	16	33	42
Aged 40 to 49	7	26	21	25	18	33	43
Aged 50 to 59	4	27	17	29	19	31	48
Aged 60 to 69	8	27	20	22	20	35	42
Aged 70 or older	3	26	14	26	19	29	45
Not a high school graduate	5	23	19	24	22	28	46
High school graduate	5	25	21	28	18	30	46
Bachelor's degree	7	34	21	28	8	41	36
Graduate degree	8	40	22	18	12	48	30

Note: Percents may not add to 100 because "can't choose" and no answer are not included.
Source: General Social Survey, National Opinion Research Center, University of Chicago

Lower Standard of Living to Protect the Environment

Americans have one of the highest standards of living in the world, and we're not about to give it up anytime soon. A plurality (43 percent) of Americans would not accept a lower standard of living in order to protect the environment. Only three in ten would.

There is an 8 percentage point gap between whites and blacks on this issue, with whites more likely to say they would accept a lower standard of living to protect the environment. Blacks, whose incomes are already low compared to whites, are not willing to see their living standard erode. Fifty-five percent say they are "not very" or "not at all" willing to lower their standard of living for the environment.

There is little difference of opinion by sex or age. The biggest disagreement on this issue is by education. Between people without a high school diploma and graduate degree holders, there is a 14 percentage point gap in the share who are willing to accept a lower standard of living to protect the environment. Agreement is lowest among people who did not complete high school (25 percent), higher among those with a high school diploma (29 percent), and highest among people with at least a bachelor's degree (38 to 39 percent).

Lower Standard of Living to Protect the Environment, 1994

"How willing would you be to accept cuts in your standard of living in order to protect the environment?"

(percent responding by sex, race, age, and education, 1994)

	very willing	fairly willing	neither	not very willing	not at all willing	very or fairly willing	not very or not at all willing
Total	4%	26%	22%	28%	15%	30%	43%
Women	5	27	21	28	15	32	43
Men	3	25	24	28	16	28	44
Black	4	20	15	29	26	24	55
White	4	28	23	28	14	32	42
Aged 18 to 29	3	29	20	32	13	32	45
Aged 30 to 39	3	25	25	30	14	28	44
Aged 40 to 49	5	27	23	28	15	32	43
Aged 50 to 59	7	26	21	25	18	33	43
Aged 60 to 69	5	22	29	22	19	27	41
Aged 70 or older	1	28	13	30	16	29	46
Not a high school graduate	4	21	20	23	25	25	48
High school graduate	4	25	22	30	16	29	46
Bachelor's degree	5	33	23	28	9	38	37
Graduate degree	7	32	32	22	6	39	28

Note: Percents may not add to 100 because "can't choose" and no answer are not included.
Source: General Social Survey, National Opinion Research Center, University of Chicago

Environmental Regulation of the Public

Given a choice between leaving it up to ordinary people to decide how best to protect the environment or passing laws to make sure they do, a slim majority of Americans (57 percent) favor the legal route. Only 21 percent would leave it up to the average person; 20 percent say they can't choose.

Men and women and blacks and whites are in agreement on this question, although blacks are slightly more likely than whites to say they can't choose, and slightly less likely to say laws are necessary.

People under age 40 are a bit less likely than their elders to favor leaving it up to the average person to figure out how to protect the environment (only 16 percent of people under age 40 want to leave it up to the average person, compared with 22 to 24 percent of those aged 40 or older). While 56 to 60 percent of people under age 60 favor passing laws to insure that the public protects the environment, the proportion drops to 54 percent among people in their 60s and to less than half (48 percent) among people aged 70 or older.

By far, the largest disagreement is found by education. Three-quarters of people with graduate degrees and two-thirds of those with bachelor's degrees favor passing laws rather than leaving environmental protection up to individuals. Only 56 percent of high school graduates and 41 percent of those without a high school diploma agree.

Environmental Regulation of the Public, 1994

"If you had to choose, which one of the following would be closest to your views? 1) Government should let ordinary people decide for themselves how to protect the environment, even if it means they don't always do the right thing, or 2) Government should pass laws to make ordinary people protect the environment, even if it interferes with people's right to make their own decisions."

(percent responding by sex, race, age, and education, 1994)

	let people decide	government pass laws	can't choose
Total	21%	57%	20%
Women	21	55	21
Men	20	58	19
Black	20	48	27
White	21	57	19
Aged 18 to 29	16	56	26
Aged 30 to 39	17	60	21
Aged 40 to 49	24	60	12
Aged 50 to 59	24	56	17
Aged 60 to 69	22	54	23
Aged 70 or older	23	48	24
Not a high school graduate	26	41	27
High school graduate	21	56	21
Bachelor's degree	17	66	16
Graduate degree	14	76	9

Note: Percents may not add to 100 because "can't choose" and no answer are not included.
Source: General Social Survey, National Opinion Research Center, University of Chicago

Environmental Regulation of Business

Americans have more confidence in the public than in business when it comes to protecting the environment. Over three-quarters say "the government should pass laws to make businesses protect the environment, even if it interferes with businesses' right to make their own decisions."

While strong majorities of all demographic segments agree with the need for government regulation, there are slight differences in opinion between women and men, blacks and whites. There is substantial disagreement by age and education.

Baby boomers (aged 30 to 49) and people in their 50s are more likely than other age groups to say laws are needed. Thirtysomethings feel most strongly that laws are needed (82 percent). Older boomers are the least ambivalent, with only 7 percent saying they "can't choose." Substantial portions of other age groups have a hard time choosing which view represents their opinion.

The smallest percentage of people who favor environmental laws regulating business is found among those without a high school diploma. This segment is also most likely to say it "can't choose." Those with the most education are least likely to say they can't choose. From 84 to 85 percent of people with college degrees believe government regulation of business is necessary to protect the environment.

Environmental Regulation of Business, 1994

"If you had to choose, which one of the following would be closest to your views? 1) Government should let businesses decide for themselves how to protect the environment, even if it means they don't always do the right thing, or 2) Government should pass laws to make businesses protect the environment, even if it interferes with businesses' right to make their own decisions."

(percent responding by sex, race, age, and education, 1994)

	let businesses decide	government pass laws	can't choose
Total	9%	76%	13%
Women	10	73	14
Men	8	79	11
Black	10	68	16
White	9	77	12
Aged 18 to 29	8	73	17
Aged 30 to 39	6	82	11
Aged 40 to 49	12	78	7
Aged 50 to 59	8	77	11
Aged 60 to 69	11	70	17
Aged 70 or older	13	64	18
Not a high school graduate	16	57	20
High school graduate	7	77	13
Bachelor's degree	7	84	9
Graduate degree	10	85	5

Note: Percents may not add to 100 because "can't choose" and no answer are not included.
Source: General Social Survey, National Opinion Research Center, University of Chicago

Will Science Save Us?

Despite a century of scientific progress, a majority of Americans (54 percent) do not believe "science will solve our environmental problems with little change to our way of life."

As is the case with most environmental questions, men and women are in agreement. Blacks are only slightly more likely than whites to believe science will save the day (24 percent of blacks and 18 percent of whites).

Most age groups are in agreement on this question, with one exception. Older boomers (aged 40 to 49) are the least likely of all age groups to believe science can painlessly solve our environmental problems (12 percent). Those aged 70 or older have the most faith in science; one-quarter believe science will ultimately save the day.

Baby boomers are the best-educated segment of the population, while older Americans are the least educated, and education plays an important role in determining attitudes on this question. While 24 percent of people who did not complete high school believe science will find the answer, only 11 percent of people with graduate degrees (the scientists themselves) agree.

Will Science Save Us? 1994

"How much do you agree or disagree: Modern science will solve our environmental problems with little change to our way of life."

(percent responding by sex, race, age, and education, 1994)

	agree strongly	agree	neither agree nor disagree	disagree	disagree strongly	agree, total	disagree, total
Total	2%	17%	22%	42%	12%	19%	54%
Women	2	16	22	41	12	18	53
Men	2	18	21	43	11	20	54
Black	2	22	24	34	8	24	42
White	2	16	21	43	12	18	55
Aged 18 to 29	3	17	28	37	11	20	48
Aged 30 to 39	1	18	25	42	10	19	52
Aged 40 to 49	1	11	21	48	14	12	62
Aged 50 to 59	3	17	18	37	16	20	53
Aged 60 to 69	3	16	16	47	8	19	55
Aged 70 or older	2	23	15	36	9	25	45
Not a high school graduate	5	19	17	34	8	24	42
High school graduate	2	19	23	41	10	21	51
Bachelor's degree	1	12	20	48	15	13	63
Graduate degree	1	10	17	53	17	11	70

Note: Percents may not add to 100 because "can't choose" and no answer are not included.
Source: General Social Survey, National Opinion Research Center, University of Chicago

Medical Testing on Animals

The proliferation of products that advertise "not tested on animals" is a sign of a growing desire among Americans to avoid inflicting unnecessary pain and suffering on animals. But when it comes to medical research that might save human lives, a majority (63 percent) of Americans are supportive.

While black and white Americans are in agreement on this issue (61 percent of blacks and 64 percent of whites), men and women stand apart. Fully 71 percent of men, but only 57 percent of women, agree that it is OK to use animals in medical tests.

The youngest adults are less supportive than others. Only 57 percent of people under age 30, compared with 62 to 68 percent of their elders, support using animals in medical tests.

People with at least a bachelor's degree are more inclined to favor using animals in medical tests than are people with less education. While only 54 percent of people without a high school diploma and 61 percent of high school graduates support medical testing, about three-quarters of those with at least a bachelor's degree are supportive.

Medical Testing on Animals, 1994

"How much do you agree or disagree: It is right to use animals for medical testing if it might save human lives."

(percent responding by sex, race, age, and education, 1994)

	agree strongly	agree	neither agree nor disagree	disagree	disagree strongly	agree, total	disagree, total
Total	14%	49%	15%	12%	6%	63%	18%
Women	11	46	17	13	8	57	21
Men	17	54	13	10	4	71	14
Black	11	50	14	15	4	61	19
White	14	50	15	11	6	64	17
Aged 18 to 29	12	45	19	13	8	57	21
Aged 30 to 39	12	51	15	12	5	63	17
Aged 40 to 49	12	53	14	13	6	65	19
Aged 50 to 59	16	46	16	11	6	62	17
Aged 60 to 69	16	52	13	8	6	68	14
Aged 70 or older	16	47	11	11	4	63	15
Not a high school graduate	13	41	17	14	5	54	19
High school graduate	13	48	16	13	7	61	20
Bachelor's degree	15	60	12	7	4	75	11
Graduate degree	19	55	10	8	6	74	14

Note: Percents may not add to 100 because "can't choose" and no answer are not included.
Source: General Social Survey, National Opinion Research Center, University of Chicago

Recycling

Most Americans seem to have learned at least one of the three R's of ecology (reduce, reuse, recycle). Fully 87 percent of adults in communities with recycling say they at least sometimes recycle; 61 percent say they recycle always or often. Only 13 percent say they never recycle.

About the same percentage of women and men recycle. Blacks are considerably less likely to always or often recycle than are whites (43 percent compared with 65 percent). But a substantial percentage of blacks say they recycle sometimes, so that the gap is much smaller among those who say they never recycle.

In spite of their green reputation, younger generations are less likely than their elders to recycle. Only half of people under age 30 always or often recycle. The proportion rises with age to more than 70 percent of people aged 60 or older saying they recycle always or often.

People with at least a bachelor's degree are far more likely to recycle than those with lower levels of education. Fully 94 percent of the best-educated Americans say they recycle at least sometimes, compared with 76 to 88 percent of those with less education.

Recycling, 1994

"How often do you make a special effort to sort glass or cans or plastic or papers and so on for recycling?"

(percent responding by sex, race, age, and education, 1994)

	always	often	sometimes	never	at least some-times	never
Total	36%	25%	26%	13%	87%	13%
Women	39	24	23	14	86	14
Men	33	26	29	12	88	12
Black	21	22	37	20	80	20
White	39	26	23	12	88	12
Aged 18 to 29	23	26	34	18	83	18
Aged 30 to 39	33	23	27	17	83	17
Aged 40 to 49	40	26	24	9	90	9
Aged 50 to 59	35	30	26	9	91	9
Aged 60 to 69	49	23	18	10	90	10
Aged 70 or older	49	20	18	12	87	12
Not a high school graduate	36	16	24	24	76	24
High school graduate	31	27	30	13	88	13
Bachelor's degree	47	31	16	6	94	6
Graduate degree	59	22	13	6	94	6

Note: Percentages were calculated after excluding respondents who indicated that recycling was not available where they live. Between 1 and 6 percent of respondents indicated that recycling was not available.
Source: General Social Survey, National Opinion Research Center, University of Chicago

Organic Food

Organic produce, once found only in health food stores, is now common in large supermarkets throughout the country. It's easy to see why: over half of adults who have organic produce available where they live say they make an effort to buy organic at least some of the time. Sixty-one percent of Americans say they look for organic food at least sometimes. Only 39 percent say they never do.

Women are more likely than men to say they look for fruits and vegetables grown without chemicals. (Women are also more likely to be the family food shoppers.) Almost two-thirds of women and 56 percent of men say they at least sometimes try to buy organic produce.

Blacks are slightly more likely than whites to buy organic, with only 34 percent saying they never buy organics, compared with 41 percent of whites.

The proportion of people who at least sometimes buy organic produce rises with age, from 57 to 58 percent of people under age 30 to a high of 64 to 67 percent among those aged 30 to 69. Only 57 percent of people aged 70 or older buy organic produce.

By education, those with the highest level of attainment are least likely to buy organics. Fifty-seven percent of people with graduate degrees, versus 62 to 63 percent of the rest of the population, say they try to buy organic food at least sometimes. These percentages exclude the 5 to 16 percent of the population who say organic produce is not available where they live. People who did not complete high school are most likely to say organic produce is not available (16 percent). It is not known how many more people would buy organic produce if it were available, or even if all respondents understood what is meant by the term "organic."

Organic Food, 1994

"How often do you make a special effort to buy fruits and vegetables grown without pesticides or chemicals?"

(percent responding by sex, race, age, and education, 1994)

	always	often	sometimes	never	at least some- times	never
Total	9%	18%	34%	39%	61%	39%
Women	11	20	34	35	65	35
Men	7	15	34	44	56	44
Black	10	20	36	34	66	34
White	9	17	33	41	59	41
Aged 18 to 29	6	16	35	44	57	44
Aged 30 to 39	6	16	36	42	58	42
Aged 40 to 49	10	19	37	34	66	34
Aged 50 to 59	10	23	34	33	67	33
Aged 60 to 69	16	22	26	35	64	35
Aged 70 or older	13	15	29	44	57	44
Not a high school graduate	12	17	33	39	62	39
High school graduate	9	19	35	38	63	38
Bachelor's degree	8	16	38	38	62	38
Graduate degree	13	15	29	44	57	44

Note: Percentages were calculated after excluding no answer and respondents who indicated that organic produce was not available where they live. Between 5 and 16 percent of respondents indicated organic produce was not available.
Source: General Social Survey, National Opinion Research Center, University of Chicago

Drive Less Often

Recycling is one thing, but doing without a car is quite another. Among Americans who drive or who have vehicles available to them, few say they always or often cut back on driving to protect the environment. Nearly two-thirds say they never do.

Women are slightly more likely than men to find alternate transportation at least some of the time. Whites are more likely than blacks to leave the car at home for the sake of the environment.

There is also some variation by age. Most likely of all age groups to say they never give up their car for environmental reasons are the oldest Americans, many of whom may find it physically difficult to use another means of transportation.

Education, however, seems to play a role—as it does on virtually every environmental question. Those with higher levels of education are more likely to say they drive less for the sake of the environment.

It is important to note that substantial proportions of the population do not drive or do not have a vehicle available to them. This includes one in five people who did not complete high school, 13 to 16 percent of people aged 60 or older, and 13 percent of blacks.

Drive Less Often, 1994

"How often do you cut back on driving a car for environmental reasons?"

(percent responding by sex, race, age, and education, 1994)

	always	often	sometimes	never	at least some-times	never
Total	2%	6%	29%	64%	37%	64%
Women	2	7	30	61	39	61
Men	1	5	27	67	33	67
Black	2	6	17	75	25	75
White	2	6	30	63	38	63
Aged 18 to 29	2	5	28	65	35	65
Aged 30 to 39	2	4	27	66	33	66
Aged 40 to 49	1	8	33	57	42	57
Aged 50 to 59	1	5	30	64	36	64
Aged 60 to 69	2	9	32	57	43	57
Aged 70 or older	0	7	21	72	28	72
Not a high school graduate	4	6	25	66	35	66
High school graduate	1	5	27	66	33	66
Bachelor's degree	1	8	34	57	43	57
Graduate degree	2	9	39	50	50	50

Note: Percentages were calculated after excluding no answer and respondents who did not have a vehicle or do not drive. Between 4 and 20 percent of respondents indicated that they do not drive or do not have a vehicle.
Source: General Social Survey, National Opinion Research Center, University of Chicago

Vegetarians

We are a nation of meat eaters. Fully 69 percent of Americans say they never "refuse to eat meat for moral or environmental reasons." (They still may skip eating meat for health reasons, however.)

Women are considerably more likely to refuse to eat meat than men, and blacks more likely to do so than whites. Over one-third of women, but only 23 percent of men, sometimes avoid meat. Thirty-seven percent of blacks compared with 27 percent of whites sometimes don't eat meat for environmental or moral reasons.

In spite of occasional stories in the media about vegetarianism among young adults, this age group is least likely to pass on the meat course for moral or environmental reasons. Only 26 percent of people under age 30 say they at least occasionally refuse to eat meat.

The proportion of people who occasionally refuse to eat meat varies by education. Graduate degree holders are more likely to say they do this, while people whose education stopped with a bachelor's degree are less likely.

Vegetarians, 1994

"How often do you refuse to eat meat for moral or environmental reasons?"

(percent responding by sex, race, age, and education, 1994)

	always	often	sometimes	never	at least some-times	never
Total	3%	7%	20%	69%	30%	69%
Women	4	9	23	63	36	63
Men	2	5	16	75	23	75
Black	3	9	25	60	37	60
White	3	6	18	71	27	71
Aged 18 to 29	5	4	17	73	26	73
Aged 30 to 39	2	7	21	69	30	69
Aged 40 to 49	2	9	21	66	32	66
Aged 50 to 59	3	10	22	64	35	64
Aged 60 to 69	4	9	18	69	31	69
Aged 70 or older	3	4	16	72	23	72
Not a high school graduate	2	8	17	68	27	68
High school graduate	3	7	21	68	31	68
Bachelor's degree	2	5	16	76	23	76
Graduate degree	6	12	23	60	41	60

Note: Percents may not add to 100 because no answer is not included.
Source: General Social Survey, National Opinion Research Center, University of Chicago

CHAPTER

3

Race and Immigration

On racial issues, we are a nation divided—not just by race, but by sex, age, and educational attainment as well. And while people's attitudes about most of the racial issues examined here have changed substantially over the last two decades, gaps between groups remain. In some cases they are wider than ever before.

Americans are strongly united on only four of the racial and immigration issues presented in this chapter. Overwhelming majorities say they:

- Would vote for a qualified black presidential candidate nominated by their party (87 percent);

- Fear more immigrants will lead to higher unemployment (85 percent);

- Do not believe interracial marriage should be illegal (84 percent);

- Do not believe blacks have worse jobs, housing, and incomes because they have less in-born ability to learn (83 percent).

On other race and immigration issues there is less agreement. Smaller majorities say they:

- Would vote for laws preventing homeowners from refusing to sell to someone because of his or her race (62 percent);

- Would try to change the rules of a segregated private club (60 percent);

- Are opposed to busing (63 percent);

- Believe the number of immigrants allowed into the U.S. should be decreased (62 percent);

- Think more immigrants will make it difficult to keep the country united (68 percent);

- Do not believe more immigrants will lead to higher economic growth (62 percent);

- Believe English should be the official language (60 percent);

- Favor bilingual education (64 percent);

- Believe election ballots should be printed in languages other than English (61 percent).

The responses to the remaining race issues reveal a divided country. Americans are strongly split on whether or not blacks are disadvantaged because of :

- Discrimination (41 percent say yes and 54 percent say no);

- Lack of a chance for education (49 percent say yes and 47 percent say no);

- Or a lack of will or motivation (49 percent say yes, 45 percent say no).

In addition, a surprisingly large number of people:

- Agree slightly or strongly (41 percent) that "blacks shouldn't push where they are not wanted." Fifty-five percent disagree with this statement.

Some Disagreement Between the Sexes

In general, women are slightly more liberal than men, but on most of the race and immigration questions, the sexes are fairly close in their opinions. Similar percentages of women and men say:

- Interracial marriage should not be illegal (83 percent of women and 86 percent of men);

- Homeowners should not be allowed to refuse to sell their homes to someone on the basis of race (64 percent of women and 61 percent of men);

- They would vote for a black presidential candidate (89 percent of women and 85 percent of men);

- They oppose busing (63 percent of women and 62 percent of men);

- The number of legal immigrants to this country should be decreased (62 percent of both women and men);

- Unemployment will probably increase if the country must absorb more immigrants (84 percent of women and 87 percent of men);

- More immigrants will make it harder to keep the nation united (68 percent of women and 67 percent of men).

Men and women are also fairly close in their assessments of why blacks, on average, have worse jobs, income, and housing than whites.

- Only 12 percent of women and 14 percent of men believe it is due to less innate ability on the part of blacks.

- Forty-seven percent of women and 51 percent of men say the cause is lack of will or motivation.

- Fifty-one percent of women and 46 percent of men say the lack of educational opportunity is the cause.

- They differ in one respect, however. Forty-three percent of women say it is due to discrimination, compared with 37 percent of men.

On the remaining questions a gender gap is apparent.

- Men are 10 percentage points more likely to agree strongly or slightly that "blacks shouldn't push themselves where they're not wanted." Forty-seven percent of men agree compared with 37 percent of women.

- Women are considerably more likely than men to say they would try to change the rules of a segregated social club (64 percent compared with 54 percent).

- Men are more likely to believe government business should be conducted in English only (64 percent of men versus 57 percent of women).

- About two-thirds of men, compared with 59 percent of women, say higher economic growth is not likely to result from an influx of immigrants.

- More women (65 percent) than men (56 percent) feel that election ballots should be available in languages other than English.

- Women are also more likely to favor bilingual education (68 percent of women compared with 60 percent of men).

Blacks and Whites Are Miles Apart

Blacks and whites disagree on most of the racial issues probed by the General Social Survey. On many questions, the opinions of blacks and whites have actually grown further apart over the years.

On only four issues do the opinions of blacks and whites not differ substantially.

- The same percentage of blacks and whites (60 percent) say they would try to change the rules of their segregated social club to allow members of the other race to join. But in this case, they have met in the middle over time, with the percentage of whites who agree increasing and the percentage of blacks who agree decreasing over the years.

- A majority of both races want to decrease immigration (61 percent of blacks and 64 percent of whites).

- Strong majorities of blacks (85 percent) and whites (86 percent) believe more immigrants will result in higher unemployment.

- Similar percentages of blacks and whites believe that socio-economic differences result from blacks' having "less ability to learn" (13 percent of whites and 10 percent of blacks).

But on other racial issues, it is apparent that strong differences of opinion between the races persist.

- Whites are more likely than blacks to say "blacks shouldn't push where they aren't wanted" (43 percent of whites compared with 31 percent of blacks).

- Virtually all blacks (98 percent) would vote for a black presidential candidate, but only 86 percent of whites say they would.

- Only 3 percent of blacks, but 15 percent of whites, would like to see laws against interracial marriage.

- Considerably more blacks than whites would support a law that would prevent a homeowner from refusing to sell on the basis of race (76 percent of blacks and 59 percent of whites).

- There is a large gap between blacks and whites on whether English should be the nation's official language. Sixty-four percent of whites, but only 45 percent of blacks, agree.

- Seventy-five percent of blacks, but only 62 percent of whites, favor bilingual education.

- There is also a gap when it comes to whether or not higher levels of immigration will make it more difficult to keep the country united. Nearly three-quarters of blacks, compared with two-thirds of whites, think it will be more difficult.

- Far more blacks (40 percent) than whites (27 percent) believe more immigrants are likely to produce higher economic growth.

- Fully 73 percent of blacks, but only 58 percent of whites, believe ballots should be printed in languages other than English.

- A majority of blacks (58 percent), but only a small minority of whites (27 percent), are in favor of busing.

- Whites and blacks differ sharply on the reasons for the differences in the socioeconomic conditions of blacks and whites. Half (51 percent) of whites, but only 29 percent of blacks, say it is because of a lack of will or motivation.

- Fully 77 percent of blacks, but only 34 percent of whites, blame discrimination.

- For both races, lack of education is the second most likely reason cited for the lower socioeconomic status of blacks. Fifty-nine percent of blacks and 47 percent of whites agree that this is the reason.

An Enduring Generation Gap

It is important to note when examining attitudes by age that each successive age group is more racially diverse. Fully 85 percent of people aged 65 or older are white, compared with only about 70 percent of people in their 20s. Within younger generations, whites do not have the numerical dominance that they do among older generations. In addition, the attitudes of young whites are influenced by the greater diversity of their peer group.

Whatever the reasons, people of different ages see things differently when it comes to questions about race. An attitudinal dividing line appears around age 50. Those above this line are members of the "Swing" and World War II generations. Below the line are baby boomers and members of Generation X. This is the "generation gap" that first became apparent in the 1960s and still persists today.

On several questions, people of different ages more or less agree. The generations find more common ground on immigration than they do on other race issues.

- Among different age groups, 35 to 46 percent say discrimination is the reason for blacks' lower socioeconomic status.

- Likewise, the percentage who cite lack of education as the reason ranges narrowly from 45 to 52 percent.

- There is not much variation in the percentage of people by age who want to decrease immigration levels (61 to 65 percent), with the exception of people under age 30 (57 percent).

- A majority of all age groups believe it will be harder to keep the country united if more immigrants come to the U.S. (62 to 73 percent).

- The generations agree that higher unemployment is likely if the nation absorbs more immigrants (82 to 89 percent of people under age 70). A smaller majority of those aged 70 or older agree (72 percent), but 11 percent of this group say they don't know.

There are, however, some wide differences of opinion by age.

- The question of whether blacks should not "push where they aren't wanted" shows a clear trend: each older age group is more likely to agree with the statement (from 30 percent of people aged 18 to 29 to 62 percent of those aged 70 or older).

- The percentage of people who favor busing generally falls with age, with the largest percentage of supporters in the 18-to-29 age group (41 percent) and the smallest percentage in the 60-to-69 age group (28 percent).

- Older age groups are more likely to favor making English the official language. Only 49 percent of the youngest age group support, this versus 77 percent of those aged 60 to 69.

- Younger Americans are more likely to support bilingual education (71 to 75 percent of people aged 18 to 39, compared with only half of those aged 70 or older).

- Younger generations also show more support for election ballots in languages other than English. The highest support is found among people under age 30 (70 percent) and the lowest among those aged 70 or older (42 percent).

On the issues described above, each ten-year age group is more (or less) likely to agree with the question. Other issues, however, reveal a single generational divide, with those under age 50 or 60 holding one opinion, while older Americans hold another.

- Traditional attitudes are apparent in the percentages of people who believe blacks have lower socioeconomic status because they have less ability to learn. Only 8 to 14 percent of people under age 60 believe this, versus 21 to 28 percent of those aged 60 or older.

- A majority (58 to 59 percent) of people aged 60 or older believe blacks' lower socioeconomic status results from a lack of will or motivation, compared with a minority (43 to 48 percent) of those under age 60.

- Similar proportions of people under age 50 say they would vote for a black presidential candidate. But from age 50 on, the proportion who would vote for a black candidate declines, with a sharp drop among those aged 70 or older.

- Fair housing laws are supported by 68 to 71 percent of people under age 50. But support declines above age 50, from 58 percent among those aged 50 to 59, to just 40 percent of those aged 70 or older.

- Fewer than 10 percent of people under age 50 believe interracial marriage should be illegal. The proportion rises from age 50 on, with 31 percent of people aged 70 or older saying it should be illegal.

- Between 62 and 68 percent of people under age 50 say they would try to change the membership rules of a segregated social club. But substantially fewer (from 49 to 54 percent) of those aged 50 or older would do so.

- Younger Americans are somewhat more likely to believe immigrants will boost the economy (34 to 35 percent of people under age 50 compared with 20 to 27 percent of people aged 50 or older).

The College-Educated Have Different Views

Education has a strong influence on attitudes toward race and immigration. It is important to remember that there is considerable overlap between age and education because younger generations are far better educated than older generations. Because of this overlap, it is not always clear whether education or age has a greater influence on attitudes toward race.

On some racial and immigration issues, education is not a clear predictor of attitudes.

- Roughly the same percentages of people favor busing, regardless of educational attainment (ranging from 30 to 34 percent).

- Regardless of education, similar percentages (61 to 67 percent) support bilingual education.

- There is also general agreement that election ballots should be available in languages other than English (60 to 66 percent).

- While there is some variation by educational level, there is no clear pattern in who favors making English the nation's official language. The lowest level of agreement is found among those with the most and least education.

- People who did not complete high school and those with graduate degrees are less likely to view immigrants as a threat to economic growth (48 and 49 percent compared with 68 percent of high school graduates and 63 percent of those with bachelor's degrees).

- The most- and-least educated are also slightly less concerned that immigrants will drive up unemployment figures (74 to 79 percent compared to 85 to 88 percent).

- There is also no clear direction in opinions regarding discrimination as a cause of the lower socioeconomic status of blacks.

On many questions, the college-educated are in the opposite camp from those with a high school diploma or less.

- Support for laws against interracial marriage is virtually nonexistent (3 to 4 percent) among people with college educations, but much greater among those with less education (ranging from 14 to 28 percent).

- With higher education comes greater support for fair housing laws. Support rises from slightly more than half (56 percent) among people without a high school diploma to 75 percent among graduate degree holders.

- Well-educated people are much more likely to say they would try to change the rules of a segregated private club (70 percent of people with college degrees, versus 49 percent of those who did not graduate from high school).

- Virtually everyone with a college degree says he or she would vote for a black presidential candidate, compared with 86 percent of people with only a high school diploma, and 79 percent of people who did not graduate from high school.

- Few of the college-educated say black people should not "push where they aren't wanted" (21 to 27 percent), but support for this position rises to 61 percent among those without a high school diploma.

- Most people who did not graduate from college believe immigration levels should be decreased (62 to 68 percent), but only a slim majority of people with bachelor's degrees (52 percent) and even fewer graduate degree holders (38 percent) agree.

- People with higher levels of education are more confident that immigrants will not divide the nation (35 to 48 percent of those with college degrees, compared with 17 to 23 percent of those with less education).

- The lower the level of education, the more likely people are to blame a lack of motivation for the lower socioeconomic status of blacks (58 percent of those without a high school diploma compared with 27 percent of graduate degree holders).

- People with higher levels of education are more likely to blame a lack of educational opportunity for the lower socioeconomic status of blacks (68 percent of those with graduate degrees compared with 42 percent of people who do not have high school diplomas).

- Few people with college degrees believe that blacks are disadvantaged because they have less innate ability (3 to 5 percent), but the percentage rises sharply among those with less education (15 percent of high school graduates and 23 percent of those who do not have a high school diploma).

Interracial Marriage

Regardless of whether they personally approve of marriage between people of different races, few Americans believe it should be illegal. Like other racial issues, opinions have changed in the past two decades so that even fewer support laws against interracial marriage today than did so in the 1970s.

About the same proportions of women and men said they would not support a law against interracial marriage in 1994. This was true in 1974 and 1984 as well.

Virtually no blacks, but 15 percent of whites, believe interracial marriage should be illegal. Blacks and whites were less likely in 1994 than in 1984 to think interracial marriage should be illegal. Older people are most likely to favor outlawing interracial marriage. Fewer than 10 percent of people under age 50 would outlaw interracial marriage, compared with 31 percent of those aged 70 or older.

The less education people have, the more likely they are to believe intermarriage should be illegal. The proportion of college graduates who think interracial marriage should be illegal has been small since 1974. The most significant change has been among those who did not graduate from high school. In 1974, over half of those who hadn't completed high school believed marriages between blacks and whites should be illegal, but the proportion with this attitude fell to 28 percent by 1994. The proportion of high school graduates who think interracial marriage should be illegal dropped from 28 to 14 percent between 1974 and 1994.

Interracial Marriage, 1994

"Do you think there should be laws against marriages between blacks and whites?"

(percent responding by sex, race, age, and education, 1994)

	yes	no
Total	13%	84%
Women	14	83
Men	13	86
Black	3	95
White	15	82
Aged 18 to 29	8	91
Aged 30 to 39	8	92
Aged 40 to 49	9	89
Aged 50 to 59	14	85
Aged 60 to 69	26	69
Aged 70 or older	31	60
Not a high school graduate	28	67
High school graduate	14	83
Bachelor's degree	3	97
Graduate degree	4	96

Note: Percents may not add to 100 because "don't know" and no answer are not included.
Source: General Social Survey, National Opinion Research Center, University of Chicago

Interracial Marriage, 1974 to 1994

"Do you think there should be laws against marriages between blacks and whites?"

(percent responding by sex, race, age, and education, 1974-94)

	yes			no		
	1994	*1984*	*1974*	*1994*	*1984*	*1974*
Total	13%	24%	34%	84%	70%	64%
Women	14	25	35	83	69	62
Men	13	22	32	86	73	66
Black	3	6	*	95	78	*
White	15	26	34	82	69	64
Aged 18 to 29	8	12	15	91	85	84
Aged 30 to 39	8	13	24	92	81	75
Aged 40 to 49	9	24	32	89	70	66
Aged 50 to 59	14	32	44	85	61	54
Aged 60 to 69	26	37	49	69	55	48
Aged 70 or older	31	46	65	60	43	29
Not a high school graduate	28	39	56	67	52	41
High school graduate	14	22	28	83	73	70
Bachelor's degree	3	7	8	97	90	92
Graduate degree	4	7	9	96	91	90

* Question not asked of blacks prior to 1980.
Note: Percents may not add to 100 because "don't know" and no answer are not included.
Source: General Social Survey, National Opinion Research Center, University of Chicago

Fair Housing Laws

In 1975, nearly two-thirds of whites believed a homeowner should have the right to refuse to sell a house to someone because of his or her race. By 1994, the proportion had dropped to one-third. While still a significant percentage, it is likely to drop further in the years ahead.

On this issue, people are more strongly divided by age than by sex, race, or education. As older generations die and are replaced by younger ones, the proportion of the total population that supports fair housing laws will rise. About half of people aged 70 or older think a homeowner should have the right to refuse to sell on the basis of race, versus fewer than 30 percent of people under age 50.

Men are slightly more likely than women to disagree with fair housing laws, although both sexes are more likely to support them than they were two decades ago. People with more education are more likely to favor fair housing laws. Support rises from only 56 percent among people who did not complete high school to 75 percent of those with graduate degrees.

Blacks are far more supportive of fair housing laws than whites. In 1975, a strong majority of whites (64 percent) felt it should be up to the owner (blacks were not asked about it that year). This proportion has fallen steadily over the years to just 35 percent in 1994. Only 26 percent of blacks favored leaving it up to the owner in 1978, a proportion that fell to 19 percent by 1994.

Fair Housing Laws, 1994

"Suppose there is a community-wide vote on the general housing issue. There are two possible laws to vote on. Which law would you vote for? 1) One law says that a homeowner can decide for himself whom to sell his house to, even if he prefers not to sell to blacks; 2) The second law says that a homeowner cannot refuse to sell to someone because of their race or color."

(percent responding by sex, race, age, and education, 1994)

	up to owner	can't refuse
Total	32%	62%
Women	31	64
Men	34	61
Black	19	76
White	35	59
Aged 18 to 29	27	70
Aged 30 to 39	25	71
Aged 40 to 49	28	68
Aged 50 to 59	37	58
Aged 60 to 69	42	50
Aged 70 or older	50	40
Not a high school graduate	36	56
High school graduate	33	62
Bachelor's degree	31	66
Graduate degree	22	75

Note: Percents may not add to 100 because "don't know," "neither," and no answer are not included.
Source: General Social Survey, National Opinion Research Center, University of Chicago

Fair Housing Laws, 1975 to 1994

"Suppose there is a community-wide vote on the general housing issue. There are two possible laws to vote on. Which law would you vote for? 1) One law says that a homeowner can decide for himself whom to sell his house to, even if he prefers not to sell to blacks; 2) the second law says that a homeowner cannot refuse to sell to someone because of their race or color."

(percent responding by sex, race, age, and education, 1975-94)

	up to owner			can't refuse		
	1994	*1984*	*1975*	*1994*	*1984*	*1975*
Total	32%	45%	64%	62%	51%	34%
Women	31	42	60	64	53	37
Men	34	49	68	61	48	30
Black	19	21	26*	76	72	71*
White	35	48	64	59	48	34
Aged 18 to 29	27	33	46	70	64	52
Aged 30 to 39	25	38	60	71	59	38
Aged 40 to 49	28	45	66	68	52	30
Aged 50 to 59	37	54	72	58	43	25
Aged 60 to 69	42	57	82	50	37	16
Aged 70 or older	50	64	74	40	27	21
Not a high school graduate	36	49	70	56	46	27
High school graduate	33	46	64	62	51	34
Bachelor's degree	31	42	51	66	55	48
Graduate degree	22	34	50	75	64	48

*Response is from 1978. This question was not asked of blacks prior to that year.
Note: Percents may not add to 100 because "don't know," "neither," and no answer are not included.
Source: General Social Survey, National Opinion Research Center, University of Chicago

Busing

Busing children between school districts to achieve racial balance has been controversial since it began. Throughout the years of the General Social Survey, a majority of the public have been opposed to busing. While there is less opposition today than in 1974, a majority still oppose busing.

People's opinions about busing differ little by sex or educational attainment. There is a large gap, however, in the opinions of whites and blacks. A majority of blacks (58 percent) favor busing. Among whites, support for busing has grown over the years, but in 1994 only 27 percent favored it.

A big difference is also found among people of different ages. Interestingly, younger respondents are far more in favor of busing than older respondents. People in their 20s and 30s, unlike their elders, actually experienced busing as a reality. Judging by their responses, they did not find it an overwhelmingly negative experience (41 percent favor it and 52 percent oppose it).

Busing, 1994

"In general, do you favor or oppose the busing of black and white school children from one school district to another?"

(percent responding by sex, race, age, and education, 1994)

	favor	*oppose*
Total	32%	63%
Women	32	63
Men	31	62
Black	58	39
White	27	67
Aged 18 to 29	41	52
Aged 30 to 39	34	60
Aged 40 to 49	30	66
Aged 50 to 59	30	66
Aged 60 to 69	20	74
Aged 70 or older	28	64
Not a high school graduate	34	57
High school graduate	30	65
Bachelor's degree	31	63
Graduate degree	34	60

Note: Percents may not add to 100 because "don't know" and no answer are not included.
Source: General Social Survey, National Opinion Research Center, University of Chicago

Busing, 1974 to 1994

"In general, do you favor or oppose the busing of black and white school children from one school district to another?"

(percent responding by sex, race, age, and education, 1974-94)

	favor			oppose		
	1994	**1985**	**1974**	**1994**	**1985**	**1974**
Total	32%	22%	20%	63%	75%	76%
Women	32	21	21	63	75	74
Men	31	22	19	62	75	78
Black	58	52	60	39	39	35
White	27	18	15	67	79	82
Aged 18 to 29	41	31	24	52	66	72
Aged 30 to 39	34	25	22	60	74	77
Aged 40 to 49	30	13	19	66	83	77
Aged 50 to 59	30	18	16	66	77	81
Aged 60 to 69	20	19	15	74	77	77
Aged 70 or older	28	18	20	64	79	74
Not a high school graduate	34	27	25	57	67	71
High school graduate	30	19	17	65	79	80
Bachelor's degree	31	25	15	63	72	79
Graduate degree	34	22	25	60	76	70

Note: Percents may not add to 100 because "don't know" and no answer are not included.
Source: General Social Survey, National Opinion Research Center, University of Chicago

Black Presidential Candidate

Fully 87 percent of Americans say they would vote for a black presidential candidate. Only 9 percent say they would not. These percentages have changed slightly since 1974, when 80 percent of respondents said they would and 16 percent said they would not vote for a black presidential candidate.

Not surprisingly, virtually all blacks would vote for a black presidential candidate. The gap between black and white opinion has remained about the same since 1974. Women and men are near agreement on this issue, as they have been for the last 20 years.

Younger generations are more accepting than older generations of the idea of a black president. Fully 16 percent of people aged 70 or older say they would not vote for a black candidate, compared with fewer than 10 percent of people under age 60. In 1974, about one-fourth of people then aged 50 or older said they would not vote for their party's nominee, if black.

People who went no further than high school are less likely to say they would vote for a black candidate than are people who have completed college. The gap between these two groups is similar to that found in 1974.

Black Presidential Candidate, 1994

"If your party nominated a black for president, would you vote for him if he were qualified for the job?"

(percent responding by sex, race, age, and education, 1994)

	yes	*no*
Total	87%	9%
Women	89	8
Men	85	11
Black	98	1
White	86	10
Aged 18 to 29	90	8
Aged 30 to 39	92	6
Aged 40 to 49	90	6
Aged 50 to 59	88	8
Aged 60 to 69	85	13
Aged 70 or older	74	16
Not a high school graduate	79	15
High school graduate	86	10
Bachelor's degree	95	4
Graduate degree	95	2

Note: Percents may not add to 100 because "don't know" and no answer are not included.
Source: General Social Survey, National Opinion Research Center, University of Chicago

Black Presidential Candidate, 1974 to 1994

"If your party nominated a black for president, would you vote for him if he were qualified for the job?"

(percent responding by sex, race, age, and education, 1974-94)

	yes			no		
	1994	*1985*	*1974*	*1994*	*1985*	*1974*
Total	87%	81%	80%	9%	14%	16%
Women	89	80	81	8	15	15
Men	85	82	78	11	14	18
Black	98	94	92	1	1	4
White	86	79	78	10	16	18
Aged 18 to 29	90	83	84	8	14	12
Aged 30 to 39	92	87	84	6	10	14
Aged 40 to 49	90	85	88	6	10	9
Aged 50 to 59	88	80	74	8	12	22
Aged 60 to 69	85	77	71	13	19	24
Aged 70 or older	74	66	67	16	25	26
Not a high school graduate	79	72	72	15	23	23
High school graduate	86	81	82	10	14	13
Bachelor's degree	95	90	89	4	5	9
Graduate degree	95	93	89	2	5	11

Note: Percents may not add to 100 because "don't know" and no answer are not included.
Source: General Social Survey, National Opinion Research Center, University of Chicago

Segregated Social Clubs

A majority of Americans say they would try to change the rules of a segregated social club to admit people of another race. But it is a small majority (60 percent) and has increased only slightly since 1985.

Remarkably, after years of strong disagreement, the proportion of blacks and whites who say they would try to change the rules is now the same (60 percent). But this is largely because blacks have become *less* inclined to say they would try to change the rules of a blacks-only club to admit whites. Whites, on the other hand, are more likely to say they would try to change the rules of a whites-only club today than they were in the past.

Women have always been more likely than men to say they would try to change the rules (perhaps cognizant of the fact that there are many clubs from which women are excluded), but the gap between men and women was wider in 1994 than in past years. Sixty-four percent of women, compared with 54 percent of men, would lobby for a rules change.

Younger people are more likely than older people to say they would try to integrate their club. As is the case on so many issues, the dividing line is age 50—baby boomers and Generation Xers versus older generations (62 to 68 percent of people under age 50 compared with 49 to 54 percent of people aged 50 or older).

Better-educated Americans have always been more inclined to say they would try to change the rules, although the educational gap was slightly smaller in 1994 than in 1977. Fully 70 percent of people with college degrees would seek a change, compared with only 49 percent of those who did not complete high school.

Segregated Social Clubs, 1994

"If you and your friends belonged to a social club that would not let whites/blacks join, would you try to change the rules so that whites/blacks could join?"

(percent responding by sex, race, age, and education, 1994)

	yes	no	don't know
Total	60%	29%	10%
Women	64	25	10
Men	54	35	10
Black	60	27	11
White	60	30	10
Aged 18 to 29	67	26	7
Aged 30 to 39	68	22	9
Aged 40 to 49	62	30	8
Aged 50 to 59	54	33	11
Aged 60 to 69	53	32	15
Aged 70 or older	49	37	14
Not a high school graduate	49	34	16
High school graduate	60	31	9
Bachelor's degree	70	22	7
Graduate degree	70	22	9

Note: Percents may not add to 100 because no answer is not included.
Source: General Social Survey, National Opinion Research Center, University of Chicago

Segregated Social Clubs, 1977 to 1994

"If you and your friends belonged to a social club that would not let whites/blacks join, would you try to change the rules so that whites/blacks could join?"

(percent responding by sex, race, age, and education, 1977-94)

	yes			no		
	1994	**1985**	**1977**	**1994**	**1985**	**1977**
Total	60%	52%	39%	29%	42%	53%
Women	64	55	40	25	39	52
Men	54	49	38	35	45	56
Black	60	74	*	27	16	*
White	60	49	39	30	45	54
Aged 18 to 29	67	65	56	26	29	37
Aged 30 to 39	68	57	46	22	39	49
Aged 40 to 49	62	52	36	30	41	55
Aged 50 to 59	54	50	32	33	46	59
Aged 60 to 69	53	40	27	32	53	67
Aged 70 or older	49	36	18	37	52	71
Not a high school graduate	49	48	31	34	43	59
High school graduate	60	51	39	31	43	55
Bachelor's degree	70	55	50	22	41	43
Graduate degree	70	71	58	22	26	33

*Question not asked of blacks prior to 1985.
Note: Percents may not add to 100 because "don't know" and no answer are not included.
Source: General Social Survey, National Opinion Research Center, University of Chicago

Socioeconomic Status of Blacks

Most Americans agree that, on average, "blacks have worse jobs, income, and housing than white people." But people are divided on the reasons for these differences. Is it due to discrimination, a lack of educational opportunity, a lack of will or motivation, or because blacks have less innate ability to learn?

Overall, people are most likely to cite lack of education or lack of motivation as causes for the lower socioeconomic status of blacks. Baby boomers (aged 30 to 49), people in their 50s, and the college-educated are most likely to cite lack of educational opportunity. Older Americans are most likely to believe a lack of motivation is behind the difference. Blacks are the only segment that cites discrimination as the biggest cause.

Discrimination

A minority of adults say they believe the lower socioeconomic status of blacks is due to discrimination. Age and education do not appear to have much influence on their response, but differences are apparent by sex and race. While 43 percent of women believe discrimination contributes to blacks' lower socioeconomic status, only 37 percent of men agree. Far more striking is the racial difference. Over three-quarters of blacks (77 percent) believe discrimination is the cause of their lower socioeconomic status, but only 34 percent of whites agree.

The percentage of people who believe discrimination is the cause has not varied much since 1977. Within some demographic segments, percentages have grown or declined over the years, but with no pattern to the change.

Lack of Education

Americans are almost evenly divided on whether or not a lack of education can be blamed for differences between blacks and whites in jobs, income, and housing. There are a few notable exceptions, however. A strong majority of blacks (59 percent) agree that this is a cause, as do majorities of people with at least a bachelor's degree. About half of women say they believe this is a cause.

As is the case with discrimination, Americans have remained close to evenly divided on this issue for years. The most interesting change has been among blacks. The percentage of blacks who blame lack of educational opportunity dropped by 11 percentage points between 1985 and 1994, from 70 to 59 percent.

Lack of Will or Motivation

The percentages of Americans who agree or disagree that a lack of will or motivation is a cause of blacks' lower socioeconomic status is close to even, but there are big differences in attitudes by race, age, and level of education.

Only 29 percent of blacks, compared with 51 percent of whites, consider lack of motivation a cause of blacks' lower socioeconomic status. By age, younger respondents are less likely than older ones to believe that blacks lack will or motivation.

The largest difference is found by educational attainment. Most of the least-educated Americans believe blacks lack the will or motivation to succeed. But this proportion drops sharply with increased years of schooling. Only 39 percent of people with bachelor's degrees and 27 percent of those with graduate degrees agree.

Americans are much less likely to believe today that blacks lack will or motivation than they were in 1977. Whether examined by sex, race, age, or educational level, the percentage of people agreeing that blacks lack will or motivation was lower in 1994 than in 1977.

Less Ability to Learn

Only 13 percent of Americans believe blacks are innately less able to learn than whites. Even in 1977, only one-quarter of whites agreed that this was a reason for blacks' lower socioeconomic status.

Older Americans and those with less education (two groups with considerable overlap) are most likely to believe that blacks have less innate ability to learn. As is the case on many issues, age 50 marks the generational divide. While only 8 to 9 percent of people under age 50 agree, 14 percent of those in their 50s, 21 percent of those in their 60s, and 28 percent of those aged 70 or older believe blacks innately have less ability to learn.

Likewise, a college education also strongly shapes attitudes on this issue. Nearly one-quarter of those without a high school diploma believe blacks have less in-born ability to learn, as do 15 percent of high school graduates. In contrast, only 3 to 5 percent of people with at least a bachelor's degree agree.

Causes of Socioeconomic Differences, 1994

"On the average blacks have worse jobs, income, and housing than white people. What do you think these differences are mainly due to?"

(percent responding by sex, race, age, and education, 1994)

	discrimination		lack of chance for education		lack of will or motivation		less ability to learn	
	yes	no	yes	no	yes	no	yes	no
Total	41%	54%	49%	47%	49%	45%	13%	83%
Women	43	51	51	45	47	46	12	85
Men	37	58	46	50	51	42	14	80
Black	77	18	59	37	29	66	10	87
White	34	60	47	49	51	42	13	83
Aged 18 to 29	46	50	46	52	48	47	9	89
Aged 30 to 39	39	56	52	45	45	49	8	89
Aged 40 to 49	40	55	51	47	43	52	8	88
Aged 50 to 59	40	54	50	44	48	45	14	82
Aged 60 to 69	35	59	45	52	59	36	21	74
Aged 70 or older	41	49	47	43	58	29	28	62
Not a high school graduate	43	48	42	50	58	32	23	67
High school graduate	38	57	45	52	53	41	15	82
Bachelor's degree	40	55	61	35	39	56	3	95
Graduate degree	47	47	68	28	27	67	5	91

Note: Responses will not add to 100 because "don't know" and no answer are not included.
Source: General Social Survey, National Opinion Research Center, University of Chicago

Causes of Socioeconomic Differences: Discrimination, 1977 to 1994

"On the average blacks have worse jobs, income, and housing than white people. Do you think these differences are mainly due to discrimination?"

(percent responding by sex, race, age, and education, 1977-94)

	yes			no		
	1994	1985	1977	1994	1985	1977
Total	41%	43%	39%	54%	52%	56%
Women	43	44	41	51	51	53
Men	37	42	36	58	54	60
Black	77	71	*	18	19	*
White	34	40	39	60	56	56
Aged 18 to 29	46	47	49	50	50	48
Aged 30 to 39	39	44	43	56	52	55
Aged 40 to 49	40	41	31	55	57	63
Aged 50 to 59	40	40	31	54	55	63
Aged 60 to 69	35	41	35	59	54	61
Aged 70 or older	41	42	40	49	49	47
Not a high school graduate	43	43	36	48	50	55
High school graduate	38	42	38	57	54	59
Bachelor's degree	40	46	50	55	51	47
Graduate degree	46	44	44	47	52	54

*Question not asked of blacks prior to 1985.
Note: Percents may not add to 100 because "don't know" and no answer are not included.
Source: General Social Survey, National Opinion Research Center, University of Chicago

Causes of Socioeconomic Differences: Lack of Education, 1977 to 1994

"On the average blacks have worse jobs, income, and housing than white people. Do you think these differences are because most blacks don't have the chance for education that it takes to rise out of poverty?"

(percent responding by sex, race, age, and education, 1977-94)

	yes			no		
	1994	**1985**	**1977**	**1994**	**1985**	**1977**
Total	49%	53%	48%	47%	45%	47%
Women	51	53	50	45	44	45
Men	46	52	47	50	46	50
Black	59	70	*	37	24	*
White	47	51	49	49	47	47
Aged 18 to 29	46	54	53	52	45	45
Aged 30 to 39	52	56	51	45	43	48
Aged 40 to 49	51	54	43	47	45	51
Aged 50 to 59	50	47	45	44	48	51
Aged 60 to 69	45	53	53	52	43	42
Aged 70 or older	47	48	45	43	47	47
Not a high school graduate	42	45	42	50	50	53
High school graduate	45	52	48	52	47	49
Bachelor's degree	61	65	69	35	33	28
Graduate degree	68	66	61	28	33	35

*Question not asked of blacks prior to 1985.
Note: Percents may not add to 100 because "don't know" and no answer are not included.
Source: General Social Survey, National Opinion Research Center, University of Chicago

Causes of Socioeconomic Differences:
Lack of Motivation, 1977 to 1994

"On the average blacks have worse jobs, income, and
housing than white people. Do you think these differences
are because most blacks just don't have the motivation or
willpower to pull themselves up out of poverty?

(percent responding by sex, race, age, and education, 1977-94)

	yes			no		
	1994	**1985**	**1977**	**1994**	**1985**	**1977**
Total	49%	55%	62%	45%	40%	32%
Women	47	54	59	46	40	34
Men	51	56	65	42	39	30
Black	29	32	*	66	59	*
White	51	58	62	42	38	32
Aged 18 to 29	48	44	52	47	53	43
Aged 30 to 39	45	53	60	49	46	37
Aged 40 to 49	43	53	65	52	45	26
Aged 50 to 59	48	61	63	45	30	29
Aged 60 to 69	59	65	69	36	28	25
Aged 70 or older	58	65	72	29	24	20
Not a high school graduate	58	66	69	32	28	24
High school graduate	53	55	63	41	40	32
Bachelor's degree	39	42	47	56	53	49
Graduate degree	27	37	35	67	61	53

*Question not asked of blacks prior to 1985.
Note: Percents may not add to 100 because "don't know" and no answer are not included.
Source: General Social Survey, National Opinion Research Center, University of Chicago

Causes of Socioeconomic Differences:
Less Innate Ability, 1977 to 1994

"On the average blacks have worse jobs, income, and housing than white people. Do you think these differences are because most blacks have less in-born ability to learn?"

(percent responding by sex, race, age, and education, 1977-94)

	yes			no		
	1994	1985	1977	1994	1985	1977
Total	13%	20%	25%	83%	75%	70%
Women	12	19	22	85	76	72
Men	14	21	28	80	75	68
Black	10	17	*	87	79	*
White	13	21	24	83	75	70
Aged 18 to 29	9	12	12	89	86	85
Aged 30 to 39	8	13	14	89	86	82
Aged 40 to 49	8	16	25	88	81	68
Aged 50 to 59	14	26	27	82	65	68
Aged 60 to 69	21	33	46	74	62	45
Aged 70 or older	28	34	43	62	58	48
Not a high school graduate	23	35	38	67	57	54
High school graduate	15	18	21	82	79	75
Bachelor's degree	3	8	12	95	91	87
Graduate degree	5	6	10	91	92	82

*Question not asked of blacks prior to 1985.
Note: Percents may not add to 100 because "don't know" and no answer are not included.
Source: General Social Survey, National Opinion Research Center, University of Chicago

Should Blacks Push Where They're Not Wanted?

Few Americans today would publicly state, "blacks should not push themselves where they are not wanted," but during the early 1960s many whites (and some blacks) frequently made this argument. While racial sensitivity has made Americans more careful of what they say, it hasn't completely changed their minds. Even today, 41 percent of Americans say they agree at least slightly with this statement.

Overall, 43 percent of whites agree strongly or slightly that "blacks shouldn't push themselves where they're not wanted," but the real surprise is that 31 percent of blacks agree.

Men are 10 percentage points more likely than women to agree with this statement. And people with different educational levels are worlds apart. Only 21 percent of graduate degree holders say blacks should not "push," compared with 61 percent of people who did not graduate from high school. In fact, people with graduate degrees were more likely than blacks to disagree strongly with this statement.

Agreement with this statement fell in every demographic segment between 1975 and 1994. The strongest sign that it will continue to decline is the large proportion of younger people who disagree (59 to 66 percent of people under age 50 disagree compared with 31 to 49 percent of those aged 50 or older).

Should Blacks Push Where They're Not Wanted? 1994

"Here is an opinion other people have expressed in connection with black-white relations: 'Blacks shouldn't push themselves where they're not wanted.' How do you feel about this statement?"

(percent responding by sex, race, age, and education, 1994)

	agree strongly	agree slightly	disagree slightly	disagree strongly	agree, total	disagree, total
Total	14%	27%	25%	30%	41%	55%
Women	14	23	25	33	37	58
Men	15	32	24	27	47	51
Black	10	21	19	48	31	67
White	15	28	26	28	43	54
Aged 18 to 29	7	23	25	41	30	66
Aged 30 to 39	10	23	26	39	33	65
Aged 40 to 49	12	26	26	33	38	59
Aged 50 to 59	18	29	28	21	47	49
Aged 60 to 69	23	30	22	19	53	41
Aged 70 or older	26	36	20	11	62	31
Not a high school graduate	30	31	18	15	61	33
High school graduate	14	29	26	28	43	54
Bachelor's degree	5	22	29	41	27	70
Graduate degree	5	16	23	56	21	79

Note: Percents may not add to 100 because "no opinion" and no answer are not included.
Source: General Social Survey, National Opinion Research Center, University of Chicago

Should Blacks Push Where They're Not Wanted? 1975 to 1994

"Here is an opinion other people have expressed in connection with black-white relations: 'Blacks shouldn't
push themselves where they're not wanted.' How
do you feel about this statement?"

(percent responding by sex, race, age, and education, 1975-94)

	agree strongly or slightly			disagree strongly or slightly		
	1994	*1984*	*1975*	*1994*	*1984*	*1975*
Total	41%	56%	72%	55%	42%	25%
Women	37	54	70	58	42	27
Men	47	58	75	51	41	22
Black	31	37	*	67	58	*
White	43	58	72	54	39	25
Aged 18 to 29	30	45	62	66	54	37
Aged 30 to 39	33	49	70	65	48	27
Aged 40 to 49	38	58	74	59	40	25
Aged 50 to 59	47	62	81	49	36	16
Aged 60 to 69	53	68	79	41	26	17
Aged 70 or older	62	72	81	31	23	14
Not a high school graduate	61	69	79	33	28	17
High school graduate	43	57	75	54	40	23
Bachelor's degree	27	36	56	70	62	43
Graduate degree	21	29	38	79	70	58

*Question not asked of blacks prior to 1980.
Source: General Social Survey, National Opinion Research Center, University of Chicago*

Immigration

Ours may be a "nation of immigrants," but in the current political climate we are a nation hostile to immigrants. Few Americans want to increase the number of immigrants to the U.S. Most would like to see the number reduced.

There is little variation by race or sex in the percentages of people who would reduce the number of immigrants to the U.S. People under age 30 are slightly less supportive than their elders of reducing the number of immigrants (57 percent compared with 61 to 65 percent). But the biggest divide is found by education. People with graduate degrees are least likely to support reducing immigration (only 38 percent do, compared with 52 percent of those with bachelor's degrees and 62 to 65 percent of people with a high school diploma or less).

While 28 percent of Americans would cut immigration "a little," a larger 34 percent would reduce it "a lot." Those most likely to say immigration should be reduced a lot are older people (aged 50 or older) and those with lower educational levels. Nearly four out of ten people in these groups want to reduce immigration a lot.

Immigration, 1994

"Do you think the number of immigrants from foreign countries who are permitted to come to the United States to live should be increased, decreased, or left the same?"

(percent responding by sex, race, age, and education, 1994)

	increase a lot	increase a little	leave the same	decrease a little	decrease a lot	increase, total	decrease, total
Total	2%	4%	27%	28%	34%	6%	62%
Women	3	3	26	29	33	6	62
Men	2	4	28	26	36	6	62
Black	3	7	22	25	36	10	61
White	2	3	27	29	35	5	64
Aged 18 to 29	2	5	33	26	31	7	57
Aged 30 to 39	2	4	25	30	35	6	65
Aged 40 to 49	3	4	28	31	30	7	61
Aged 50 to 59	1	3	28	24	38	4	62
Aged 60 to 69	3	3	25	25	39	6	64
Aged 70 or older	2	2	19	27	38	4	65
Not a high school graduate	5	5	20	24	38	10	62
High school grad.	2	4	23	30	38	6	68
Bachelor's degree	2	3	38	26	26	5	52
Graduate degree	3	2	50	24	14	5	38

Note: Percents may not add to 100 because "don't know" and no answer are not included.
Source: General Social Survey, National Opinion Research Center, University of Chicago

Will More Immigration Bring Economic Growth?

Americans don't believe that more immigrants will bring economic growth. A majority (62 percent) says this is not too likely or not at all likely.

Men are more likely than women to say immigration is not likely to fuel economic growth. Blacks and whites also diverge on the question of economic growth. While 66 percent of whites believe it is unlikely that immigrants will help the economy grow, only about half of blacks agree.

The generations divide around age 50 on whether economic growth will result from immigration. About one-third of Americans under age 50 feel it is at least somewhat likely that the economy will grow, but only 20 to 27 percent of those aged 50 or older agree. Fully 20 percent of people aged 70 or older and 11 percent of those in their 60s say they do not know whether higher economic growth will result.

People with graduate degrees are most likely to think that immigration could result in economic growth (45 percent). Those without a high school diploma are most likely to say they "don't know" the answer to this question (19 percent).

Will More Immigration Bring Economic Growth? 1994

"If more immigrants come to this country, is higher economic growth very likely, somewhat likely, not too likely, or not at all likely?"

(percent responding by sex, race, age, and education, 1994)

	very likely	somewhat likely	not too likely	not at all likely	don't know	very or somewhat likely	not too or not at all likely
Total	8%	21%	41%	21%	7%	29%	62%
Women	9	22	40	19	10	31	59
Men	8	21	42	24	4	29	66
Black	16	24	33	16	10	40	49
White	7	20	44	22	7	27	66
Aged 18 to 29	7	26	47	15	4	33	62
Aged 30 to 39	10	24	40	21	5	34	61
Aged 40 to 49	8	27	41	20	4	35	61
Aged 50 to 59	6	16	45	27	6	22	72
Aged 60 to 69	12	15	36	27	11	27	63
Aged 70 or older	7	13	35	22	20	20	57
Not a high school graduate	15	17	26	22	19	32	48
High school grad.	8	18	44	24	5	26	68
Bachelor's degree	4	30	49	14	4	34	63
Graduate degree	9	36	42	7	5	45	49

Note: Numbers may not add to 100 because no answer is not included.
Source: General Social Survey, National Opinion Research Center, University of Chicago

Will More Immigrants Increase Unemployment?

Many Americans have lost confidence in the economy, so it isn't surprising that most would worry about the economic impact on the nation of absorbing additional immigrants. An overwhelming majority (85 percent) believe that the likely result will be higher unemployment.

Men and women share the same opinion on this issue. Blacks and whites also agree that unemployment is likely to increase if more immigrants come to this country.

Most age groups are in rough agreement on the affect of immigration on unemployment, with one exception. While 82 to 89 percent of Americans under age 70 think immigration will increase unemployment, a smaller 72 percent of people aged 70 or older agree. However, a substantial percentage of people aged 70 or older (11 percent) say they don't know whether more unemployment is likely or not.

People with different levels of education also differ in their opinions. High school graduates and those with bachelor's degrees agree that more immigration is likely to lead to higher unemployment (88 and 85 percent, respectively). People with graduate degrees are less certain, with only 74 percent believing that unemployment will result.

Will More Immigrants Increase Unemployment? 1994

"If more immigrants come to this country, is
higher unemployment very likely, somewhat likely,
not too likely, or not at all likely?"

(percent responding by sex, race, age, and education, 1994)

	very likely	somewhat likely	not too likely	not at all likely	don't know	very or somewhat likely	not too or not at all likely
Total	54%	31%	8%	2%	4%	85%	10%
Women	54	30	8	2	6	84	10
Men	54	33	8	2	3	87	10
Black	53	32	6	1	8	85	7
White	55	31	8	2	4	86	10
Aged 18 to 29	48	39	7	2	4	87	9
Aged 30 to 39	54	35	5	2	3	89	7
Aged 40 to 49	54	31	11	2	2	85	13
Aged 50 to 59	60	28	6	2	4	88	8
Aged 60 to 69	56	26	10	3	6	82	13
Aged 70 or older	53	19	11	5	11	72	16
Not a high school graduate	58	21	8	2	11	79	10
High school graduate	61	27	6	3	3	88	9
Bachelor's degree	38	47	11	2	2	85	13
Graduate degree	31	43	20	1	4	74	21

Note: Numbers may not add to 100 because no answer is not included.
Source: General Social Survey, National Opinion Research Center, University of Chicago

Will Increased Immigration Divide the Nation?

It is ironic that a nation as diverse as the United States would oppose the influx of new immigrants. But 68 percent of Americans fear that more immigrants will make it harder to keep the country united.

About the same proportions of men and women agree on this question. Blacks are somewhat more concerned than whites. About three-quarters of blacks feel more immigrants will increase divisions in the nation, compared with two-thirds of whites.

Opinions do not vary much by age, although there are differences in the percentages who feel it is "very likely" that increased immigration will further divide the nation. People under age 50 are less likely than older Americans to say it is very likely that more immigrants will make it difficult to keep the country united.

There is a clear difference of opinion by education. Those with a college degree are not as worried as those with less education. As is the truth with other questions about immigration, substantial percentages of people admit they just don't know. People aged 30 or older and people who did not complete high school are most likely to say they do not know if more immigrants will make it difficult to keep the country united.

Will Increased Immigration Divide the Nation? 1994

"If more immigrants come to this country, is it very likely, somewhat likely, not too likely, or not at all likely that this will make it harder to keep the country united?"

(percent responding by sex, race, age, and education, 1994)

	very likely	somewhat likely	not too likely	not at all likely	don't know	very or somewhat likely	not too or not at all likely
Total	34%	34%	18%	8%	6%	68%	26%
Women	34	34	17	7	8	68	24
Men	34	33	20	8	4	67	28
Black	35	39	11	7	9	74	18
White	34	33	19	8	6	67	27
Aged 18 to 29	27	43	20	7	4	70	27
Aged 30 to 39	33	36	19	7	5	69	26
Aged 40 to 49	29	33	22	12	5	62	34
Aged 50 to 59	38	32	17	6	6	70	23
Aged 60 to 69	45	28	12	8	7	73	20
Aged 70 or older	41	23	13	5	16	64	18
Not a high school graduate	41	28	12	5	14	69	17
High school graduate	37	34	16	7	6	72	23
Bachelor's degree	25	37	26	9	3	62	35
Graduate degree	11	34	32	16	6	45	48

Note: Numbers may not add to 100 because no answer is not included.
Source: General Social Survey, National Opinion Research Center, University of Chicago

English as the Official Language

A majority of Americans (60 percent) say they favor a law that would require government business to be conducted only in English. But levels of support vary by demographic group, with a minority of blacks and young adults in favor of making English the official language.

Only 45 percent of blacks and 49 percent of people under age 30 favor such a law. There is a gap of 19 percentage points between whites and blacks on this issue, with 64 percent of whites in favor.

Support is strongest among older Americans. Fully 77 percent of people aged 60 to 69 support English as the official language compared with only 60 percent of Americans as a whole. Support declines steadily with each younger age group, but only among the youngest adults (aged 18 to 29) does support fall below a majority.

There is less variation in support among people by education. Those with the highest and lowest levels of education are least likely to favor an English-only law.

A majority of women (57 percent) say they would support an English-only law, but women are less likely than men (64 percent) to favor such a law.

English as the Official Language, 1994

"Do you favor a law making English the official language of the United States, meaning government business would be conducted in English only, or do you oppose such a law?"

(percent responding by sex, race, age, and education, 1994)

	favor	oppose	neither
Total	60%	27%	9%
Women	57	29	10
Men	64	24	9
Black	45	37	15
White	64	24	8
Aged 18 to 29	49	39	10
Aged 30 to 39	57	27	10
Aged 40 to 49	57	30	11
Aged 50 to 59	65	24	8
Aged 60 to 69	77	15	6
Aged 70 or older	71	14	7
Not a high school graduate	53	29	12
High school graduate	63	26	8
Bachelor's degree	62	27	10
Graduate degree	51	33	11

Note: Percents may not add to 100 because "don't know" and no answer are not included.
Source: General Social Survey, National Opinion Research Center, University of Chicago

Bilingual Education

Americans support bilingual education, but not by an overwhelming margin. Only 30 percent oppose bilingual education, while 64 percent are in favor.

Women are slightly more likely than men to support bilingual education. There is little variation in the level of support by education. But by race and age, there is considerable disagreement on this issue.

Blacks are more likely than whites to favor bilingual education. Three-quarters of blacks say they are in favor compared with only 62 percent of whites. But the gap is greatest by age. A higher level of support for bilingual education is found among America's most racially diverse adults: people under age 30, fully 75 percent of whom favor it. People in their 30s are also supportive, with seven out of ten favoring bilingual education. Support drops somewhat among people aged 40 to 59, continues to slide among those in their 60s, and plunges below 50 percent among people aged 70 or older.

Bilingual Education, 1994

"How do you feel about bilingual education?"

(percent responding by sex, race, age, and education, 1994)

	strongly favor	somewhat favor	somewhat oppose	strongly oppose	don't know	strongly/ somehat favor	strongly / somewhat oppose
Total	26%	38%	16%	14%	5%	64%	30%
Women	29	39	16	11	5	68	27
Men	23	37	17	19	4	60	36
Black	35	40	7	7	11	75	14
White	24	38	18	16	4	62	34
Aged 18 to 29	29	46	15	9	1	75	24
Aged 30 to 39	30	41	15	12	2	71	27
Aged 40 to 49	28	34	17	17	3	62	34
Aged 50 to 59	24	37	15	18	6	61	33
Aged 60 to 69	23	35	19	16	8	58	35
Aged 70 or older	18	31	19	18	12	49	37
Not a high school graduate	27	34	15	12	12	61	27
High school graduate	26	41	16	13	4	67	29
Bachelor's degree	26	36	18	18	2	62	36
Graduate degree	29	36	15	19	1	65	34

Note: Numbers may not add to 100 because no answer is not included.
Source: General Social Survey, National Opinion Research Center, University of Chicago

Bilingual Ballots

A majority of Americans (61 percent) believe that election ballots should be printed in languages other than English in areas of the country with large non-English-speaking populations. But there is considerable division on this issue by demographic segment.

Women are more receptive than men to ballots in languages other than English. A slim majority of men (56 percent) believe ballots should be printed in languages other than English compared with 65 percent of women.

Blacks and whites are further apart on the issue. Nearly three-quarters of blacks, but only a small majority of whites, feel ballots should be printed in other languages.

The racial diversity and tolerance of younger generations is apparent in the sharp differences between young and old on this issue. With each older age group, the percent favoring non-English ballots falls. Fully 70 percent of people under age 30 feel ballots should be printed in languages other than English, compared with fewer than half of those aged 70 or older.

Age is a far stronger predictor of opinion on this issue than educational attainment. The most educated Americans are slightly more inclined than the least educated to accept non-English ballots, but the difference is minimal.

Bilingual Ballots, 1994

"Do you believe that election ballots should be printed only in English, or in areas where lots of people don't speak English should they also be printed in some other languages?"

(percent responding by sex, race, age, and education, 1994)

	English only	other languages
Total	36%	61%
Women	31	65
Men	41	56
Black	22	73
White	38	58
Aged 18 to 29	28	70
Aged 30 to 39	31	66
Aged 40 to 49	36	62
Aged 50 to 59	36	58
Aged 60 to 69	43	55
Aged 70 or older	49	42
Not a high school graduate	33	60
High school graduate	36	61
Bachelor's degree	36	62
Graduate degree	30	66

Note: Numbers may not add to 100 because "don't know" and no answer are not included.
Source: General Social Survey, National Opinion Research Center, University of Chicago

4

Religion

Although most Americans are religious, we are a religiously diverse nation. While there is strong consensus on the big questions—Do you believe in God? Is there life after death?—on most other questions there is difference of opinion and practice.

- Only 2 percent of Americans don't believe in God. A majority (62 percent) believe in God and have no doubt.

- Fully 72 percent of Americans believe in life after death.

- A majority of people (55 percent) say they pray at least once a day.

- Only about one-third of Americans attend religious services at least once a week, but 49 percent attend services at least once a month.

- Half of adults say the Bible is the inspired word of God but is not to be taken literally in everything it says. Thirty-one percent believe in a literal interpretation, while 15 percent view the Bible as an ancient book of fables.

- A majority (59 percent) of Americans identify themselves as Protestant, while one-quarter are Catholic. This is virtually unchanged from 20 years ago, but if current trends among younger generations continue, there will soon be no majority religious viewpoint.

- Sixty-two percent say they were raised as Protestants and 30 percent as Catholics.

- About half of Americans say they have "only some" confidence in the leaders of the nation's religious institutions. Roughly equal percentages have a great deal or hardly any confidence in religious leaders.

- There is no consensus on the nature of nature, either. One-third of Americans say nature is sacred because it was created by God. Another third say nature is not sacred at all. And to 21 percent of adults, nature is sacred in itself.

- About half of Americans say "we believe too often in science, and not enough in feelings and faith."

Women Are More Religious Than Men

While women and men agree on almost all of the religious issues examined here, there are significant differences in opinion and behavior. Conventional wisdom holds that women are more religious than men and this is supported by the results of the General Social Survey.

- Women are more likely than men to believe in God and have no doubts (68 percent of women and 55 percent of men). Only 7 percent of women, but 13 percent of men, say they believe in a "higher power" rather than a personal God.

- Women are slightly more likely than men to believe in life after death (74 percent of women and 69 percent of men).

- Similar percentages of men and women are Catholic or Jewish. But women are slightly more likely to be Protestant; men are more likely than women to say they have no religious preference.

- There is little difference, however, in the percentages of men and women who were raised in the different religions.

Women and men make similar assessments of religious leaders, with only 24 percent of either sex saying they have a "great deal of confidence" in them. But women are more likely than men to:

- Attend religious services at least once a month (54 percent of women and 41 percent of men), or attend services at least weekly (36 percent of women compared with 26 percent of men);

- Pray at least once a day (65 percent of women versus 41 percent of men);

- Believe the Bible should be taken literally (35 percent of women compared with 26 percent of men);

- Believe we put too much faith in science (55 percent of women and 48 percent of men);

- Believe "nature is sacred because it is created by God" (37 percent of women and 28 percent of men). Fully 41 percent of men believe that nature is not sacred at all, compared with only 28 percent of women.

Whites Are Less Religious Than Blacks

Black and white Americans differ considerably in their religious beliefs and practices. On one issue, they are in complete agreement, however.

- Similar percentages of blacks and whites believe there is life after death (74 and 72 percent, respectively).

Blacks are more likely than whites to:

- Say they are Protestant (81 percent of blacks and 58 percent of whites);

- Have been raised as Protestants (84 percent of blacks compared with 60 percent of whites);

- Believe without a doubt in the existence of God (77 percent of blacks versus 59 percent of whites);

- Pray at least once a day (78 percent of blacks and 52 percent of whites);

- Attend religious services at least once a month (60 percent of blacks, but only 46 percent of whites). Only 8 percent of blacks, compared with 18 percent of whites, say they never attend religious services;

- Believe we rely too much on science and not enough on faith and feelings (67 percent of blacks, but only 50 percent of whites);

- Interpret the Bible literally (53 percent of blacks and 27 percent of whites);

- Believe that nature is sacred because it was created by God (45 percent of blacks compared with 31 percent of whites). Blacks are much less likely than whites to say nature is not at all sacred (28 percent of blacks, compared with 41 percent of whites);

- Have a great deal of confidence in the leaders of organized religion (31 percent of blacks and 24 percent of whites).

Are Younger Generations Losing Their Faith?

Depending on which headline you read, baby boomers and younger generations are either returning to the fold or seeking spiritual guidance from nontraditional religions. The General Social Survey shows distinct differences in religious beliefs and practices by age.

- People under age 40 are most likely to believe in God with some doubts (19 to 21 percent compared with 9 to 13 percent of other age groups). Older Americans are most likely to say they believe in God without a doubt (65 to 69 percent of people aged 50 or older versus 53 to 62 percent of people under age 50). Baby boomers, who popularized Eastern and "New Age" religions, are most likely to view God as a "higher power" (12 percent).

- Sixteen percent of young adults have no religious preference compared with just 2 percent of people aged 70 or older. Religious diversity is also greater among younger generations. Nearly three-quarters of people aged 70 or older, but only 47 percent of those aged 30 or younger, are Protestant. The younger group is more likely to be Catholic (29 percent, compared with 20 percent of the oldest Americans).

- Adults under age 30 are not only more likely than older generations to have no religious preference now, they were more likely to be raised with no religion (8 percent compared with 1 percent of the oldest Americans).

- Surprisingly, older Americans are less likely than younger people to believe in life after death (64 to 67 percent of those aged 60 or older compared with 72 to 77 percent of people under age 60).

- Older people are most likely to say they are unsure about it (13 to 15 percent, compared with 8 to 10 percent of younger age groups).

- The likelihood of attending religious services at least weekly increases with age, from 22 percent of those under age 30 to 42 percent of those aged 70 or older. But similar percentages of all age groups say they never attend.

- Younger people are less likely to pray every day (ranging from 40 percent of those under age 30 to 75 percent of those aged 70 or older).

- People aged 50 or older are slightly more likely than younger people to have a great deal of confidence in the leaders of organized religion (28 to 33 percent of people aged 50 or older compared to 19 to 22 percent of those under age 50).

- Older generations are more inclined to feel that people believe too much in science and not enough in faith.

- People aged 60 or older are most likely to believe nature is sacred because it was created by God, while those under age 30 are most likely to feel nature is sacred in itself. Most likely to say nature is not sacred are those aged 40 to 59.

- Older Americans, especially those aged 70 or older, are more likely to say the Bible is the actual word of God.

Better-Educated Adults Are Less Certain

People with lower levels of education are more confident in their religious faith than are those with more education. The well-educated are less certain about religion.

- Fourteen percent of people with graduate degrees have no religious preference, versus 9 percent of less-educated Americans.

- People with college degrees are more likely than those with less education to have been raised in religions other than Protestant. Only 50 to 53 percent of those with college degrees were raised Protestant, compared to 65 to 67 percent of those with less education.

- People without a high school diploma are most likely to believe in God without any doubts (69 percent), while those with graduate degrees are least likely to believe without doubt (49 percent). The best-educated Americans are most likely to say they are believers, but have doubts (22 percent).

- Americans who did not complete high school are less likely than those with more education to say they do not believe in or are uncertain about life after death.

- People with at least a bachelor's degree are slightly more likely than those with less education to attend religious services at least once a month. This may be, in part, because the least-educated Americans tend to be older and may have mobility problems that prevent them from attending church services.

- Less-educated Americans are more likely to pray once a day or more. More than half (58 percent) of people without a high school diploma pray at least once a day. Only 23 percent pray less than once a week or never. In contrast, only 46 percent of people with graduate degrees pray at least once a day, while 33 percent pray less than once a week or never.

- People without a high school diploma are more likely than better-educated Americans to have a great deal of confidence in the leaders of organized religion.

- The most striking difference among people by education is in the percentage who believe in a literal interpretation of the Bible. Fully half of those without a high school diploma say the Bible should be taken literally, compared with one-third of high school graduates, 18 percent of people with bachelor's degrees, and just 8 percent of those with graduate degrees.

- The tendency to view nature as sacred because it is God's creation falls with increased education. While 44 percent of people without a high school diploma hold this view, only 22 percent of those with graduate degrees agree.

- Not surprisingly, those with the least education are most likely to feel "we believe too much in science, and not enough in feelings and faith." The proportion who agree with this statement falls with increasing education. Only 38 to 47 percent of people with at least a bachelor's degree agree.

Religious Preference

A majority (59 percent) of Americans are Protestant, while one-quarter are Catholic. Although the Protestant proportion has declined slightly since 1974, the religious makeup of America has not changed significantly in the past 20 years. But as older generations die, the religious mix will change because young adults have decidedly different religious preferences.

Men and women differ only slightly in their religious preference. Women are somewhat more likely to be Protestant, while men are slightly more likely to have no religious preference.

There is more of a difference between blacks and whites. Fully 81 percent of blacks are Protestant, compared with 58 percent of whites. While 27 percent of whites are Catholic, among blacks the proportion is only 8 percent.

The most significant difference in religious preference is by age. Catholicism has been growing among younger generations, in part because of the immigration of Hispanics to the United States. The percentage with no religion is also growing among young adults. Only 47 percent of people under age 30 are Protestant, compared with 73 percent of people aged 70 or older. Twenty-nine percent of young adults are Catholic, compared with 20 percent of the oldest Americans. Fully 16 percent of people under age 30 have no religion, versus just 2 percent of those aged 70 or older.

While there has been some speculation on whether baby boomers and younger generations would return to the church as they got older, the evidence so far indicates they will not. The same proportion of boomers reported they had no religion in 1994 as did in 1974.

Religious Preference, 1994

"What is your religious preference? Is it Protestant, Catholic, Jewish, some other religion, or no religion?"

(percent responding by sex, race, age, and education, 1994)

	Protestant	Catholic	Jewish	other	none
Total	59%	25%	2%	4%	9%
Women	63	24	2	4	7
Men	55	27	2	4	12
Black	81	8	1	5	6
White	58	27	2	3	9
Aged 18 to 29	47	29	2	6	16
Aged 30 to 39	56	25	2	5	11
Aged 40 to 49	58	26	2	4	11
Aged 50 to 59	65	25	2	2	5
Aged 60 to 69	65	25	2	2	5
Aged 70 or older	73	20	3	1	2
Not a high school graduate	64	22	1	3	9
High school graduate	62	24	1	4	9
Bachelor's degree	51	31	5	5	9
Graduate degree	47	27	7	5	14

Note: Percents may not add to 100 because "don't know" and no answer are not included.
Source: General Social Survey, National Opinion Research Center, University of Chicago

Religious Preference, 1974 to 1994

"What is your religious preference? Is it Protestant, Catholic, Jewish, some other religion, or no religion?"

(percent responding by sex, race, age, and education, 1974-94)

	Protestant			Catholic			Jewish			other			none		
	1994	1984	1974	1994	1984	1974	1994	1984	1974	1994	1984	1974	1994	1984	1974
Total	59%	63%	64%	25%	26%	25%	2%	2%	3%	4%	1%	1%	9%	7%	7%
Women	63	66	65	24	25	27	2	2	4	4	1	1	7	5	4
Men	55	59	64	27	26	24	2	2	2	4	1	1	12	10	10
Black	81	85	86	8	9	8	1	0	1	5	1	1	6	4	5
White	58	61	62	27	27	28	2	2	3	3	1	0	9	8	7
Aged 18 to 29	47	60	55	29	26	30	2	2	3	6	1	1	16	11	11
Aged 30 to 39	56	57	64	25	28	24	2	2	4	5	2	0	11	10	8
Aged 40 to 49	58	67	64	26	27	29	2	2	1	4	0	0	11	5	6
Aged 50 to 59	65	65	67	25	26	25	2	3	3	2	2	0	5	4	5
Aged 60 to 69	65	67	75	25	24	19	2	1	3	2	2	0	5	5	4
Aged 70 or older	73	75	72	20	18	19	3	3	5	1	1	0	2	3	4
Not a high school graduate	64	68	71	22	22	22	1	1	2	3	1	0	9	9	6
High school graduate	62	63	62	24	28	29	1	1	2	4	2	1	9	5	7
Bachelor's degree	51	59	60	31	25	22	5	5	7	5	1	1	9	9	10
Graduate degree	47	58	59	27	25	16	7	5	11	5	1	1	14	10	12

Source: General Social Survey, National Opinion Research Center, University of Chicago

Religious Background

A majority (62 percent) of Americans were raised as Protestants, while a substantial minority (30 percent) were raised as Catholics. Four percent were raised with no religion, 2 percent were raised Jewish, and 3 percent with some other religion.

Black Americans were more likely than whites to have been raised as Protestants (84 percent compared with 60 percent) and considerably less likely to be raised Catholic. This was also true in 1974.

Each successive generation of Americans is more likely to have been raised Catholic and less likely to have been raised Protestant. Fewer than one-quarter of people aged 60 or older were raised in the Catholic religion, compared with 35 percent of people under age 30. While 72 percent of the oldest Americans were raised as Protestants, this is true for only 52 percent of the youngest adults.

The proportion of people who were raised Jewish or in other religions does not vary much by age. A relatively large percentage of people under age 30 (8 percent) say they were not raised in any religion.

People with graduate degrees are more likely to have been raised Jewish than are those with less education. They are also more likely to have been raised in some other religion, reflecting the large share of first- and second-generation immigrants from Hindu, Moslem, and other faiths among the best-educated Americans.

Religious Background, 1994

"In what religion were you raised?"

(percent responding by sex, race, age, and education, 1994)

	Protestant	Catholic	Jewish	other	none
Total	62%	30%	2%	3%	4%
Women	63	29	2	2	4
Men	60	31	2	3	4
Black	84	10	0	2	4
White	60	32	2	2	4
Aged 18 to 29	52	35	2	3	8
Aged 30 to 39	59	32	2	3	5
Aged 40 to 49	60	32	1	2	4
Aged 50 to 59	67	27	1	2	2
Aged 60 to 69	67	24	3	2	4
Aged 70 or older	72	22	2	2	1
Not a high school graduate	67	26	0	2	5
High school graduate	65	27	1	2	5
Bachelor's degree	53	37	4	3	3
Graduate degree	50	34	7	6	3

Note: Percents may not add to 100 because "don't know" and no answer are not included.
Source: General Social Survey, National Opinion Research Center, University of Chicago

Religious Background, 1974 to 1994

"In what religion were you raised?"

(percent responding by sex, race, age, and education, 1974-94)

	Protestant			Catholic		
	1994	*1984*	*1974*	*1994*	*1984*	*1974*
Total	62%	65%	66%	30%	27%	27%
Women	63	67	65	29	27	28
Men	60	62	68	31	28	26
Black	84	87	92	10	11	8
White	60	63	63	32	29	30
Aged 18 to 29	52	60	58	35	31	34
Aged 30 to 39	59	59	66	32	33	27
Aged 40 to 49	60	69	66	32	25	27
Aged 50 to 59	67	66	69	27	25	26
Aged 60 to 69	67	68	76	24	25	21
Aged 70 or older	72	79	73	22	15	20
Not a high school graduate	67	69	71	26	23	25
High school graduate	65	64	64	27	29	30
Bachelor's degree	53	61	66	37	29	25
Graduate degree	50	65	62	34	25	16

Note: Percents may not add to 100 because "Jewish," "none," "other," "don't know," and no answer are not included.
Source: General Social Survey, National Opinion Research Center, University of Chicago

Belief in God

Most Americans believe in God. A majority (62 percent) say they have no doubts that God really exists. But one-quarter have some doubts, or believe in a "higher power" rather than a "personal God."

Women are more certain than men that God exists (68 percent of women compared with 55 percent of men). Men are considerably more likely to believe God is a higher power or to have some doubts.

Blacks are much stronger believers than are whites. While 77 percent of blacks say they have no doubts about the existence of God, only 59 percent of whites agree. Fully 27 percent of whites have some doubts or see God as a higher power, beliefs shared by only 12 percent of blacks.

The generations also disagree about the existence and nature of God. People aged 40 to 69 are those most likely to view God as some kind of higher power. Those under age 40 are most likely to say they believe, but have doubts. The proportion saying they are certain of God's existence rises with age.

The most striking difference in beliefs about God is found by education. While 69 percent of people who did not complete high school say they have no doubts about God, the proportion declines with rising educational attainment. Only 49 percent of graduate degree holders believe in God without a doubt. Fully 35 percent of the most-educated say they have doubts or view God as a higher power of some kind.

Belief in God, 1994

"Which statement comes closest to expressing what you believe about God? 1) I don't believe in God; 2) I don't know whether there is a God and I don't believe there is any way to find out; 3) I don't believe in a personal God, but I do believe in a Higher Power of some kind; 4) I find myself believing in God some of the time, but not at others; 5) While I have doubts, I feel that I do believe in God; 6) I know God really exists and I have no doubts about it."

(percent responding by sex, race, age, and education, 1994)

	no doubts	believe, but have doubts	believe sometimes	higher power	don't know, no way to find out	don't believe
Total	62%	15%	4%	10%	3%	2%
Women	68	14	3	7	2	2
Men	55	18	5	13	3	3
Black	77	7	2	5	2	0
White	59	17	4	10	3	3
Aged 18 to 29	53	21	4	8	6	4
Aged 30 to 39	60	19	4	9	3	1
Aged 40 to 49	62	13	3	12	3	4
Aged 50 to 59	68	13	3	10	2	1
Aged 60 to 69	69	9	4	11	0	3
Aged 70 or older	65	13	4	6	1	3
Not a high school graduate	69	9	4	5	2	4
High school graduate	64	16	3	8	2	2
Bachelor's degree	52	16	4	17	5	3
Graduate degree	49	22	6	13	6	3

Note: Percents may not add to 100 because "don't know" and no answer are not included.
Source: General Social Survey, National Opinion Research Center, University of Chicago

Life After Death

Most Americans (72 percent) believe in life after death. The percentage who believe in the afterlife has not changed much over the past two decades.

There is little disagreement among Americans on this issue by sex, race, age, or educational attainment. The biggest difference is by education. While three-quarters of high school graduates and those with bachelor's degrees believe in life after death, only 64 percent of those without a high school diploma agree.

Interestingly, older people are slightly less likely than younger Americans to believe in an afterlife. While 77 percent of people in their 40s say they believe, only 64 to 67 percent of those aged 60 or older agree. Thirteen to 15 percent of people aged 60 or older are unsure about life after death.

Life After Death, 1994

"Do you believe there is a life after death?"

(percent responding by sex, race, age, and education, 1994)

	yes	no	undecided
Total	72%	17%	10%
Women	74	15	10
Men	69	18	12
Black	74	15	10
White	72	17	11
Aged 18 to 29	72	19	8
Aged 30 to 39	72	17	10
Aged 40 to 49	77	14	8
Aged 50 to 59	75	13	10
Aged 60 to 69	67	20	13
Aged 70 or older	64	19	15
Not a high school graduate	64	21	14
High school graduate	74	16	9
Bachelor's degree	75	15	11
Graduate degree	70	19	10

Note: Percents may not add to 100 because no answer is not included.
Source: General Social Survey, National Opinion Research Center, University of Chicago

Life After Death, 1975 to 1994

"Do you believe there is a life after death?"

(percent responding by sex, race, age, and education, 1975-94)

	yes			no			undecided		
	1994	*1984*	*1975*	*1994*	*1984*	*1975*	*1994*	*1984*	*1975*
Total	72%	73%	67%	17%	19%	23%	10%	8%	10%
Women	74	76	70	15	16	21	10	7	9
Men	69	69	64	18	23	25	12	8	11
Black	74	65	58	15	26	26	10	9	16
White	72	75	68	17	17	22	11	7	9
Aged 18 to 29	72	73	65	19	19	25	8	8	10
Aged 30 to 39	72	75	67	17	16	21	10	7	12
Aged 40 to 49	77	69	72	14	24	19	8	8	8
Aged 50 to 59	75	73	66	13	20	24	10	6	9
Aged 60 to 69	67	74	66	20	18	24	13	6	10
Aged 70 or older	64	73	66	19	16	23	15	10	10
Not a high school graduate	64	69	64	21	22	26	14	9	10
High school grad.	74	76	69	16	17	21	9	6	9
Bachelor's degree	75	76	66	15	15	23	11	7	11
Graduate degree	70	61	70	19	21	22	10	18	8

Note: Percents may not add to 100 because no answer is not included.
Source: General Social Survey, National Opinion Research Center, University of Chicago

Attend Religious Services

In a busy world, it is not surprising that most Americans do not attend religious services each week. Only one-third say they attend at least once a week. But most people attend religious services at least occasionally during the year. Only 16 percent say they never do. The overall percentages of people who attend religious services occasionally, regularly, or never has not changed much over the past 20 years.

Men are more likely than women to never attend religious services (20 percent of men versus 13 percent of women); women are more likely to go to religious services weekly or more (36 percent of women versus 26 percent of men). Whites are more likely than blacks to never attend religious services (18 percent of whites compared with 8 percent of blacks).

Many religious institutions have noticed a drop in attendance among younger generations. While 42 percent of people aged 60 or older say they attend religious services at least weekly, only 33 to 35 percent of people aged 40 to 59 do so. Regular attendance is lowest among the young, with only 22 to 25 percent of people aged 18 to 39 attending at least weekly. About the same percentage of people of all ages say they never attend religious services.

People who did not complete high school are most likely to say they never attend church (24 percent). This is a much higher proportion for this age group than in 1974, when only 15 percent said they never attend.

Attend Religious Services, 1994

"How often do you attend religious services?"

(percent responding by sex, race, age, and education, 1994)

	weekly or more	1 to 3 times a month	up to several times a year	never
Total	32%	17%	34%	16%
Women	36	18	32	13
Men	26	15	37	20
Black	36	24	31	8
White	31	15	35	18
Aged 18 to 29	22	18	43	16
Aged 30 to 39	25	18	39	17
Aged 40 to 49	33	18	32	16
Aged 50 to 59	35	18	30	15
Aged 60 to 69	42	11	30	16
Aged 70 or older	42	12	27	17
Not a high school graduate	32	12	30	24
High school graduate	30	16	38	15
Bachelor's degree	34	21	32	12
Graduate degree	35	19	28	17

Note: Percents may not add to 100 because "don't know" and no answer are not included.
Source: General Social Survey, National Opinion Research Center, University of Chicago

Attend Religious Services, 1974 to 1994

"How often do you attend religious services?"

(percent responding by sex, race, age, and education, 1974-94)

	weekly or more			once a month or more			less than once a month			never		
	1994	1984	1974	1994	1984	1974	1994	1984	1974	1994	1984	1974
Total	32%	37%	36%	48%	53%	53%	34%	33%	35%	16%	13%	12%
Women	36	44	40	53	60	58	32	29	32	13	10	10
Men	26	28	32	41	43	47	37	40	38	20	17	15
Black	36	39	34	60	61	51	31	32	41	8	7	7
White	31	37	36	46	52	53	35	33	34	18	14	13
Aged 18 to 29	22	26	26	40	47	42	43	41	45	16	12	13
Aged 30 to 39	25	37	36	44	51	51	39	32	37	17	16	12
Aged 40 to 49	33	32	35	51	50	55	32	36	32	16	14	12
Aged 50 to 59	35	50	41	52	65	57	30	24	31	15	11	12
Aged 60 to 69	42	46	42	54	59	60	30	28	28	16	11	12
Aged 70 or older	42	51	49	53	58	62	27	27	24	17	13	14
Not a high school graduate	32	38	33	45	39	49	30	33	36	24	16	15
High school graduate	30	37	37	45	53	53	38	35	36	15	11	11
Bachelor's degree	34	36	38	55	55	59	32	30	32	12	13	9
Graduate degree	35	46	45	54	55	59	28	22	26	17	17	15

Note: Percents may not add to 100 because "don't know" and no answer are not included.
Source: General Social Survey, National Opinion Research Center, University of Chicago

Prayer

A majority of Americans say they pray at least once a day (55 percent). Women are much more likely to pray than men. Fully 65 percent of women say they pray at least daily, compared with only 41 percent of men. One-third of men say they pray less than once a week, versus 15 percent of women.

Blacks are more likely than whites to pray daily (78 percent of blacks compared with 52 percent of whites). One-quarter of whites, but only 9 percent of blacks, say they pray less than once a week.

Not surprisingly, the proportion of people who pray at least daily rises with age, from only 40 percent of people under age 30 to 75 percent of people aged 70 or older.

Frequent prayers are also more likely to be found among the less-educated (who are also disproportionately older). While 58 percent of people without a high school diploma pray at least once a day, only 46 percent of people with graduate degrees join in.

Prayer, 1994

"About how often do you pray?"

(percent responding by sex, race, age, and education, 1994)

	several times a day	once a day	several times a week	once a week	less than once a week	never
Total	23%	32%	11%	8%	22%	1%
Women	29	36	10	8	15	1
Men	14	27	13	10	33	2
Black	40	38	10	3	9	0
White	20	32	12	9	25	1
Aged 18 to 29	16	24	13	16	30	2
Aged 30 to 39	16	30	13	8	30	2
Aged 40 to 49	23	35	12	7	20	1
Aged 50 to 59	28	33	11	7	18	1
Aged 60 to 69	30	37	10	7	15	1
Aged 70 or older	35	40	6	4	11	1
Not a high school graduate	24	34	9	8	22	1
High school graduate	24	32	11	9	22	1
Bachelor's degree	20	35	13	9	20	1
Graduate degree	19	27	12	8	30	3

Note: Percents may not add to 100 because "don't know" and no answer are not included.
Source: General Social Survey, National Opinion Research Center, University of Chicago

Confidence in Religious Leaders

The leaders of organized religion do not inspire the confidence they undoubtedly wish to, or once did. Only one-quarter of Americans say they have a great deal of confidence in organized religion's leaders, down from 44 percent in 1974. About one-half say they have only some confidence. Twenty-two percent say they have hardly any confidence in religious leaders.

Men and women are in agreement on this issue. Blacks, however, are slightly more likely to say they have a great deal of confidence in religious leaders than are whites (31 percent of blacks compared with 24 percent of whites). In 1974, whites were more likely to have a great deal of confidence.

Confidence in the leaders of organized religion is greater among older Americans. While 28 to 33 percent of people aged 50 or older say they have a great deal of confidence in religious leaders, only 19 to 22 percent of people under age 50 agree. Older Americans placed more confidence in religious leaders in 1974 as well, but confidence has fallen among all age groups since then.

People without a high school diploma are more likely to say they have a great deal of confidence in religious leaders (32 percent) than are better-educated people. People with graduate degrees are those most likely to say they have hardly any confidence in them (26 percent).

Confidence in Religious Leaders, 1994

"As far as the people running organized religion are
concerned, would you say you have a great deal
of confidence, only some confidence, or
hardly any confidence at all in them?"

(percent responding by sex, race, age, and education, 1994)

	a great deal	only some	hardly any
Total	24%	52%	22%
Women	24	52	22
Men	24	51	22
Black	31	50	17
White	24	52	22
Aged 18 to 29	22	56	22
Aged 30 to 39	19	54	24
Aged 40 to 49	20	53	24
Aged 50 to 59	28	51	20
Aged 60 to 69	33	46	20
Aged 70 or older	32	42	17
Not a high school graduate	32	42	22
High school graduate	23	53	22
Bachelor's degree	21	57	20
Graduate degree	24	47	26

Note: Percents may not add to 100 because "don't know" and no answer are not included.
Source: General Social Survey, National Opinion Research Center, University of Chicago

Confidence in Religious Leaders, 1974 to 1994

"As far as the people running organized religion are concerned, would you say you have a great deal of confidence, only some confidence, or hardly any confidence at all in them?"

(percent responding by sex, race, age, and education, 1974-94)

	a great deal			only some			hardly any		
	1994	1984	1974	1994	1984	1974	1994	1984	1974
Total	24%	30%	44%	52%	46%	43%	22%	19%	11%
Women	24	31	46	52	46	43	22	18	9
Men	24	30	42	51	47	43	22	20	13
Black	31	28	39	50	51	44	17	18	16
White	24	31	45	52	46	43	22	19	10
Aged 18 to 29	22	31	40	56	47	49	22	20	10
Aged 30 to 39	19	28	39	54	52	47	24	16	13
Aged 40 to 49	20	27	42	53	47	46	24	23	11
Aged 50 to 59	28	29	49	51	48	40	20	20	9
Aged 60 to 69	33	31	50	46	44	34	20	19	13
Aged 70 or older	32	39	54	42	36	32	17	16	9
Not a high school graduate	32	28	47	42	40	38	22	25	12
High school graduate	23	30	45	53	49	43	22	18	11
Bachelor's degree	21	41	36	57	43	56	20	12	7
Graduate degree	24	28	38	47	55	45	26	11	14

Note: Percents may not add to 100 because "don't know" and no answer are not included.
Source: General Social Survey, National Opinion Research Center, University of Chicago

What Is the Bible?

One-half of Americans view the Bible as "the inspired word of God," not to be taken literally. Only 31 percent say it should be taken literally. Fifteen percent feel it is an ancient book of fables "recorded by men." Disagreements on how the Bible should be interpreted are found in every demographic segment.

Men and women disagree, although not as much as do other demographic segments. Women are more likely than men to say the Bible is the actual word of God and is to be taken literally. Women were less likely to believe this in 1994 (35 percent), than they were in 1984 (44 percent).

Blacks and whites disagree sharply on this topic. Fully 53 percent of blacks, but only 27 percent of whites, believe the Bible is the actual word of God. Whites are considerably more likely than blacks to say it is inspired by God, but not to be taken literally. These differences of opinion by race also existed in 1984.

Generational differences of opinion are less pronounced, but still apparent. Least likely to believe the Bible should be taken literally are people under age 30 (28 percent), while people aged 70 or older are most likely to believe the Bible is the literal word of God (40 percent).

The widest gaps are found by education. While half of people who did not complete high school believe the Bible should be taken literally, only 8 percent of those with graduate degrees agree. This group is most likely to view the Bible as a book of ancient fables (31 percent of those with graduate degrees compared with 12 percent of those with a high school diploma or less). The education gap is not as large as it was in 1984, when fully 62 percent of people without a high school diploma said the Bible was the actual word of God.

What Is the Bible? 1994

"Which of these statements comes closest to describing your feelings about the Bible? 1)The Bible is the actual word of God and is to be taken literally, word for word; 2) The Bible is the inspired word of God, but not everything in it should be taken literally, word for word; or 3) The Bible is an ancient book of fables, legends, history, and moral precepts recorded by men."

(percent responding by sex, race, age, and education, 1994)

	actual word	inspired word	ancient book
Total	31%	51%	15%
Women	35	51	11
Men	26	50	20
Black	53	36	7
White	27	54	16
Aged 18 to 29	28	52	16
Aged 30 to 39	30	53	15
Aged 40 to 49	27	51	18
Aged 50 to 59	34	51	13
Aged 60 to 69	32	52	13
Aged 70 or older	40	44	11
Not a high school graduate	50	32	12
High school graduate	34	52	12
Bachelor's degree	18	62	19
Graduate degree	8	58	31

Note: Percents may not add to 100 because "don't know" and no answer are not included.
Source: General Social Survey, National Opinion Research Center, University of Chicago

What Is the Bible? 1984 to 1994

"Which of these statements comes closest to describing
your feelings about the Bible? 1)The Bible is the actual
word of God and is to be taken literally, word for word;
2) The Bible is the inspired word of God, but not
everything in it should be taken literally, word for word;
or 3) The Bible is an ancient book of fables, legends,
history, and moral precepts recorded by men."

(percent responding by sex, race, age, and education, 1984-94)

	actual word		inspired word		ancient book	
	1994	**1984**	**1994**	**1984**	**1994**	**1984**
Total	31%	37%	51%	45%	15%	14%
Women	35	44	51	43	11	11
Men	26	28	50	49	20	19
Black	53	60	36	32	7	6
White	27	34	54	48	16	15
Aged 18 to 29	28	35	52	46	16	16
Aged 30 to 39	30	28	53	52	15	17
Aged 40 to 49	27	39	51	42	18	17
Aged 50 to 59	34	36	51	44	13	18
Aged 60 to 69	32	43	52	47	13	6
Aged 70 or older	40	53	44	35	11	6
Not a high school graduate	50	62	32	26	12	9
High school grad.	34	35	52	49	12	14
Bachelor's degree	18	12	62	60	19	24
Graduate degree	8	8	58	68	31	24

Note: Question not asked prior to 1984.
Source: General Social Survey, National Opinion Research Center, University of Chicago

Is Nature Sacred?

Americans are divided on the nature of nature. Nearly the same percentage (33 percent) say nature is sacred because it was created by God as say nature is not sacred at all (34 percent). Another 21 percent believe nature is sacred in and of itself.

Men are considerably more likely than women to say there is nothing sacred about nature (41 percent of men versus 28 percent of women). Women are more likely to believe nature is sacred because it was created by God.

Blacks and whites also differ strongly in their opinions about nature. Fully 45 percent of blacks, but only 31 percent of whites, say nature is sacred because it was created by God. Whites are more likely to say nature is not sacred. People of different ages hold different opinions about nature. Most likely to consider nature sacred in and of itself are people under age 30. Those aged 70 or older are most likely to view nature as sacred because it was created by God. People in their 40s and 50s are more likely than average to say there's nothing sacred about it.

The biggest differences are found by education. Fully 44 percent of people who did not complete high school believe nature was created by God and is, therefore, sacred. Among graduate degree holders, 45 percent say nature is not sacred.

Is Nature Sacred? 1994

"Which statement is closest to your views? 1) Nature is sacred because it is created by God. 2) Nature is spiritual or sacred in itself. 3) Nature is important, but not spiritual or sacred."

(percent responding by sex, race, age, and education, 1994)

	sacred because created by God	sacred in itself	not sacred
Total	33%	21%	34%
Women	37	21	28
Men	28	20	41
Black	45	15	21
White	31	22	36
Aged 18 to 29	31	30	26
Aged 30 to 39	33	22	30
Aged 40 to 49	33	19	39
Aged 50 to 59	30	20	39
Aged 60 to 69	36	20	32
Aged 70 or older	40	8	35
Not a high school graduate	44	14	24
High school graduate	33	19	35
Bachelor's degree	26	27	36
Graduate degree	22	25	45

Note: Percents may not add to 100 because "can't choose" and no answer are not included.
Source: General Social Survey, National Opinion Research Center, University of Chicago

Faith or Science?

A majority (52 percent) of Americans agree that "we believe too often in science, and not enough in feelings and faith." About a quarter say they neither agree nor disagree with this statement, while 20 percent disagree.

Women and men are not far apart on this question, although women are slightly more likely to believe we put too much faith in science. Black and white Americans, however, are far apart on this issue, with blacks considerably more likely to believe that science is overrated (67 percent of blacks versus 50 percent of whites).

The generations are not in agreement on this issue, but the differences by age are not large. The gap is greatest between people under age 40 and those in their 60s. Less than half of the younger group agree that we place too much faith in science, compared to 65 percent of those in their 60s.

Not surprisingly, the scientists themselves (people with graduate degrees) are far more likely than average to disagree with this notion. Fully 38 percent disagree that we rely too much on science. In contrast, only 12 percent of people who did not complete high school, 17 percent of high school graduates, and 27 percent of college graduates disagree with the statement.

Faith or Science? 1994

"We believe too often in science, and not enough in feelings and faith. How much do you agree or disagree?"

(percent responding by sex, race, age, and education, 1994)

	strongly agree	agree	neither agree nor disagree	disagree	strongly disagree	agree, total	disagree, total
Total	12%	40%	23%	17%	3%	52%	20%
Women	13	42	22	14	2	55	16
Men	10	38	23	21	4	48	25
Black	22	45	15	10	2	67	12
White	10	40	24	18	3	50	21
Aged 18 to 29	8	39	22	24	3	47	27
Aged 30 to 39	12	36	26	19	3	48	22
Aged 40 to 49	11	41	25	15	4	52	19
Aged 50 to 59	15	40	20	15	3	55	18
Aged 60 to 69	19	46	20	8	2	65	10
Aged 70 or older	8	47	16	14	1	55	15
Not a high school graduate	15	48	13	11	1	63	12
High school graduate	13	41	24	15	2	54	17
Bachelor's degree	6	34	28	22	5	40	27
Graduate degree	3	34	23	29	9	38	38

Note: Percents may not add to 100 because "can't choose" and no answer are not included.
Source: General Social Survey, National Opinion Research Center, University of Chicago

5

Work and Money

While Americans are sometimes divided in their opinions about work and money, they are surprisingly optimistic about their financial situation despite corporate downsizing, a sluggish economy, and an uncertain future. Most (three out of four) adults are "pretty well" or "more or less" satisfied with their current financial situation. Only 26 percent say they are not at all satisfied. These responses are similar to those from 1974 and 1984, although our society has changed enormously during those two decades. Majorities of Americans agree that:

- Working women should receive paid maternity leave (71 percent).

- Hard work rather than luck is the key to getting ahead (69 percent).

- They would keep working even if they had enough money to live comfortably for the rest of their lives (65 percent).

- Their standard of living is at least somewhat better than their parents' was at the same age (63 percent).

Less agreement is found on other questions, however.

- A 47 percent plurality of Americans say a feeling of accomplishment is most important in a job, compared with high income (most important to 22 percent), a chance for advancement (17 percent), job security (8 percent), or short working hours (2 percent).

- Fewer than half (45 percent) of Americans believe their children's future standard of living will be at least somewhat better than theirs is today. Twenty percent believe it will be the same and 21 percent fear it will be worse.

- The largest percentage (41 percent) say their financial situation has stayed the same over the last few years. Thirty-six percent say it has improved, while only one-quarter say it has gotten worse.

- Only 42 percent say child care benefits should be available to parents if both work.

Men and Women Have Similar Opinions

Couples may fight about the family finances, but on the issues examined here men and women have little to fight about. Similar percentages of both men and women:

- Think hard work, rather than luck, is how people get ahead (70 percent of women and 68 percent of men);

- Would continue working even if they didn't need the money (64 percent of women and 65 percent of men);

- Believe their standard of living is better than that of their parents at the same age (61 percent of women and 65 percent of men);

- Believe their children's future standard of living will be better than theirs is now (46 percent of women and 44 percent of men);

- Are "more or less" satisfied with their financial situation (45 percent of women, 46 percent of men); the remainder are split between "pretty well" or "not at all" satisfied;

- Say that over the last few years their financial situation has stayed about the same (41 percent of women and 40 percent of men), improved (35 percent of women and 38 percent of men), or gotten worse (24 percent of women and 21 percent of men).

Where the opinions of men and women differ, the differences are slight.

- Women are slightly more likely to say a feeling of accomplishment is most important in a job (50 percent of women versus 43 percent of men). Men are more likely to say high income is more important (25 percent versus 19 percent).

- Women are somewhat more likely to support maternity leave for working women (75 percent compared with 65 percent of men).

- Women are also more likely to support child care benefits for dual-income families (46 percent of women compared with 37 percent of men).

Blacks Feel Like They've Lost Ground

Blacks and whites agree about many financial issues. Similar percentages of blacks and whites say:

- People get ahead through hard work rather than luck (66 percent of blacks and 69 percent of whites);

- They would continue working even if they were financially well-off (67 percent of blacks and 64 percent of whites);

- Their standard of living is better than that of their parents at their age (68 percent of blacks and 62 percent of whites).

Whites are slightly more likely than blacks to say their financial situation has improved over the past few years (37 percent, compared to 31 percent of blacks). But blacks are considerably more likely than whites to say:

- They support paid maternity leave for working women (81 percent of blacks compared with 69 percent of whites);

- Their children will enjoy a better standard of living (63 percent of blacks compared with 41 percent of whites);

- Parents should receive child care benefits if both work (52 percent of blacks compared with 40 percent of whites);

- They are not at all satisfied with their present financial situation (38 percent of blacks compared with 24 percent of whites).

There are distinct differences between blacks and whites in how they rank various job characteristics.

- Blacks rank high income as the most important job characteristic (36 percent), followed by chance for advancement (28 percent), and a feeling of accomplishment (22 percent). Whites rank a feeling of accomplishment first (52 percent), followed by high income (18 percent), and chance for advancement (15 percent).

Differences by Age Linked to Life Stage

On many work and money issues, differences in attitudes are strongly associated with age. Behind this association is life stage. Young adults are in entry-level jobs and generally have low incomes. The middle-aged are at the peak of their careers and incomes. Older Americans are retired and dependent on pensions and Social Security. These experiences shape attitudes.

- Young adults are considerably more likely than their elders to say their financial situation has improved in the last few years (47 to 48 percent of people under age 40). This is predictable, since incomes rise with age until people are in their 40s and 50s. Among people in their 40s and 50s, a smaller 33 to 36 percent say their finances have improved. Among those in the post-retirement age groups, only 14 to 20 percent say their situation has improved.

- Young adults are more likely to be dissatisfied with their current financial situation than older people. From 26 to 32 percent of those under age 60 are dissatisfied, compared with 13 to 18 percent of those aged 60 or over.

- Younger generations are far more likely than older ones to support paid maternity leave for working women. Three-quarters of adults under age 50 and two-thirds of those in their 50s support maternity leave, but only 59 to 60 percent of people aged 60 or older agree.

- Support for child care benefits for working parents also divides along generational lines. A majority of people under age 40 support child care benefits, but support is lower in each older age group. Only 18 percent of people aged 70 or older feel child care benefits should be provided.

- The percentage of workers who would continue to work if they had as much money as they needed declines through the working years, from 71 percent of people under age 30 to 56 percent of those in their 50s. It rises again, however, among older workers.

- People under age 60 say the most important job characteristic is a feeling of accomplishment, followed by high income and the chance for advancement. Workers in their 60s rank advancement slightly higher than income. But workers aged 70 or older say the most important characteristic is advancement, followed by a feeling of accomplishment.

- Among the age groups, about the same percentages believe their children will be better off (43 to 46 percent) with two exceptions. People in their 40s are less likely to think so (39 percent) and those in their 20s are more likely to think so (54 percent).

- Older Americans are most likely to say they are better off than their parents were at the same age (69 to 77 percent of those aged 50 or older). The percentage is considerably lower among younger people. Only a bare majority (53 percent) of people in their 30s say they are better off than their parents were.

- There is some variation by age in the percentage of people who believe hard work is the route to success, although there is no discernible age-related pattern. Seventy-three percent of people under age 30 say hard work is the ticket to success, compared with 63 percent of people in their 60s. The other age groups fall in between.

More Education, Fewer Complaints

As a rule, the higher the educational level, the more money people make. This accounts for the higher levels of financial satisfaction found among the college-educated. On only two issues are responses similar by education. Regardless of education, majorities say:

- Working women should receive paid maternity leave (66 to 72 percent);

- They have a better standard of living than their parents did at the same age (61 to 65 percent).

People with college degrees are more likely than those with lower levels of education to:

- Rank a feeling of accomplishment first out of five job characteristics (66 to 71 percent of people with college degrees). While a 46 percent plurality of high school graduates rank accomplishment first, only 29 percent of people who did not complete high school agree;

- Say their financial situation has improved in the last few years. From 46 to 49 percent of people with at least a bachelor's degree say this, compared with 23 to 34 percent of those with a high school diploma or less;

- Say they are satisfied with their current financial situation. From 35 to 38 percent of people with college degrees say this, compared with 25 to 26 percent of those with less education;

- Say luck is equally or more important than hard work in getting ahead (33 to 38 percent of people with a college degree say luck is a major factor, compared with 28 percent of those with a high school diploma or less).

Perhaps because of their relatively high standard of living, only a small percentage of people with college degrees:

- Believe their children's future standard of living will be better than their own (27 to 33 percent of those with at least a bachelor's degree say this, compared with 47 to 50 percent of people with less education).

Responses varied by education on the two remaining issues.

- Workers with high school diplomas are least likely to say they would continue working if they had enough money to live comfortably (62 percent). Those with graduate degrees are most likely to say they would continue to work (74 percent).

- People with graduate degrees are mavericks on the issue of child care benefits for working couples. While 41 to 43 percent of people with a bachelor's degree or less education support these benefits, only 35 percent of those with graduate degrees agree.

Satisfaction With Financial Situation

While most Americans don't say their finances are lousy, most aren't thrilled with their bank accounts, either. Only 28 percent of adults say they are "pretty well" satisfied with their finances. A similar proportion (26 percent) say they are "not at all" satisfied. Slightly fewer than half (46 percent) take the middle ground, saying they are "more or less" satisfied.

The percentage taking the middle ground does not vary much by demographic segment. But several groups are more likely than average to say they are "pretty well" or "not at all" satisfied.

Blacks are more likely than whites to say they are "not at all" satisfied (38 percent). Only 24 percent of whites say they are unhappy with their finances.

Younger adults are also more likely to be financially unhappy. This is not surprising, since most are entry-level workers with low incomes. The proportion of Americans who are not satisfied with their finances drops with age, from 32 percent of those under age 30 to 13 percent of those aged 70 or older.

People aged 60 or older are far more likely than average to say they are "pretty well" satisfied with their finances (41 to 43 percent). They should be. This generation has been more successful in building retirement savings (thanks in large measure to rapid gains in home values and generous pension and Social Security benefits) than any previous generation. Future generations of retirees may have less reason to be so sanguine.

Because education is directly related to earnings, people with higher levels of education are more likely than others to say they are "pretty well" satisfied with their financial situation.

Satisfaction With Financial Situation, 1994

"So far as you and your family are concerned, would you say that you are pretty well satisfied with your present financial situation, more or less satisfied, or not satisfied at all?"

(percent responding by sex, race, age, and education, 1994)

	pretty well satisfied	more or less satisfied	not at all satisfied
Total	28%	46%	26%
Women	27	45	27
Men	28	46	25
Black	18	44	38
White	30	46	24
Aged 18 to 29	20	47	32
Aged 30 to 39	21	48	31
Aged 40 to 49	26	46	28
Aged 50 to 59	30	44	26
Aged 60 to 69	41	41	18
Aged 70 or older	43	42	13
Not a high school graduate	26	42	31
High school graduate	25	46	28
Bachelor's degree	35	44	21
Graduate degree	38	49	13

Note: Numbers may not add to 100 because "don't know" and no answer are not included.
Source: General Social Survey, National Opinion Research Center, University of Chicago

Satisfaction With Financial Situation, 1974 to 1994

"So far as you and your family are concerned,
would you say that you are pretty well satisfied
with your present financial situation, more or
less satisfied, or not satisfied at all?"

(percent responding by sex, race, age, and education, 1974-94)

	pretty well satisfied			more or less satisfied			not at all satisfied		
	1994	*1984*	*1974*	*1994*	*1984*	*1974*	*1994*	*1984*	*1974*
Total	28%	28%	31%	46%	45%	45%	26%	26%	23%
Women	27	28	31	45	47	46	27	25	23
Men	28	29	32	46	43	45	25	27	23
Black	18	17	22	44	38	46	38	44	32
White	30	29	32	46	47	45	24	24	22
Aged 18 to 29	20	20	22	47	50	51	32	28	27
Aged 30 to 39	21	19	26	48	49	45	31	31	29
Aged 40 to 49	26	26	30	46	44	51	28	30	19
Aged 50 to 59	30	32	36	44	44	40	26	24	24
Aged 60 to 69	41	47	41	41	37	39	18	16	19
Aged 70 or older	43	43	47	42	39	40	13	18	13
Not a high school graduate	26	27	33	42	42	41	31	31	25
High school grad.	25	26	27	46	48	49	28	25	24
Bachelor's degree	35	35	35	44	45	45	21	19	19
Graduate degree	38	47	43	49	35	47	13	18	10

Note: Numbers may not add to 100 because "don't know" and no answer are not included.
Source: General Social Survey, National Opinion Research Center, University of Chicago

Changes in Financial Situation

Americans are more likely to say their financial situation has gotten better (36 percent) than gotten worse (23 percent) during the past few years. But the largest percentage (41 percent) say their situation has not changed. Overall, Americans' assessment of short-term changes in their financial situation was about the same in 1994 as it was in 1974.

There are only small differences in the proportions of blacks and whites who say their financial situation has gotten better or worse. There is almost no difference between men's and women's assessment of their financial situation.

The young and the old are miles apart, however. Older people are more likely to say their situation has remained the same or gotten worse. Younger people are more likely to say their financial situation has improved. Nearly half of people under age 40 say they've seen improvements, compared with 20 percent or fewer of those aged 60 or older. Some of this difference is due to the rising incomes of younger adults as they gain job experience. Most people aged 60 or older, on the other hand, have incomes that, at best, rise at the rate of inflation.

People in their 30s in 1994 (younger baby boomers) were slightly less likely than were people in this age group in 1974 (pre-boomers) to say their financial situation had gotten worse. But people aged 70 or older were more likely to say their financial situation had deteriorated than did the oldest age group in 1974.

People who did not complete high school were more likely to say in 1994 than in 1974 that their financial situation had gotten worse in the past few years. Changes in the economy have reduced the wages of less-educated workers, leaving those without a high school diploma in a difficult situation.

Changes in Financial Situation, 1994

"During the last few years, has your financial situation been getting better, worse, or has it stayed the same? "

(percent responding by sex, race, age, and education, 1994)

	gotten better	stayed the same	gotten worse
Total	36%	41%	23%
Women	35	41	24
Men	38	40	21
Black	31	47	20
White	37	40	23
Aged 18 to 29	48	34	17
Aged 30 to 39	47	34	19
Aged 40 to 49	36	35	29
Aged 50 to 59	33	41	25
Aged 60 to 69	20	56	24
Aged 70 or older	14	61	23
Not a high school graduate	23	22	54
High school graduate	34	25	41
Bachelor's degree	49	18	32
Graduate degree	46	20	33

Note: Percents may not add to 100 because "don't know" and no answer are not included.
Source: General Social Survey, University of Chicago, National Opinion Research Center

Changes in Financial Situation, 1974 to 1994

"During the last few years, has your financial situation been getting better, worse, or has it stayed the same?"

(percent responding by sex, race, age, and education, 1974-94)

	gotten better			stayed the same			gotten worse		
	1994	1984	1974	1994	1984	1974	1994	1984	1974
Total	36%	39%	39%	41%	39%	39%	23%	22%	22%
Women	35	36	39	41	41	38	24	22	22
Men	38	42	40	40	37	39	21	21	21
Black	31	27	35	47	45	41	20	27	24
White	37	40	40	40	39	38	23	21	21
Aged 18 to 29	48	51	46	34	29	34	17	18	19
Aged 30 to 39	47	46	44	34	31	30	19	22	25
Aged 40 to 49	36	33	40	35	37	37	29	29	22
Aged 50 to 59	33	32	37	41	42	38	25	26	24
Aged 60 to 69	20	28	28	56	51	50	24	21	22
Aged 70 or older	14	18	30	61	68	52	23	14	16
Not a high school graduate	23	24	31	22	50	24	54	26	45
High school grad.	34	41	42	25	38	21	41	21	36
Bachelor's degree	49	57	52	18	25	17	32	18	30
Graduate degree	46	49	47	20	35	18	33	14	34

Note: Percents may not add to 100 because "don't know" and no answer are not included.
Source: General Social Survey, National Opinion Research Center, University of Chicago

Standard of Living Relative to Parents'

Most adults believe that their current standard of living is better than their parents enjoyed at the same age. A 63 percent majority say they have a better standard of living, with 31 percent saying it is much better.

Sixty-one percent of women and 65 percent of men say they have a better standard of living than their parents did. By race, 68 percent of blacks and 62 percent of whites say they have it better than their parents. The proportions do not vary much by education either.

The only significant variation is by age because the generations have different points of reference. About three-quarters of people aged 60 or older say they are better off than their parents were at their age. Today's elderly have been spared the extreme poverty experienced by a substantial portion of elderly in the past—thanks in large part to Social Security. Current retirees also benefited from unique economic circumstances, such as the rapid rise in home values during the 1970s and 1980s as the baby-boom generation bid up the price of homes. This has left today's older Americans better off in retirement than any previous generation.

Younger Americans, on the other hand, have been struggling since the early 1970s with stagnating or declining wages. Only 5 percent of people aged 70 or older say they are worse off than their parents were at their age. In comparison, fully 22 percent of people in their 30s, and 19 percent of those under age 30, say they are worse off than their parents were at their age.

Standard of Living Relative to Parents', 1994

"Compared to your parents when they were the age you
are now, do you think your own standard of living now
is much better, somewhat better, about the same,
somewhat worse, or much worse than theirs was?"

(percent responding by sex, race, age, and education, 1994)

	much better	somewhat better	about the same	somewhat worse	much worse	better, total	worse, total
Total	31%	32%	21%	11%	3%	63%	14%
Women	29	32	22	11	4	61	15
Men	34	31	19	12	3	65	15
Black	34	34	14	12	5	68	17
White	30	32	22	11	3	62	14
Aged 18 to 29	25	34	21	14	5	59	19
Aged 30 to 39	21	32	24	18	4	53	22
Aged 40 to 49	27	34	25	9	4	61	13
Aged 50 to 59	37	32	16	12	2	69	14
Aged 60 to 69	47	30	16	3	2	77	5
Aged 70 or older	43	28	17	4	1	71	5
Not a high school graduate	34	30	19	10	4	64	14
High school graduate	30	31	21	12	3	61	15
Bachelor's degree	27	34	25	10	3	61	13
Graduate degree	32	33	19	12	2	65	14

Note: Percents may not add to 100 because "don't know" and no answer are not included.
Source: General Social Survey, National Opinion Research Center, University of Chicago

Children's Future Standard of Living

All parents want their children to have a life that is as good or better than theirs. Overall, 45 percent of Americans believe their children will live better than they themselves do today. Only 21 percent believe their children's standard of living will be somewhat or much worse.

The percentage who say their children will do better depends on the circumstances of each demographic segment. Among Americans who now have a below-average standard of living, a relatively large percentage expect a better life for their children. Blacks, for example, have the greatest expectations for their children's future. Fully 63 percent believe their children's standard of living will be at least somewhat better than their own. Only 42 percent of whites feel this way.

People with graduate degrees, who command above-average salaries, are least likely to believe their children's standard of living will be better than their own. Instead, they are most likely to think their children will achieve about the same standard of living as they now enjoy.

Children's Future Standard of Living, 1994

"When your children are at the age you are now,
do you think their standard of living will be much better,
somewhat better, about the same, somewhat worse,
or much worse than yours is now?"

(percent responding by sex, race, age, and education, 1994)

	much better	somewhat better	about the same	somewhat worse	much worse	better, total	worse, total
Total	17%	28%	21%	16%	5%	45%	21%
Women	17	29	21	15	5	46	20
Men	16	28	20	16	5	44	21
Black	30	33	11	11	5	63	16
White	14	28	22	17	5	42	22
Aged 18 to 29	22	32	17	15	5	54	20
Aged 30 to 39	15	30	21	16	5	45	21
Aged 40 to 49	13	26	21	15	6	39	21
Aged 50 to 59	15	30	24	16	5	45	21
Aged 60 to 69	22	23	22	15	4	45	19
Aged 70 or older	16	27	19	16	2	43	18
Not a high school graduate	21	26	16	18	6	47	24
High school graduate	19	31	18	15	6	50	21
Bachelor's degree	9	24	31	16	3	33	19
Graduate degree	6	21	28	16	3	27	19

Note: Numbers may not add to 100 because "don't know" and no answer are not included.
Source: General Social Survey, National Opinion Research Center, University of Chicago

Would You Work If You Were Rich?

About one-third of working Americans would lay down their pencils or tools if they had enough money to live comfortably for the rest of their lives. But two-thirds say they would go on working, even if they didn't need the money. Money may be a major reason for working, but it is clearly not the only one.

About the same proportions of working men and women, blacks and whites, say they would continue to work even if they had as much money as they needed. But there are significant differences by age. Seventy-one percent of young adults, with the enthusiasm of those just entering the work force, say they would keep working. Among workers in their 40s—with two decades of work under their belt—the proportion drops to 62 percent. Only 56 percent of workers in their 50s, when many people are beginning to think about retirement, would continue to work if they didn't need the money. But the proportion rises again among workers in their 60s and peaks among those aged 70 or older. Most of these older workers obviously want to work or they would already be retired.

Workers with graduate degrees are more likely than those with less education to say they would continue to work even if they didn't need to. This is no surprise, since graduate degree holders would not have invested so much money and time in getting a degree if they did not intend to use it.

Would You Work If You Were Rich? 1994

"If you were to get enough money to live as comfortably as you would like for the rest of your life, would you continue to work or would you stop working?"

(percent of workers responding by sex, race, age, and education, 1994)

	continue to work	stop working
Total	65%	34%
Women	64	34
Men	65	33
Black	67	31
White	64	34
Aged 18 to 29	71	28
Aged 30 to 39	67	32
Aged 40 to 49	62	37
Aged 50 to 59	56	42
Aged 60 to 69	64	34
Aged 70 or older	78	9
Not a high school graduate	67	33
High school graduate	62	37
Bachelor's degree	68	29
Graduate degree	74	24

Note: Asked of people who were currently working or temporarily out of work at the time of the survey. Numbers may not add to 100 because "don't know" and no answer are not included.
Source: General Social Survey, National Opinion Research Center, University of Chicago

Would You Work If You Were Rich? 1974 to 1994

"If you were to get enough money to live as comfortably as you would like for the rest of your life, would you continue to work or would you stop working?"

(percent of workers responding by sex, race, age, and education, 1974-94)

	continue to work			stop working		
	1994	1984	1974	1994	1984	1974
Total	65%	75%	63%	34%	24%	34%
Women	64	73	55	34	26	41
Men	65	77	68	33	21	30
Black	67	70	55	31	29	40
White	64	75	64	34	23	34
Aged 18 to 29	71	81	69	28	18	29
Aged 30 to 39	67	80	63	32	19	34
Aged 40 to 49	62	74	64	37	24	34
Aged 50 to 59	56	65	62	42	34	37
Aged 60 to 69	64	52	46	34	47	53
Aged 70 or older	78	71	53	9	24	40
Not a high school graduate	67	65	56	33	31	43
High school graduate	62	76	61	37	24	37
Bachelor's degree	68	77	79	29	21	17
Graduate degree	74	81	82	24	17	15

Note: Asked of people who were currently working or temporarily out of work at the time of the survey. Percents may not add to 100 because "don't know" and no answer are not included.
Source: General Social Survey, National Opinion Research Center, University of Chicago

Hard Work or Luck?

A majority of Americans believe it is by the sweat of their brows that they get ahead. But a substantial minority (30 percent) believe luck plays an equal or more important role.

Men and women, blacks and whites, are in agreement on this issue. While there is some variation by age, only one age group stands in sharp contrast on this issue. Fully 37 percent of people aged 60 to 69 believe luck is as or more important than hard work, versus 30 percent of all Americans.

Interestingly, people with higher levels of education are less likely to believe that hard work is the key to success. Thirty-eight percent of people with graduate degrees believe luck is at least as important as hard work, compared with 28 percent of those with a high school diploma or less.

The proportion of Americans saying hard work is more important increased from 1974 to 1994 in every demographic segment, but especially among men, young adults, and people in their 50s. The public's strong and growing belief in hard work calls into question the claim that Americans have become jaded and cynical.

Hard Work or Luck? 1994

"Some people say that people get ahead by their
own hard work; others say that lucky breaks or
help from other people are more important.
Which do you think is most important?"

(percent responding by sex, race, age, and education, 1994)

	hard work	hard work, luck equally important	luck
Total	69%	19%	11%
Women	70	20	9
Men	68	19	12
Black	66	22	12
White	69	19	11
Aged 18 to 29	73	18	8
Aged 30 to 39	67	19	13
Aged 40 to 49	69	19	11
Aged 50 to 59	70	22	9
Aged 60 to 69	63	25	12
Aged 70 or older	71	16	10
Not a high school graduate	70	16	12
High school graduate	71	18	10
Bachelor's degree	66	22	11
Graduate degree	61	32	6

Note: Percents may not add to 100 because "don't know" and no answer are not included.
Source: General Social Survey, National Opinion Research Center, University of Chicago

Hard Work or Luck? 1974 to 1994

Some people say that people get ahead by their own hard work; others say that lucky breaks or help from other people are more important. Which do you think is most important?"

(percent responding by sex, race, age, and education, 1974-94)

	hard work			hard work, luck equally important			luck		
	1994	*1984*	*1974*	*1994*	*1984*	*1974*	*1994*	*1984*	*1974*
Total	69%	66%	61%	19%	18%	29%	11%	15%	9%
Women	70	68	64	20	18	27	9	13	8
Men	68	64	57	19	18	30	12	17	10
Black	66	63	58	22	15	32	12	20	9
White	69	67	61	19	18	28	11	14	9
Aged 18 to 29	73	71	61	18	16	25	8	13	12
Aged 30 to 39	67	64	60	19	20	33	13	17	6
Aged 40 to 49	69	65	63	19	17	29	11	17	6
Aged 50 to 59	70	69	57	22	17	31	9	13	9
Aged 60 to 69	63	60	61	25	24	28	12	15	8
Aged 70 or older	71	66	64	16	15	25	10	16	10
Not a high school graduate	70	66	62	16	15	26	12	18	10
High school grad.	71	68	60	18	18	31	10	14	8
Bachelor's degree	66	64	63	22	20	23	11	15	10
Graduate degree	61	65	55	32	22	36	6	12	7

Note: Percents may not add to 100 because "don't know" and no answer are not included.
Source: General Social Survey, National Opinion Research Center, University of Chicago

Maternity Leave

Americans strongly support paid maternity leave for working women. Fully 71 percent say it should be provided, while only 12 percent disagree.

Women are more supportive than men (75 versus 65 percent). Blacks are much more supportive than whites (81 versus 69 percent).

As with most issues involving working women, the generations disagree. Younger people are more supportive of paid leave than their elders. Three-quarters of people under age 50 believe women should receive paid maternity leave, but the proportion drops to around 60 percent among people aged 60 or older.

There is less disagreement by educational, though people with graduate degrees are surprisingly less supportive of paid maternity leave than others. Eighteen percent are opposed, versus 9 to 14 percent of those with less education.

Maternity Leave, 1994

"Working women should receive paid maternity leave when they have a baby—do you agree or disagree?"

(percent responding by sex, race, age, and education, 1994)

	strongly agree	agree	neither	disagree	strongly disagree	agree, total	disagree, total
Total	27%	44%	10%	10%	2%	71%	12%
Women	31	44	10	8	1	75	9
Men	21	44	11	14	3	65	17
Black	35	46	5	2	1	81	3
White	25	43	11	12	2	69	14
Aged 18 to 29	39	37	8	4	1	76	5
Aged 30 to 39	32	43	10	7	2	75	9
Aged 40 to 49	26	48	9	11	1	74	12
Aged 50 to 59	22	44	11	12	4	66	16
Aged 60 to 69	13	46	13	19	3	59	22
Aged 70 or older	14	46	12	16	2	60	18
Not a high school graduate	23	49	8	8	1	72	9
High school graduate	26	43	11	11	2	69	13
Bachelor's degree	26	45	11	11	3	71	14
Graduate degree	26	40	11	13	5	66	18

Note: Numbers may not add to 100 because "can't choose" and no answer are not included.
Source: General Social Survey, National Opinion Research Center, University of Chicago

Child Care Benefits for Working Parents

A plurality of Americans (42 percent) agree that "families should receive financial benefits for child care when both parents work." About one-third disagree, while 18 percent say they neither agree nor disagree with the statement.

Those most likely to agree are also most likely to have a personal stake in the issue. Women are somewhat more likely than men to feel child care benefits should be provided (46 percent of women compared with 37 percent of men). A larger disparity is found between blacks and whites, with over half of blacks in favor compared with 40 percent of whites.

The group most supportive of child care benefits are people in their 30s (57 percent), who are most likely to have young children at home. People under age 30 are almost equally supportive of child care benefits (54 percent). But as the need declines, so does support for benefits. Only 34 percent of people in their 50s and 18 percent of those aged 70 or older think that benefits should be provided.

By education, about the same proportion of people favor child care benefits (41 to 43 percent), but those with graduate degrees are least supportive (35 percent).

Child Care Benefits for Working Parents, 1994

"Families should receive financial benefits for child care
when both parents work—do you agree or disagree?"

(percent responding by sex, race, age, and education, 1994)

	strongly agree	agree	neither	disagree	strongly disagree	agree, total	disagree, total
Total	14%	28%	18%	27%	5%	42%	32%
Women	17	29	18	24	4	46	28
Men	10	27	19	31	6	37	37
Black	19	33	15	19	3	52	22
White	13	27	19	28	5	40	33
Aged 18 to 29	24	30	19	14	3	54	17
Aged 30 to 39	22	35	13	19	4	57	23
Aged 40 to 49	11	33	21	26	4	44	30
Aged 50 to 59	9	25	19	34	8	34	42
Aged 60 to 69	5	19	18	43	6	24	49
Aged 70 or older	3	15	21	41	8	18	49
Not a high school graduate	13	28	16	29	3	41	32
High school graduate	14	28	19	27	4	42	31
Bachelor's degree	14	29	19	24	7	43	31
Graduate degree	11	24	17	32	9	35	41

Note: Percents may not add to 100 because "can't choose" and no answer are not included.
Source: General Social Survey, National Opinion Research Center, University of Chicago

Most Important Job Characteristic

Americans work for different reasons. When asked to rank five different job characteristics (feeling of accomplishment, high income, chance for promotion, job security, and short working hours), people have different ideas about their order of importance. Nearly half choose "a feeling of accomplishment" as the most important of five different job characteristics. High income is most important to 22 percent, while 17 percent say they most want a chance for advancement.

Given the current economic climate and the time pressure most people feel, it is remarkable that only 8 percent choose job security as the most important characteristic and that only 2 percent choose short working hours. This is not to say, however, that people do not want secure jobs or lots of time off from work. But most people would not choose to be secure in a miserable dead-end job or choose to have lots of free time without enough income to make ends meet.

Both men and women are more likely to choose "feeling of accomplishment" over other characteristics as the most important aspect of a job. Blacks and whites rank job characteristics differently, however. The largest percentage of blacks (36 percent) choose high income as the most important characteristic, followed by chance for promotion (28 percent), and feeling of accomplishment (22 percent). Whites are far more likely to say a feeling of accomplishment (52 percent) is most important. Only 18 percent of whites say a high income is most important. At least some of this disparity results from the fact that blacks are more likely than whites to have low incomes.

In almost every age group, a feeling of accomplishment is the most important job characteristic, followed by a high income for those under age 60 and a chance for advancement among people aged 60 or older. People aged 70 or older, however, rank chance for advancement as most important.

The higher the level of education, the greater the percentage of people who rank a sense of accomplishment as the most important job characteristic. Among people who did not complete high school, a high income is just as important as a feeling of accomplishment.

Most Important Job Characteristic, 1994

"Which one thing would you most prefer in a job?

(percent ranking each job characteristic as most important by sex, race, age, and education, 1994)

	feeling of accomplishment	high income	chance for advancement	job security	short working hours
Total	47%	22%	17%	8%	2%
Women	50	19	19	6	1
Men	43	25	14	10	4
Black	22	36	28	11	0
White	52	18	15	8	3
Aged 18 to 29	43	23	19	6	2
Aged 30 to 39	52	25	12	5	3
Aged 40 to 49	51	23	12	9	1
Aged 50 to 59	49	26	12	8	3
Aged 60 to 69	52	13	19	10	2
Aged 70 or older	31	13	34	13	2
Not a high school graduate	29	29	20	12	4
High school graduate	46	21	19	9	2
Bachelor's degree	71	16	10	0	0
Graduate degree	66	17	7	3	0

Source: General Social Survey, National Opinion Research Center, University of Chicago

Most Important Job Characteristic, 1974 to 1994

"Which one thing would you most prefer in a job?

(percent ranking each characteristic as most important by sex, race, age, and education, 1974-94)

	feeling of accomplishment			high income			chance for advancement		
	1994	*1984*	*1974*	*1994*	*1984*	*1974*	*1994*	*1984*	*1974*
Total	47%	50%	50%	22%	19%	18%	17%	19%	18%
Women	50	52	55	19	18	18	19	18	15
Men	43	47	45	25	20	18	14	20	20
Black	22	24	27	36	36	39	28	21	18
White	52	54	53	18	17	16	15	19	18
Aged 18 to 29	43	43	49	23	23	13	19	23	22
Aged 30 to 39	52	55	54	25	15	24	12	20	13
Aged 40 to 49	51	54	57	23	22	20	12	14	13
Aged 50 to 59	49	54	48	26	20	19	12	10	16
Aged 60 to 69	52	52	46	13	17	18	19	16	20
Aged 70 or older	31	45	41	13	11	16	34	24	22
Not a high school graduate	29	39	36	29	24	26	20	17	19
High school grad.	46	49	53	21	19	17	19	22	19
Bachelor's degree	71	65	70	16	13	7	10	14	10
Graduate degree	66	75	81	17	10	3	7	7	8

(continued)

(continued from previous page)

	job security			short working hours		
	1994	*1984*	*1974*	*1994*	*1984*	*1974*
Total	8%	7%	8%	2%	3%	5%
Women	6	7	5	1	3	5
Men	10	8	10	4	3	5
Black	11	12	9	0	4	6
White	8	7	7	3	3	5
Aged 18 to 29	6	6	10	2	2	4
Aged 30 to 39	5	6	4	3	4	4
Aged 40 to 49	9	5	6	1	2	4
Aged 50 to 59	8	12	7	3	4	8
Aged 60 to 69	10	9	9	2	2	4
Aged 70 or older	13	10	10	2	3	6
Not a high school graduate	12	14	12	4	3	6
High school grad.	9	6	5	2	2	4
Bachelor's degree	0	2	4	0	4	7
Graduate degree	3	3	1	0	4	3

Source: General Social Survey, National Opinion Research Center, University of Chicago

6

Marriage and Family

Most people say they are happily married and that their family life is satisfying. Americans' attitudes regarding marriage and divorce are upbeat within most demographic segments. But there are dramatic differences in attitude by generation that underscore the changing nature of marriage and family in American society.

On average, Americans are in agreement on most of the issues considered here. Majorities of Americans say they:

- Get a great or very great deal of satisfaction from family life (75 percent);

- Do not believe a bad marriage is better than no marriage (89 percent);

- Do think it's sometimes necessary to spank a child (72 percent);

- Agree that watching children grow up is life's greatest joy (78 percent);

- Do not believe having children interferes too much with the freedom of parents (72 percent);

- Do not believe a childless couple should stay together even if they don't get along (78 percent);

- Believe people who want children should marry (71 percent);

- Do not feel parents should stay together just for the sake of the children (63 percent);

- Have a very happy marriage (60 percent);

- Do not believe the main purpose of marriage these days is to have children (67 percent);

- Don't agree that the main advantage of marriage is financial security (60 percent).

Smaller majorities or pluralities say:

- Family life often suffers because men concentrate too much on their work (56 percent);

- Two is the ideal number of children (53 percent);

- It is most important for children to learn to think for themselves (53 percent);

- They don't believe people who do not have children lead empty lives (50 percent);

- One parent cannot bring up a child as well as two parents together (49 percent);

- Divorce is usually the best solution when a couple can't work out problems (47 percent);

- Married people are happier than unmarried people (45 percent).

Women Enjoy Family Life More

Women and men share the same outlook on marriage, divorce, and the joys of parenting. Similar percentages of women and men say:

- Their marriages are very happy (59 percent of women and 61 percent of men);

- Watching children grow up is life's greatest joy (80 percent of women and 76 percent of men);

- Two children is the ideal number (54 percent of women and 52 percent of men);

- If people want children, they should marry (70 percent of women and 72 percent of men);

- They don't believe childless couples should remain together if they don't get along (79 percent of women and 74 percent of men);

- Even couples with children should not have to stay together if they are unhappy (69 percent of women and 55 percent of men);

- Men focus too much on work and it takes a toll on the family (54 percent of women and 60 percent of men);

- Divorce is usually best if marital problems can't be worked out (46 percent of women and 47 percent of men);

- The main advantage of marriage is not financial security (62 percent of women compared with 57 percent of men).

The differences of opinion between the sexes are telling, however. Women are more satisfied with family life than men, but they are also more confident that they could live without it. Women are more likely than men to say:

- They get a great or very great deal of satisfaction from family life (79 percent of women compared with 70 percent of men);

- One parent can raise a child as well as two (43 percent of women compared with 25 percent of men);

- They do not believe a bad marriage is better than no marriage (93 percent of women compared with 84 percent of men);

- They don't believe having children interferes too much with parents' freedom (75 percent of women compared with 68 percent of men);

- They don't agree that life is empty without children (53 percent of women compared with 46 percent of men);

- They do not believe the main reason people marry is to have kids (73 percent of women compared with 60 percent of men);

- The most important thing children should learn is to think for themselves (56 percent of women compared with 49 percent of men).

Men are more likely to say:

- Married people are happier than the unmarried (49 percent of men compared with 42 percent of women);

- It is sometimes necessary to discipline a child with a "good, hard spanking" (78 percent of men compared with 69 percent of women).

Many Differences by Race

While there are many differences of opinion on marriage and family issues by race, similar proportions of blacks and whites say:

- They get a great or very great deal of satisfaction from family life (75 percent of blacks and 74 percent of whites);

- Watching children grow up is life's greatest joy (80 percent of blacks and 78 percent of whites);

- A bad marriage is not preferable to no marriage (86 percent of blacks and 90 percent of whites);

- The don't agree that childless couples should stay together even if they don't get along (77 percent of blacks and 78 percent of whites);

- Even if children are present, unhappy couples should not have to stay together (60 percent of blacks and 64 percent of whites);

- They do not feel too much freedom is lost when people have children (72 percent of whites and 69 percent of blacks);

- They do not believe that people who don't have children lead empty lives (53 percent of blacks and 49 percent of whites);

- They don't believe the main purpose of marriage is to have children (65 percent of blacks and 68 percent of whites).

On a few questions, the differences of opinion between blacks and whites are small. But on other issues, there are wide gaps in opinion. Whites are more likely than blacks to say:

- Men often focus too much on work, to the detriment of their families (58 percent of whites compared with 46 percent of blacks);

- Two children is the ideal number (56 percent of whites compared with 35 percent of blacks);

- Their marriages are very happy (62 percent of whites compared with 37 percent of blacks);

- Married people are happier than the unmarried (47 percent of whites compared with 28 percent of blacks);

- People who want children should marry (74 percent of whites compared with 54 percent of blacks);

- The most important quality to instill in children is independent thinking (55 percent of whites compared with 47 percent of blacks).

Blacks, on the other hand, are more likely than whites to say:

- Sparing the rod spoils the child. Fully 86 percent of blacks, compared with 70 percent of whites, say a spanking is sometimes necessary;

- The main advantage of marriage is financial security (33 percent of blacks compared with 14 percent of whites);

- One parent can do as good a job as two (52 percent of blacks compared with 32 percent of whites);

- Divorce is the best solution if a couple can't work out their problems (52 percent of blacks compared with 46 percent of whites);

- The most important quality to instill in children is obedience (28 percent of blacks say this, compared with 16 percent of whites).

Marriage Is Less Important to Younger Generations

While there are some marriage and family issues where the generations see eye-to-eye, there are sharp differences on most of the
fundamental questions. Marriage is not as important to younger
generations as it is to older ones.

On a few questions, there is little or no debate. Similar proportions of the different age groups:

- Don't view a bad marriage as better than none (ranging from 83 to
  92 percent);

- Agree that spanking is sometimes necessary to discipline children
  (ranging from 68 to 77 percent);

- Don't think childless couples should remain together if they don't
  get along (from 74 to 79 percent).

A difference of opinion—but no generational trend—can be found
in the proportions of people who say:

- They do not believe the main advantage of marriage is financial
  security (ranging from nearly two-thirds of people aged 30 to 49 and
  60 to 69 to just over half of the other age groups);

- Two is the ideal number of children (from over half of people aged
  30 to 59 compared with slightly less than half of those younger or
  older).

Sometimes, stage of life influences point of view.

- Most age groups agree that children are life's greatest joy, ranging
  from 78 to 80 percent of all but two age groups. The two exceptions:
  those in their 40s—who are likely to be parents of teenagers—are
  least likely to agree (71 percent); those aged 70 or older—who are
  likely to be grandparents—are most likely to agree (87 percent).

- Similar percentages of most age groups say their marriages are very
  happy (58 to 62 percent), but the happiest are the relative newcom-

ers to marriage. Sixty-six percent of people under age 30 say their marriages are very happy.

- Those under age 50 (who are most likely to be raising children) are less likely than older people to disagree with the statement, "having children interferes too much with the freedom of parents" (67 to 71 percent of those under age 50 compared with 77 percent of people aged 50 or older).

- Similar percentages of people under age 60 say they get a great or very great deal of satisfaction from family life (72 to 77 percent). But the percentage is slightly higher among people in their 60s (82 percent) and slightly lower among people aged 70 or older (68 percent).

The changing attitudes of younger generations are apparent in responses to many of the questions. Younger people are more likely than older ones to say they:

- Have a positive view of single parenting. Fifty percent of people under age 30 say one parent can do as good a job as two. Agreement is much lower in the older age groups, with only 16 percent of people aged 70 or older agreeing that one parent is as good;

- Don't believe married people are happier than the unmarried. The proportion saying married people are happier falls with each older age group, from 64 percent of those aged 70 or older to only 27 percent of those under age 30;

- Disagree that people who never had children lead empty lives (ranging from 56 percent of those under age 40 to 40 percent of those aged 70 or older);

- Don't believe the main purpose of marriage these days is to have children (ranging from 72 percent of people under age 30 to 58 percent of those aged 70 or older);

- Disagree that people who want children should marry (ranging from 26 percent of people under age 30 to only 4 to 5 percent of those aged 60 or older);

- Don't believe that men concentrate too much on work, causing family life to suffer (46 to 50 percent of people under age 40 compared with 59 to 66 percent of older adults).

Divorce is a great concern to the generations most affected by it.

- People aged 50 or older (who are less likely to be divorced or to have had their parents divorce) are most likely to say divorce is usually best when a couple can't work out problems. While 52 to 56 percent believe this, only 43 to 47 percent of baby boomers (aged 30 to 49) agree. Agreement is lowest among people under age 30 (35 percent).

- Even if they don't view divorce as the best solution, younger generations aren't willing to say unhappy couples should stay together. Among people under age 60, 62 to 68 percent say they don't believe unhappy couples should stay together, even if they have kids. A smaller 59 percent of people in their 60s and 49 percent of those aged 70 or older don't think parents should stay together if they are unhappy.

One question highlights the personality differences of Generation Xers, baby boomers, and older Americans.

- Older Americans (aged 50 or older) are more likely than younger ones to say it is most important for children to learn to be obedient (20 to 24 percent of people aged 50 to 69 and 34 percent of those aged 70 or older say this, compared with just 12 percent of people aged 30 to 49). Baby boomers (aged 30 to 49) are the ones most likely to say children should learn to think for themselves (59 to 60 percent compared with 35 to 54 percent of other age groups).

Education Splits Opinions

Differences of opinion on marriage and family issues by education are common. Some of the disagreement may be due to socioeco-

nomic differences (people with higher levels of education earn more, on average) or age differences (younger people generally have more education than older generations).

There are some areas of agreement, however. For example, there is little difference in the proportions of people who say:

- Family life often suffers because men concentrate too much on their work (ranging from 54 to 62 percent);

- People who want children should marry (ranging from 70 to 76 percent);

- Their marriages are very happy (ranging from 57 to 68 percent);

- They do not feel that a major reason to marry these days is to have kids (ranging from 63 to 71 percent).

College graduates are more likely than those with less education to say:

- They don't believe the main advantage of marriage is financial security (65 to 70 percent compared with 59 percent of those with a high school diploma and 47 percent of people who did not complete high school);

- The most important thing for children to learn is to think for themselves (65 to 68 percent of college graduates compared with 53 percent of high school graduates and just 33 percent of people who did not complete high school). Those with the least education are far more likely than others to believe it is most important that children learn to obey;

- People with graduate degrees are more likely than those with less education to say married people are happier than the unmarried (53 percent compared with 43 to 48 percent of those with a bachelor's degree or less).

People with less education are more likely to say they:

- Get a great or very great deal of satisfaction from family life (77 percent of people who did not complete high school, 74 percent of those with a high school diploma or bachelor's degree, and 69 percent of people with graduate degrees);

- Believe one parent can raise a child as well as two parents (36 to 38 percent of people with a high school diploma or less compared with 27 to 30 percent of the college-educated);

- Feel it is sometimes necessary to spank a child (61 to 63 percent of college graduates compared with 75 to 76 percent of those with less education);

- Think children are the greatest joy in life (81 to 82 percent of people who did not complete college compared with 60 to 69 percent of college graduates).

On several questions, those with the least education stand apart from the others.

- They are more likely to believe that life is empty without children (35 percent compared with 9 to 17 percent of people with at least a high school diploma).

- People who did not complete high school are more likely to say divorce is the best solution when a couple can't work out their problems (52 percent compared with 42 to 47 percent of people with at least a high school diploma).

- Although the least educated are more likely than others to think divorce is the best solution, in a seeming contradiction they are also more likely to think couples should stay together if they have children (27 percent compared with 11 to 15 percent of those with a high school diploma or more).

- The least-educated are also more likely to think unhappy childless couples should stay together. While 78 to 80 percent of people with at least a high school diploma do not believe unhappy childless couples should stay together, only 70 percent of people who did not complete high school agree.

- People with at least a high school diploma are more likely to reject the idea that a bad marriage is preferable to no marriage (91 to 93 percent compared with 79 percent of people who did not complete high school).

- Those who did not complete high school are slightly less likely to say the ideal family has two children (46 percent compared with 53 to 55 percent of those with at least a high school diploma).

- The least-educated are most likely to say children interfere too much with the freedom of parents (14 percent compared with 4 to 8 percent of people with more education).

Satisfaction With Family

Social observers may worry that the family is in trouble, but most Americans are happy with family life. Three-quarters of Americans get great or very great satisfaction from family life. Only 8 percent say they get only some, a little, or no satisfaction.

Women are slightly more likely than men to say they get a great deal of satisfaction from family life (79 percent of women compared with 70 percent of men). While the satisfied proportion has stayed about the same for women since 1974, it has declined for men— perhaps because of the rise in divorce and the loss of child custody for many men. About the same proportions of blacks and whites get a great deal of satisfaction from their families (74 and 75 percent, respectively).

Similar proportions of people under age 60 say family life is very satisfying (72 to 77 percent). The extremes are found among the elderly: fully 82 percent of people in their 60s get a great deal of satisfaction from family, versus only 68 percent of people aged 70 or older. At the oldest ages, the rise of widowhood dampens satisfaction with family life.

People who did not complete high school are slightly more likely than those with graduate degrees to say family life is very satisfying (77 percent compared with 69 percent).

The percentage of all Americans who say they get great satisfaction from family life has not changed over the past two decades. But among those aged 70 or older, the proportion has dropped from 77 percent in 1974 to 68 percent in 1994. Even more, the proportion of people with graduate degrees who find family life greatly satisfying has declined from 90 percent in 1974 to just 69 percent in 1994.

Satisfaction With Family, 1994

"How much satisfaction do you get from your family life?"

(percent responding by sex, race, age, and education, 1994)

	a very great deal	a great deal	quite a bit	a fair amount	some	a little	none	very/ great	quite/ fair	some/ little/ none
Total	40%	35%	10%	7%	3%	3%	2%	75%	17%	8%
Women	46	33	10	6	3	2	1	79	16	6
Men	32	38	11	8	4	4	3	70	19	11
Black	37	38	11	8	2	2	2	75	19	6
White	40	34	11	7	4	3	2	74	18	9
Aged 18 to 29	42	30	10	9	5	2	2	72	19	9
Aged 30 to 39	39	38	7	10	4	0	2	77	17	6
Aged 40 to 49	46	28	12	7	2	3	2	74	19	7
Aged 50 to 59	37	38	8	5	3	5	3	75	13	11
Aged 60 to 69	40	42	16	2	0	0	0	82	18	0
Aged 70 or older	31	37	14	6	3	7	1	68	20	11
Not a high school graduate	43	34	6	3	6	3	3	77	9	12
High school graduate	33	41	12	7	2	3	2	74	19	7
Bachelor's degree	50	24	11	10	0	3	3	74	21	6
Graduate degree	38	31	11	9	9	0	2	69	20	11

Note: Numbers may not add to 100 because no answer is not included.
Source: General Social Survey, National Opinion Research Center, University of Chicago

Satisfaction With Family, 1974 to 1994

"How much satisfaction do you get from your family life?"

(percent responding by sex, race, age, and education, 1974-94)

	very great/great deal			quite a bit/fair amount			some/a little/none		
	1994	**1984**	**1974**	**1994**	**1984**	**1974**	**1994**	**1984**	**1974**
Total	75%	76%	77%	17%	17%	18%	8%	6%	6%
Women	79	78	77	16	17	18	6	5	5
Men	70	74	76	19	18	17	11	6	7
Black	75	66	73	19	24	17	6	9	10
White	74	78	77	18	16	17	9	6	5
Aged 18 to 29	72	75	71	19	18	21	9	7	8
Aged 30 to 39	77	74	82	17	19	15	6	6	3
Aged 40 to 49	74	77	78	19	18	16	7	5	5
Aged 50 to 59	75	80	78	13	16	17	11	4	5
Aged 60 to 69	82	77	76	18	15	18	0	6	7
Aged 70 or older	68	77	77	20	14	18	11	8	5
Not a high school graduate	77	73	75	9	18	19	12	9	6
High school grad.	74	78	78	19	17	17	7	5	6
Bachelor's degree	74	78	72	21	19	22	6	3	7
Graduate degree	69	81	90	20	14	10	11	5	0

Note: Numbers may not add to 100 because no answer is not included.
Source: General Social Survey, National Opinion Research Center, University of Chicago

Marital Happiness

Most married people describe their marriages as very happy (60 percent). Few say their marriages are not too happy. Since 1974, however, there has been a decline in the percentage of people saying their marriages are very happy (from 69 percent in 1974 to 60 percent in 1994).

Twenty years ago, men and women were equally likely to say their marriages were very happy, and this was still true in 1994. There are no big differences by age, either, although people under age 30 (who are still relatively new to marriage) are slightly more likely to say they have very happy marriages.

There is not much difference in marital happiness by education. People with bachelor's degrees are slightly more likely than those with more or less education to say their marriages are very happy (68 percent of those with a bachelor's degree compared with 57 to 61 of people with higher or lower levels of education). In 1974, the proportion of people saying they had very happy marriages rose with each higher level of education.

The sharpest difference of opinion is between blacks and whites. Whites are far more likely than blacks to say their marriages are very happy (62 percent of whites compared with 37 percent of blacks). The gap between the races was much smaller in 1974, but since then there has been an enormous decline in the percentage of blacks who say their marriages are very happy (from 60 percent in 1974 to only 37 percent in 1994).

Marital Happiness, 1994

"Taking all things together, how would you describe your marriage? Would you say that your marriage is very happy, pretty happy, or not too happy?"

(percent responding by sex, race, age, and education, 1994)

	very happy	pretty happy	not too happy
Total	60%	36%	3%
Women	59	36	4
Men	61	36	2
Black	37	53	9
White	62	35	3
Aged 18 to 29	66	31	3
Aged 30 to 39	58	37	4
Aged 40 to 49	61	36	3
Aged 50 to 59	58	39	3
Aged 60 to 69	61	34	4
Aged 70 or older	62	36	1
Not a high school graduate	61	37	2
High school graduate	57	39	3
Bachelor's degree	68	29	2
Graduate degree	59	37	3

Note: Asked of people who were currently married at the time of the survey. Percents may not add to 100 because "don't know" and no answer are not included.
Source: General Social Survey, National Opinion Research Center, University of Chicago

Marital Happiness, 1974 to 1994

"Taking all things together, how would you describe your marriage? Would you say that your marriage is very happy, pretty happy, or not too happy?"

(percent responding by sex, race, age, and education, 1974-94)

	very happy			pretty happy			not too happy		
	1994	1984	1974	1994	1984	1974	1994	1984	1974
Total	60%	65%	69%	36%	32%	27%	3%	3%	4%
Women	59	65	68	36	31	27	4	3	5
Men	61	65	69	36	33	28	2	3	2
Black	37	49	60	53	46	31	9	5	8
White	62	66	70	35	31	27	3	3	3
Aged 18 to 29	66	67	69	31	30	27	3	2	4
Aged 30 to 39	58	64	67	37	32	29	4	3	4
Aged 40 to 49	61	61	65	36	35	29	3	3	4
Aged 50 to 59	58	65	77	39	33	21	3	2	3
Aged 60 to 69	61	64	64	34	30	31	4	6	5
Aged 70 or older	62	68	74	36	31	26	1	2	0
Not a high school graduate	61	60	66	37	34	29	2	7	4
High school grad.	57	65	69	39	33	28	3	2	3
Bachelor's degree	68	70	74	29	27	21	2	2	4
Graduate degree	59	75	77	37	23	23	3	2	0

Note: Asked of people who were currently married at the time of the survey. Percents may not add to 100 because "don't know" and no answer are not included.
Source: General Social Survey, National Opinion Research Center, University of Chicago

Are Married People Happier?

A plurality of Americans (44 percent) agree that married people are generally happier than unmarried people. Twenty-one percent disagree, and 30 percent neither agree nor disagree.

There are small differences of opinion between the sexes and by education. Men are more likely than women to say married people are happier (49 percent of men compared with 42 percent of women). People with graduate degrees are slightly more likely than those with less education to say marriage is a happier state (53 percent of those with graduate degrees compared with 43 to 48 percent of others).

There is a wide gap in the opinions of whites and blacks. Whites are much more likely than blacks to say that married people are happier (47 percent of whites compared with 28 percent of blacks). Opinions also differ by age, with each older age group more likely to link marriage with happiness. Only 27 percent of people under age 30 agree that married people are happier than those who are not married. The proportion rises to 40 and 44 percent for people aged 30 to 49. Among those aged 50 to 69, an even higher 51 to 54 percent agree, as do 64 percent of those aged 70 or older.

Are Married People Happier? 1994

"Married people are generally happier than
unmarried people—do you agree or disagree?"

(percent responding by sex, race, age, and education, 1994)

	strongly agree	agree	neither	disagree	strongly disagree	agree, total	disagree, total
Total	10%	34%	30%	17%	4%	44%	21%
Women	10	32	32	18	5	42	23
Men	11	38	28	16	3	49	19
Black	5	23	28	28	7	28	35
White	11	36	30	16	4	47	20
Aged 18 to 29	7	20	39	25	5	27	30
Aged 30 to 39	9	31	33	17	7	40	24
Aged 40 to 49	11	33	28	20	3	44	23
Aged 50 to 59	13	38	29	16	2	51	18
Aged 60 to 69	8	46	27	13	2	54	15
Aged 70 or older	15	49	22	7	1	64	8
Not a high school graduate	10	38	24	17	4	48	21
High school graduate	11	32	31	19	3	43	22
Bachelor's degree	10	36	34	13	4	46	17
Graduate degree	12	41	28	8	8	53	16

Note: Percents may not add to 100 because "can't choose" and no answer are not included.
Source: General Social Survey, National Opinion Research Center, University of Chicago

Is a Bad Marriage Better Than None?

Americans do not favor marriage at any cost. Fully 89 percent disagree with the statement, "It is better to have a bad marriage than no marriage at all." Nearly half (48 percent) disagree strongly.

In their responses to this question, men seem more anxious about marriage than women. They are less likely to disagree that a bad marriage is better than no marriage (93 percent of women disagree compared with 84 percent of men).

The generations all disagree that a bad marriage is better than no marriage. The proportions who disagree range from 83 percent of people aged 70 or older to between 88 and 92 percent of younger people.

The only people who stand apart on this question are those who did not complete high school. Only 79 percent disagree that a bad marriage is better than no marriage, compared with 91 to 93 percent of people with at least a high school diploma.

Is a Bad Marriage Better Than None? 1994

"It is better to have a bad marriage than no marriage
at all—do you agree or disagree?"

(percent responding by sex, race, age, and education, 1994)

	strongly agree	agree	neither	disagree	strongly disagree	agree, total	disagree, total
Total	1%	2%	5%	41%	48%	3%	89%
Women	0	2	3	42	51	2	93
Men	2	3	8	39	45	5	84
Black	1	1	4	44	42	2	86
White	1	2	5	41	49	3	90
Aged 18 to 29	1	3	5	32	57	4	89
Aged 30 to 39	1	2	3	36	56	3	92
Aged 40 to 49	0	2	5	38	53	2	91
Aged 50 to 59	1	1	5	45	45	2	90
Aged 60 to 69	1	2	7	56	32	3	88
Aged 70 or older	1	5	5	53	30	6	83
Not a high school graduate	2	7	6	47	32	9	79
High school graduate	1	1	5	41	50	2	91
Bachelor's degree	0	1	4	42	51	1	93
Graduate degree	1	2	4	33	60	3	93

Note: Numbers may not add to 100 because "can't choose" and no answer are not included.
Source: General Social Survey, National Opinion Research Center, University of Chicago

Do People Marry to Have Children?

Given that a substantial number of women now have children without getting married, it isn't surprising that 67 percent of Americans say parenthood is not the main reason for marrying. The responses to this question show that some demographic segments are more likely than others to separate marriage from parenthood.

Women are much more likely than men to say they don't believe the main purpose of marriage is to have children (73 percent of women compared with 60 percent of men). Sixteen percent of men, but only 11 percent of women, agree with this assertion.

Similar proportions of blacks and whites don't think parenthood is the primary reason for marriage (65 percent of blacks and 68 percent of whites). But there is a substantial generation gap on this issue. Younger generations are more likely than older people to say they don't believe the primary purpose of marriage is parenthood. Fully 72 percent of people under age 30 disagree that people marry to have kids, but this falls to only 58 percent among people aged 70 or older.

No trend is apparent by education. People with the most and least education are slightly less likely than others to disagree that people marry primarily to have kids (63 percent of people who did not complete high school or who have graduate degrees disagree, compared with 69 to 71 percent of high school graduates and those with bachelor's degrees).

People Marry to Have Children, 1994

"The main purpose of marriage these days is to have children—do you agree or disagree?"

(percent responding by sex, race, age, and education, 1994)

	strongly agree	agree	neither	disagree	strongly disagree	agree, total	disagree, total
Total	2%	11%	17%	53%	14%	13%	67%
Women	2	9	14	57	16	11	73
Men	1	15	21	48	12	16	60
Black	2	8	15	49	16	10	65
White	1	11	17	53	15	12	68
Aged 18 to 29	2	6	16	56	16	8	72
Aged 30 to 39	2	8	17	51	19	10	70
Aged 40 to 49	1	12	18	50	17	13	67
Aged 50 to 59	2	15	14	55	12	17	67
Aged 60 to 69	0	12	19	59	8	12	67
Aged 70 or older	2	17	18	51	7	19	58
Not a high school graduate	2	15	15	50	13	17	63
High school graduate	2	11	16	55	14	13	69
Bachelor's degree	1	8	18	54	17	9	71
Graduate degree	2	14	21	46	17	16	63

Note: Numbers may not add to 100 because "can't choose" and no answer are not included.
Source: General Social Survey, National Opinion Research Center, University of Chicago

Do People Marry for Financial Security?

These days, most families need two incomes to make ends meet. But a majority of Americans (60 percent) don't believe that financial security is the main advantage of marriage. Some people feel more strongly about this than others, however.

Women and men essentially agree about this issue. Sixty-two percent of women and 57 percent of men say they don't believe the main advantage of marriage is financial security.

Blacks and whites see things differently, however. Among whites, 62 percent disagree that the primary advantage of marriage is financial security. But only 43 percent of blacks disagree. Blacks are far more likely than whites to agree (33 percent compared with 14 percent of whites).

There is no age-related trend in responses to this question, although there are differences by age. People aged 30 to 49 and those in their 60s are more likely than others to disagree that financial security is the main advantage of marriage (62 to 65 percent of those aged 30 to 49 or 60 to 69, compared with 53 to 56 percent of other age groups).

There are substantial differences of opinion by education. People with higher levels of education are more likely to disagree that financial security is the main advantage of marriage (65 to 70 percent of college graduates compared with 59 percent of high school graduates and 47 percent of people who did not complete high school). People with less education are more likely to need two incomes to pay their bills—which explains why 35 percent of those without a high school degree say financial security is the main advantage of marriage, compared with only 5 to 16 percent of those with higher levels of education.

People Marry for Financial Security, 1994

"The main advantage of marriage is that it gives financial security—do you agree or disagree?"

(percent responding by sex, race, age, education, 1994)

	strongly agree	agree	neither	disagree	strongly disagree	agree, total	disagree, total
Total	3%	13%	21%	48%	12%	16%	60%
Women	3	13	20	49	13	16	62
Men	4	14	23	46	11	18	57
Black	6	27	16	35	8	33	43
White	3	11	22	49	13	14	62
Aged 18 to 29	5	15	21	42	13	20	55
Aged 30 to 39	3	10	21	49	16	13	65
Aged 40 to 49	2	11	23	48	14	13	62
Aged 50 to 59	2	16	24	47	9	18	56
Aged 60 to 69	2	12	21	55	8	14	63
Aged 70 or older	5	20	16	47	6	25	53
Not a high school graduate	8	27	14	37	10	35	47
High school graduate	3	13	22	49	10	16	59
Bachelor's degree	1	4	23	53	17	5	70
Graduate degree	2	8	24	50	15	10	65

Note: Percents may not add to 100 because "can't choose" and no answer are not included.
Source: General Social Survey, National Opinion Research Center, University of Chicago

Do Families Suffer When Men Work too Much?

A small majority of Americans (56 percent) believe that family life often suffers because men concentrate too much on their work. Twenty percent disagree with this statement, while 20 percent neither agree nor disagree.

There is no real disagreement between the sexes on this issue. Fifty-four percent of women and 60 percent of men agree that family life is often the victim of men's focus on work.

Whites are slightly more likely than blacks to agree with the notion that family life suffers because men focus too much on their work (58 percent of whites and 46 percent of blacks).

People under age 40 are considerably less likely than older Americans to believe family life suffers because men concentrate too much on their work. Slightly fewer than half (46 to 50 percent) of people under age 40 agree, compared with 57 to 66 percent of older adults.

Baby boomers in their 40s are more likely than other age groups to believe men work too much and the family suffers; they are most likely to say they strongly agree with this statement. This opinion probably springs directly from their personal experience. This is the age when people are most likely to have children at home and careers reaching their peak.

There is little difference of opinion by education. People with a high school diploma or less are only slightly less likely than those with at least a bachelor's degree to agree that family life suffers because men focus too much on their work.

Do Families Suffer When Men Work too Much? 1994

"Family life often suffers because men concentrate too
much on their work—do you agree or disagree?"

(percent responding by sex, race, age, and education, 1994)

	strongly agree	agree	neither	disagree	strongly disagree	agree, total	disagree, total
Total	8%	48%	20%	17%	3%	56%	20%
Women	8	46	21	17	3	54	20
Men	9	51	19	16	2	60	18
Black	9	37	19	19	7	46	26
White	8	50	20	17	2	58	19
Aged 18 to 29	6	40	26	20	5	46	25
Aged 30 to 39	9	41	22	21	5	50	26
Aged 40 to 49	11	55	15	12	3	66	15
Aged 50 to 59	7	52	19	17	1	59	18
Aged 60 to 69	9	48	21	19	0	57	19
Aged 70 or older	8	58	15	11	1	66	12
Not a high school graduate	9	45	17	19	3	54	22
High school graduate	8	47	22	16	3	55	19
Bachelor's degree	9	53	15	17	2	62	19
Graduate degree	9	50	22	13	3	59	16

Note: Percents may not add to 100 because "can't choose" and no answer are not included.
Source: General Social Survey, National Opinion Research Center, University of Chicago

Is Divorce the Best Solution?

A plurality of Americans (47 percent) believe divorce is usually the best solution when a couple cannot solve their marriage problems. But a substantial 31 percent disagree.

Men and women are equally likely to agree that divorce is sometimes the best solution. But there is less agreement within other demographic segments.

Blacks are only slightly more likely than whites to say divorce is the best solution when there are irreconcilable differences (52 percent of blacks compared with 46 percent of whites). People who did not complete high school are more likely than those with higher levels of education to feel divorce is sometimes the best solution (52 percent compared with 42 to 47 percent of people with at least a high school diploma).

The most surprising finding is the difference of opinion by age. Over half of people aged 50 or older say divorce is sometimes the best solution (52 to 56 percent). Baby boomers, aged 30 to 49, are less likely to agree—though they are more likely to have experienced divorce than older people. Only 43 percent of people in their 30s and 47 percent of those in their 40s agree that divorce is the best solution. Growing up in the era of divorce has left its mark on the youngest adults. Only 35 percent believe divorce is the best solution when a couple can't work out their problems, while 42 percent disagree.

Is Divorce the Best Solution? 1994

"Divorce is usually the best solution when a couple
can't seem to work out their marriage problems—
do you agree or disagree?"

(percent responding by sex, race, age, and education, 1994)

	strongly agree	agree	neither	disagree	strongly disagree	agree, total	disagree, total
Total	9%	38%	19%	23%	8%	47%	31%
Women	10	36	20	22	8	46	30
Men	7	40	18	24	8	47	32
Black	16	36	14	19	9	52	28
White	7	39	20	23	8	46	31
Aged 18 to 29	9	26	21	28	14	35	42
Aged 30 to 39	8	35	20	26	8	43	34
Aged 40 to 49	9	38	20	20	10	47	30
Aged 50 to 59	11	45	18	22	2	56	24
Aged 60 to 69	9	43	17	22	3	52	25
Aged 70 or older	8	46	16	18	5	54	23
Not a high school graduate	12	40	13	22	6	52	28
High school graduate	8	39	20	22	8	47	30
Bachelor's degree	6	36	16	30	8	42	38
Graduate degree	9	36	23	22	6	45	28

Note: Percents may not add to 100 because "can't choose" and no answer are not included.
Source: General Social Survey, National Opinion Research Center, University of Chicago

Should Parents Stay Together?

Most Americans (63 percent) do not believe parents who don't get along should stay together for the sake of the children. Only 15 percent believe they should stay together no matter what.

Women are more likely than men to disagree that parents should stay together just for the kids (69 percent of women and 55 percent of men). Similar percentages of blacks and whites disagree that parents should stay together (60 percent of blacks and 64 percent of whites).

Americans aged 70 or older are traditionalists. They are more likely to agree that parents should stay together even if they don't get along (24 percent). Only 49 percent of the oldest age group think parents who don't get along should split up, versus 59 percent of people in their 60s and from 64 to 68 percent of people younger than age 60.

People who did not complete high school (a group that includes a large percentage of older people) are far more likely than those with at least a high school diploma to say parents should stay together even if they don't get along (27 percent). Only 11 to 15 percent of people with at least a high school diploma agree.

Should Parents Stay Together? 1994

"When there are children in the family, parents
should stay together even if they don't get along—
do you agree or disagree?"

(percent responding by sex, race, age, and education, 1994)

	strongly agree	agree	neither	disagree	strongly disagree	agree, total	disagree, total
Total	3%	12%	16%	46%	17%	15%	63%
Women	2	9	14	48	21	11	69
Men	4	16	19	43	12	20	55
Black	2	14	13	39	21	16	60
White	2	11	17	47	17	13	64
Aged 18 to 29	2	12	15	43	19	14	62
Aged 30 to 39	2	10	15	46	22	12	68
Aged 40 to 49	3	11	14	48	19	14	67
Aged 50 to 59	3	9	16	50	14	12	64
Aged 60 to 69	3	13	17	48	11	16	59
Aged 70 or older	4	20	20	40	9	24	49
Not a high school graduate	7	20	13	37	12	27	49
High school graduate	1	10	17	48	18	11	66
Bachelor's degree	2	13	14	48	17	15	65
Graduate degree	2	9	16	46	22	11	68

Note: Percents may not add to 100 because "can't choose" and no answer are not included.
Source: General Social Survey, National Opinion Research Center, University of Chicago

Should Childless Couples Stay Together?

Few Americans believe childless couples should remain married if they don't get along. Over three-quarters say childless couples who are unhappily married should not have to stay together.

This is one of the few questions where there is little disagreement by demographic segment. Similar proportions of women and men, blacks and whites, say they don't believe childless couples should remain married if they are unhappy.

By age, similar proportions disagree that unhappily married people should stay together (ranging from 74 to 79 percent). But there is some difference of opinion in the oldest age group. While only 4 to 9 percent of people under age 70 feel childless couples should not divorce, 12 percent of those aged 70 or older believe these couples should stay together.

People without a high school diploma (many of them older) are more likely to think childless couples should stay together (13 percent compared with 5 to 9 percent of those with more education).

Should Childless Couples Stay Together? 1994

"Even when there are no children in the family, a married couple should stay together even if they don't get along— do you agree or disagree?"

(percent responding by sex, race, age, and education, 1994)

	strongly agree	agree	neither	disagree	strongly disagree	agree, total	disagree, total
Total	2%	6%	10%	50%	28%	8%	78%
Women	1	5	9	50	29	6	79
Men	2	6	10	49	25	8	74
Black	1	8	6	45	32	9	77
White	2	5	10	50	28	7	78
Aged 18 to 29	2	5	11	46	28	7	74
Aged 30 to 39	1	5	10	46	33	6	79
Aged 40 to 49	2	6	8	48	31	8	79
Aged 50 to 59	2	7	7	52	27	9	79
Aged 60 to 69	1	3	15	55	20	4	75
Aged 70 or older	3	9	7	58	18	12	76
Not a high school graduate	4	9	8	49	21	13	70
High school graduate	1	4	10	50	28	5	78
Bachelor's degree	1	8	10	50	26	9	76
Graduate degree	1	4	11	45	35	5	80

Note: Percents may not add to 100 because "can't choose" and no answer are not included.
Source: General Social Survey, National Opinion Research Center, University of Chicago

Is One Parent as Good as Two?

Single parents are common today, but half of Americans say one parent is not as good as two. Only 36 percent agree that "one parent can bring up a child as well as two parents together." But there is significant disagreement by demographic segment.

Women are far more likely than men to be single parents and blacks more likely than whites. Their different experiences clearly result in different attitudes about single parents.

Men are much more likely than women to believe two parents are better than one: 58 percent of men say two are better, while only 25 percent say one is just as good. Women are more divided in their opinions, with 43 percent saying one parent is as good as two and another 42 percent saying two are better than one.

Half of blacks say one parent is as good as two; just one-third of whites agree. Conversely, half of whites say two parents are necessary, while only one-third of blacks agree.

A generational trend is also clear on this issue. Younger people are more likely to believe one parent can raise a child as well as two. The proportion who think one parent can do just as good a job as two stands at 50 percent among people under age 30, and falls steadily with age to a low of 16 percent among people aged 70 or older.

The college-educated are less likely to agree that one parent is as good as two. While 36 to 38 percent of people who did not complete college say this, only 27 to 30 percent of people with at least a bachelor's degree agree.

Is One Parent as Good as Two? 1994

"One parent can bring up a child as well as two parents together—do you agree or disagree?"

(percent responding age sex, race, age, and education, 1994)

	strongly agree	agree	neither	disagree	strongly disagree	agree, total	disagree, total
Total	9%	27%	14%	38%	11%	36%	49%
Women	11	32	14	33	9	43	42
Men	5	20	15	44	14	25	58
Black	25	27	9	24	9	52	33
White	6	26	15	40	11	32	51
Aged 18 to 29	16	34	16	26	8	50	34
Aged 30 to 39	12	32	13	32	10	44	42
Aged 40 to 49	4	27	15	38	13	31	51
Aged 50 to 59	9	28	13	41	10	37	51
Aged 60 to 69	3	19	13	48	12	22	60
Aged 70 or older	4	12	15	51	14	16	65
Not a high school graduate	13	23	12	40	8	36	48
High school graduate	9	29	15	35	11	38	46
Bachelor's degree	4	23	13	42	16	27	58
Graduate degree	5	25	21	41	8	30	49

Note: Numbers may not add to 100 because "can't choose" and no answer are not included.
Source: General Social Survey, National Opinion Research Center, University of Chicago

Should Marriage Come Before Parenthood?

A majority of Americans believe people who want children should get married (71 percent). Similar proportions of men and women agree that marriage should come before parenthood (70 percent of women and 72 percent of men). By education, people are also more or less in agreement on this question, ranging from 70 to 76 percent.

But there are striking differences of opinion between blacks and whites and among age groups. Three-quarters of whites, but only 54 percent of blacks, say couples who want kids should marry.

People under age 50 (Generation Xers and baby boomers) see things differently than older generations. Among people aged 50 or older, fully 83 to 88 percent think people who want children should get married. But agreement drops with age, from 73 percent among people in their 40s and 64 percent among those in their 30s to only 53 percent among people under age 30.

People under age 40 are considerably more likely than older people to disagree that marriage is a prerequisite for parenthood. The individualistic attitudes of younger generations are apparent in the larger percentages who say they neither agree nor disagree with the question—in other words, they're not willing to tell other people what they should or should not do.

Should Marriage Come Before Parenthood? 1994

"People who want children ought to get married—
do you agree or disagree?"

(percent responding by sex, race, age, and education, 1994)

	strongly agree	agree	neither	disagree	strongly disagree	agree, total	disagree, total
Total	30%	41%	10%	12%	4%	71%	16%
Women	31	39	10	13	5	70	18
Men	28	44	11	12	3	72	15
Black	24	30	10	20	10	54	30
White	31	43	10	11	3	74	14
Aged 18 to 29	17	36	17	19	7	53	26
Aged 30 to 39	25	38	11	18	6	64	24
Aged 40 to 49	34	39	10	10	3	73	13
Aged 50 to 59	34	49	5	8	2	83	10
Aged 60 to 69	34	51	8	4	0	85	4
Aged 70 or older	44	44	4	5	0	88	5
Not a high school graduate	31	43	8	10	3	74	13
High school graduate	29	41	11	12	5	70	17
Bachelor's degree	32	43	10	11	3	75	14
Graduate degree	36	40	8	12	1	76	13

Note: Percents may not add to 100 because "can't choose" and no answer are not included.
Source: General Social Survey, National Opinion Research Center, University of Chicago

Ideal Number of Children

For a majority of Americans (53 percent), the ideal family has two children. Another 22 percent think three is best. While the proportion saying three is ideal has not changed since 1974, people were more likely to say two is the perfect number in 1994 than they were in 1974 (55 percent compared with 44 percent). Few Americans in either 1994 or 1974 considered fewer than two children to be ideal. And while large families might have been popular earlier in this century, the proportion who think four or more children is ideal stood at just 12 percent in 1994.

Similar proportions of men and women say two is the ideal number of children (54 percent of women and 52 percent of men). Men and women were also in agreement on this issue in 1974.

Blacks and whites have different perspectives on the ideal number of children. Whites are more likely to say two is ideal (56 percent of whites compared with 35 percent of blacks). Blacks are more likely to say four is ideal (17 percent of blacks compared with 8 percent of whites).

People who are just starting families (under age 30) and those whose children are grown (aged 60 or older) are slightly more likely than those in the prime childrearing ages to view larger families as ideal. Among people aged 30 to 59, a 54 to 59 percent majority say two is the perfect number, compared with 47 to 49 percent of younger and older adults.

People who did not complete high school (many of whom are older) are less likely than those with more education to say two is the ideal number of children (46 percent compared with 53 to 55 percent of people with at least a high school education).

Ideal Number of Children, 1994

"What do you think is the ideal number of children for a family to have?"

(percent responding by sex, race, age, and education, 1994)

	none	one	two	three	four	five or more	"as many as you want"
Total	1%	3%	53%	22%	10%	2%	6%
Women	1	3	54	22	10	1	6
Men	2	2	52	23	8	2	6
Black	1	3	35	26	17	3	12
White	1	2	56	21	8	1	5
Aged 18 to 29	1	3	48	29	12	2	4
Aged 30 to 39	2	3	56	23	7	1	5
Aged 40 to 49	2	4	59	18	7	1	7
Aged 50 to 59	1	3	54	20	10	2	8
Aged 60 to 69	2	2	49	23	13	0	6
Aged 70 or older	1	0	47	21	13	3	8
Not a high school graduate	2	2	46	21	14	5	7
High school graduate	1	3	55	22	10	1	5
Bachelor's degree	1	2	53	26	8	1	5
Graduate degree	1	4	53	19	7	1	11

Note: Percents may not add to 100 because "don't know" and no answer are not included.
Source: General Social Survey, National Opinion Research Center, University of Chicago

Ideal Number of Children, 1974 to 1994

"What do you think is the ideal number of children for a family to have?"

(percent responding by sex, race, age, and education, 1974-94)

	two			three			four		
	1994	**1985**	**1974**	**1994**	**1985**	**1974**	**1994**	**1985**	**1974**
Total	53%	55%	44%	22%	21%	23%	10%	11%	16%
Women	54	56	43	22	20	22	10	11	18
Men	52	54	44	23	22	25	8	10	13
Black	35	45	22	26	20	24	17	20	27
White	56	57	47	21	21	23	8	10	14
Aged 18 to 29	48	59	55	29	22	23	12	9	10
Aged 30 to 39	56	60	45	23	20	20	7	7	15
Aged 40 to 49	59	66	41	18	19	26	7	7	17
Aged 50 to 59	54	56	43	20	16	22	10	13	16
Aged 60 to 69	49	47	37	23	25	28	13	12	18
Aged 70 or older	47	38	29	21	25	24	13	21	25
Not a high school graduate	46	48	38	21	16	19	14	19	21
High school grad.	55	58	46	22	22	26	10	8	13
Bachelor's degree	53	59	56	26	25	22	8	7	11
Graduate degree	53	60	47	19	22	27	7	7	10

Note: Percents may not add to 100 because "none," "one," "as many as you want," "don't know," and no answer are not included.
Source: General Social Survey, National Opinion Research Center, University of Chicago

Are Children Life's Greatest Joy?

Few Americans argue with the assertion that "watching children grow up is life's greatest joy." Fully 78 percent of Americans agree with this statement.

There's no argument between men and women on this question—80 percent of women and 76 percent of men agree. Likewise, blacks and whites are in agreement (80 percent of blacks and 78 percent of whites).

There is close agreement by age, with only two exceptions that can be explained by lifestage. Among people aged 18 to 39 and those aged 50 to 69, 78 to 80 percent say children are life's greatest joy. People aged 70 or older (who are most likely to be grandparents) are most likely to agree (87 percent). People in their 40s (many of whom have teenagers at home) are least likely to agree (71 percent).

Interestingly, college graduates are less enamored of children than are those with less education. Over 80 percent of people who did not complete college say children are life's greatest joy, compared with 69 percent of those with a bachelor's degree and just 60 percent of people with graduate degrees.

Are Children Life's Greatest Joy? 1994

"Watching children grow up is life's greatest joy—
do you agree or disagree? "

(percent responding by sex, race, age, and education, 1994)

	strongly agree	agree	neither	disagree	strongly disagree	agree, total	disagree, total
Total	33%	45%	13%	4%	0%	78%	4%
Women	36	44	12	4	0	80	4
Men	30	46	15	4	1	76	5
Black	41	39	11	1	1	80	2
White	32	46	14	4	0	78	4
Aged 18 to 29	36	44	12	2	0	80	2
Aged 30 to 39	38	40	13	4	1	78	5
Aged 40 to 49	27	44	17	6	0	71	6
Aged 50 to 59	36	42	14	3	1	78	4
Aged 60 to 69	26	52	12	4	0	78	4
Aged 70 or older	35	52	7	2	1	87	3
Not a high school graduate	43	39	7	2	0	82	2
High school graduate	34	47	11	3	0	81	3
Bachelor's degree	27	42	21	5	0	69	5
Graduate degree	16	44	25	8	2	60	10

Note: Percents may not add to 100 because "can't choose" and no answer are not included.
Source: General Social Survey, National Opinion Research Center, University of Chicago

Is Life Empty Without Children?

Americans think kids are great, but they don't believe life is empty without them. One-half disagree with the statement "people who have never had children lead empty lives."

Similar proportions of blacks and whites do not agree that the childless lead empty lives (53 percent of blacks and 49 percent of whites). But there is some disagreement by sex, age, and education.

The most interesting difference of opinion is between men and women. Although (or perhaps because) women still assume a larger role in raising children, they are more likely than men to disagree with the assertion that the childless lead empty lives (53 percent of women compared with 46 percent of men).

There is also a pronounced generation gap on this issue. Older generations are more likely to agree that life is empty without children while younger generations are more likely to disagree. Only 40 to 43 percent of people aged 50 or older disagree that childless people lead empty lives, but disagreement rises to 51 percent among people in their 40s and to 55 to 56 percent among people under age 40.

The opinions of people who did not complete high school are very different on this issue from the opinions of those with more education. Fully 35 percent of the least educated say life without children is empty, compared with only 17 percent of high school graduates and just 9 to 11 percent of college graduates.

Is Life Empty Without Children? 1994

"People who have never had children lead empty lives—
do you agree or disagree? "

(percent responding by sex, race, age, and education, 1994)

	strongly agree	agree	neither	disagree	strongly disagree	agree, total	disagree, total
Total	3%	15%	26%	37%	13%	18%	50%
Women	3	14	24	40	13	17	53
Men	4	16	28	34	12	20	46
Black	6	13	21	39	14	19	53
White	3	15	27	37	12	18	49
Aged 18 to 29	1	10	25	40	16	11	56
Aged 30 to 39	2	11	25	38	17	13	55
Aged 40 to 49	3	11	30	38	13	14	51
Aged 50 to 59	5	19	27	36	6	24	42
Aged 60 to 69	4	15	30	37	6	19	43
Aged 70 or older	7	30	16	31	9	37	40
Not a high school graduate	6	29	22	25	9	35	34
High school graduate	3	14	26	39	12	17	51
Bachelor's degree	2	9	26	42	14	11	56
Graduate degree	2	7	29	38	20	9	58

Note: Percents may not add to 100 because "can't choose" and no answer are not included.
Source: General Social Survey, National Opinion Research Center, University of Chicago

Do Children Interfere With Freedom?

Americans have become more individualistic (and self centered) over the last few decades. Most would agree that having children prevents parents from "doing their own thing." But a majority of Americans (72 percent) say children do not exact too high a price in foregone freedom. Only 8 percent think children interfere too much with parents' freedom.

Men are less likely than women to agree, however. Fully three-quarters of women, but only two-thirds of men, don't believe children interfere too much with the freedom of parents.

Blacks and whites are in agreement on this issue, with 69 percent of blacks and 72 percent of whites saying people do not lose too much freedom when they become parents.

Younger generations are slightly more likely than their elders to feel too much freedom is lost when children are added to the equation. Among people aged 50 or older, 77 percent disagree with the statement, compared with a somewhat smaller 67 to 71 percent of those aged 18 to 49. The younger generations are the ones currently raising children. Once their children are grown, they may look back on childrearing with a kinder eye.

People who did not complete high school are most likely to agree that children interfere too much with freedom (14 percent compared with 4 to 8 percent of people with more education).

Do Children Interfere With Freedom? 1994

"Having children interferes too much with the freedom of parents—do you agree or disagree? "

(percent responding by sex, race, age, and education, 1994)

	strongly agree	agree	neither	disagree	strongly disagree	agree, total	disagree, total
Total	1%	7%	15%	52%	20%	8%	72%
Women	1	6	13	54	21	7	75
Men	1	9	17	49	19	10	68
Black	2	7	17	52	17	9	69
White	1	7	15	52	20	8	72
Aged 18 to 29	3	8	16	51	16	11	67
Aged 30 to 39	1	10	17	47	21	11	68
Aged 40 to 49	0	8	16	49	22	8	71
Aged 50 to 59	1	4	12	58	19	5	77
Aged 60 to 69	0	5	11	55	22	5	77
Aged 70 or older	0	5	12	58	19	5	77
Not a high school graduate	2	12	13	46	17	14	63
High school graduate	1	7	13	55	21	8	76
Bachelor's degree	0	4	18	52	22	4	74
Graduate degree	1	7	25	45	19	8	64

Note: Percents may not add to 100 because "can't choose" and no answer are not included.
Source: General Social Survey, National Opinion Research Center, University of Chicago

Spanking Children

While "time out" has become the discipline of choice for many parents in recent years, spanking remains popular. Seventy-two percent of Americans say a "good, hard spanking" is sometimes necessary for disciplining children.

Women are more likely than men to want to spare the rod. While 78 percent of men say a spanking is sometimes necessary, a smaller percentage of women (69 percent) agree.

Blacks are far more in favor of spanking than whites. Fully 86 percent of blacks say a spanking is sometimes necessary, compared with 70 percent of whites.

People under age 30 and those in their 40s are less likely than other age groups to believe spanking is sometimes necessary (68 to 69 percent compared with 74 to 77 percent of other age groups).

College graduates are also less enthusiastic about spanking as a disciplinary method. Among people with a high school diploma or less education, three-quarters say a spanking is sometimes needed. Among college graduates, only 61 to 63 percent agree.

Spanking Children, 1994

"It is sometimes necessary to discipline a child with a good, hard spanking—do you agree or disagree?"

(percent responding by sex, race, age, and education, 1994)

	strongly agree	agree	disagree	strongly disagree	agree, total	disagree, total
Total	26%	46%	18%	8%	72%	26%
Women	25	44	20	10	69	30
Men	29	49	15	6	78	21
Black	41	45	11	3	86	14
White	24	46	19	9	70	28
Aged 18 to 29	24	44	23	8	68	31
Aged 30 to 39	26	48	17	8	74	25
Aged 40 to 49	24	45	20	10	69	30
Aged 50 to 59	28	47	15	8	75	23
Aged 60 to 69	27	50	15	6	77	21
Aged 70 or older	31	42	16	8	74	24
Not a high school graduate	34	42	16	6	76	22
High school graduate	27	48	17	6	75	23
Bachelor's degree	19	44	23	14	63	37
Graduate degree	18	43	23	14	61	37

Note: Numbers may not add to 100 because "don't know" and no answer are not included.
Source: General Social Survey, National Opinion Research Center, University of Chicago

Most Important Qualities in Children

Half of Americans (53 percent) believe the most important quality children need to learn is to think for themselves. People are more likely to choose "think for him or herself" over "work hard," "help others," "obey," or "be popular." Overall, pluralities of Americans rank to work hard as the second-most important quality (38 percent), to help others as third-most important (36 percent), and to obey, as fourth (38 percent). An overwhelming majority (76 percent) put popularity last.

Women are more likely than men to put the highest value on independent thinking (56 percent compared with 49 percent of men). Whites are more likely than blacks to say thinking for themselves is most important (55 percent compared with 47 percent); blacks are more likely to say it is most important that children learn to obey (28 percent of blacks compared with 16 percent of whites).

There is a striking generational difference in the rankings of obedience and independent thought. Baby boomers (aged 30 to 49) are more likely than older age groups to say teaching children to think for themselves is most important (59 to 60 percent say this compared with 49 to 54 of people aged 50 to 69 and just 35 percent of those aged 70 or older). Older Americans are more likely to say obedience is most important (20 to 34 percent say so compared with just 12 percent of baby boomers).

Interestingly, people under age 30 are less likely than boomers to say independent thought is most important (49 percent). They are also less likely than older Americans to value obedience (17 percent). They are more likely than most other age groups to believe children should be taught to work hard (20 percent say this compared with 11 to 15 percent of most other age groups).

People with college degrees have substantially different views on what children need to succeed. Among college graduates, 65 to 68 percent say it's most important that they learn to think for themselves. In contrast, only 53 percent of high school graduates and 33 percent of people who did not complete high school agree. The less-educated are considerably more likely to say obedience is most important.

Responses to this question have not changed much since 1986 (the first year this question was included in the General Social Survey), except for a decline in the proportion of people saying obedience is the most important quality. The proportion who think obedience is most important dropped from 23 percent in 1986 to 18 percent in 1994. Younger generations, in particular, were less likely to value obedience in 1994 than they were in 1986. As younger generations replace older ones, the overall value placed on obedience will continue to decline.

Most Important Qualities in Children, 1994

"If you had to choose, which thing on this list would you pick as the most important for a child to learn to prepare him or her for life?"

(percent choosing quality as most important, by sex race, age, and education, 1994)

	to think for himself or herself	to obey	to work hard	to help others	to be popular
Total	53%	18%	15%	13%	0%
Women	56	18	13	11	0
Men	49	18	18	15	1
Black	47	28	14	8	1
White	55	16	14	13	0
Aged 18 to 29	49	17	20	14	0
Aged 30 to 39	59	12	15	13	0
Aged 40 to 49	60	12	14	12	0
Aged 50 to 59	49	20	18	11	2
Aged 60 to 69	54	24	11	10	1
Aged 70 or older	35	34	12	16	1
Not a high school graduate	33	33	13	18	1
High school graduate	53	20	15	12	0
Bachelor's degree	65	6	16	12	0
Graduate degree	68	2	19	9	0

Source: General Social Survey, National Opinion Research Center, University of Chicago

Most Important Qualities in Children, 1986 to 1994

"If you had to choose, which thing on this list would you pick as the most important for a child to learn to prepare him or her for life?"

(percent choosing quality as most important, by sex race, age, and education, 1986-94)

	to think for himself or herself		to obey		to work hard		to help others		to be popular	
	1994	1986	1994	1986	1994	1986	1994	1986	1994	1986
Total	53%	51%	18%	23%	15%	11%	13%	14%	0%	1%
Women	56	52	18	26	13	9	11	12	0	1
Men	49	50	18	18	18	14	15	16	1	1
Black	47	48	28	23	14	14	8	14	1	1
White	55	52	16	23	14	11	13	14	0	0
Aged 18 to 29	49	49	17	18	20	14	14	18	0	0
Aged 30 to 39	59	61	12	13	15	13	13	11	0	1
Aged 40 to 49	60	59	12	24	14	10	12	7	0	0
Aged 50 to 59	49	46	20	26	18	10	11	15	2	1
Aged 60 to 69	54	46	24	35	11	5	10	13	1	1
Aged 70 or older	35	34	34	31	12	12	16	20	1	1
Not a high school graduate	33	28	33	36	13	14	18	18	1	2
High school graduate	53	53	20	22	15	10	12	13	0	0
Bachelor's degree	65	67	6	11	16	11	12	11	0	0
Graduate degree	68	88	2	2	19	6	9	2	0	0

Source: General Social Survey, National Opinion Research Center, University of Chicago

7

Women's Roles

Opinions about the appropriate roles of women have changed dramatically over the past two decades—perhaps more so than opinions about any other topic. Most Americans no longer believe women should follow traditional roles. Majorities say they:

- Would vote for a woman for president (89 percent);

- Do not agree that women should run the home and men should run the country (83 percent);

- Do not believe men are better suited emotionally for politics than are women (74 percent);

- Believe most women have to work to support their families (83 percent);

- Don't agree that it is more important for a wife to help her husband's career than to have one herself (76 percent);

- Approve of a married woman working even if her husband can support her (79 percent);

- Do not agree that it's best for wives to handle hearth and home and let husbands be the breadwinners (63 percent);

- Believe working mothers can have as good a relationship with their children as mothers who do not work (69 percent).

Smaller majorities say they:

- Do not agree that preschool children are likely to suffer if their mothers work (56 percent);

- Do not believe it is bad for a man to stay home with his children while his wife goes off to work (55 percent).

Traditional sex roles are still evident in who does what around the house, but a growing share of couples say both the man and woman share responsibility for household chores. Majorities of American couples (either married or cohabiting) say:

- The woman usually or always does the laundry (65 percent);

- The woman plans dinner (52 percent);

- The man handles repairs (67 percent).

But some chores are shared.

- Forty-seven percent say the woman cares for sick family members, while 45 percent share this responsibility.

- Grocery shopping is the woman's job according to 47 percent of respondents, but both the man and woman shop according to another 42 percent.

Women and Men Agree About Women's Issues

Although one might assume that men and women would diverge in their opinions about appropriate roles for women, on most of the issues examined here this is not the case. Similar percentages of men and women say they:

- Would vote for a woman for president (90 percent of women and 88 percent of men);

- Believe most women have to work to support families (86 percent of women and 80 percent of men);

- Do not believe women should stick to hearth and home and leave running the country up to men (84 percent of women and 81 percent of men);

- Feel it is fine for a woman to earn money even if her husband can support her (80 percent of women and 79 percent of men);

- Do not agree that men are better suited emotionally for politics (76 percent of women and 72 percent of men);

- Do not believe a husband's career should take precedence over his wife's (76 percent of women and 74 percent of men).

Women are more likely than men to say:

- A working mother can have as good a relationship with her children as a mother who does not work (75 percent of women compared with 60 percent of men);

- They do not feel preschool children are likely to suffer if their mother works (63 percent of women compared with 48 percent of men);

- They do not believe it is better for everyone involved if the man is the achiever outside the home and the woman takes care of the home and family (65 percent of women compared with 59 percent of men);

- They do not think it is bad for a man to stay home with the kids while his wife goes to work (57 percent of women compared with 50 percent of men).

Men and women disagree somewhat on who does the chores. Each sex tends to see themselves doing more. Women are more likely to say they:

- Plan dinner (59 percent), but only 46 percent of men say the woman usually or always does this;

- Care for sick family members (52 percent), but only 40 percent of men say this is mostly the woman's chore;

- Shop for groceries (50 percent), but only 44 percent of men say this is the case.

Men are more likely to take credit for:

- Handling small repairs around the house. Fully 76 percent of men, but only 60 percent of women, say the man always or usually handles repairs.

There is near agreement on only one chore:

- Sixty-eight percent of women and 63 percent of men say the woman usually does the laundry.

Blacks and Whites Agree on Most Issues

Black and white Americans disagree about many issues. But when it comes to women's roles, there is little argument. Both races are about equally likely to say they:

- Would vote for a woman presidential candidate (90 percent of blacks and 89 percent of whites);

- Do not believe men are better suited emotionally for politics (70 percent of blacks and 75 percent of whites);

- Do not believe women should stick to running the home and let men handle running the country (78 percent of blacks and 83 percent of whites);

- Feel most women have to work because their families need the money (85 percent of blacks and 83 percent of whites);

- Say they approve of a married woman working even if her husband can support her (77 percent of blacks and 80 percent of whites);

- Believe a working mother can have as good a relationship with her children as a mother who does not work (72 percent of blacks and 69 percent of whites);

- Do not feel it is best for men to be breadwinners and women to be homemakers (64 percent of blacks and whites);

- Do not agree that a husband's career should take precedence over his wife's (72 percent of blacks and 75 percent of whites).

Black Americans are more likely than whites to say:

- A working mother can have as good a relationship with her children as a non-working mother (74 percent of blacks, compared to 67 percent of whites).

Whites are slightly more likely than blacks to say:

- They do not think it is a bad idea for the man to stay home and care for the children while his wife works (56 percent of whites compared with 48 percent of blacks);

- Believe preschool children are likely to suffer if their mothers work (42 percent of whites compared with 37 percent of blacks).

White couples are more likely than black couples to divide household chores along traditional lines.

- Sixty-eight percent of whites, but only 55 percent of blacks, say the woman usually or always does the laundry.

- A majority of whites (53 percent) but only 40 percent of blacks say the woman plans dinner.

- Almost half of whites (49 percent) but only 32 percent of blacks say grocery shopping is up to the woman.

- Whites are only slightly more likely than blacks to say caring for sick family members falls to the woman (46 percent of blacks and 41 percent of whites).

- Repairs are the man's job according to 69 percent of whites, but only 58 percent of blacks.

Older Generations Support Traditional Roles

The generation gap is wide on almost all the women's role issues examined here. There is little disagreement by age on only one question:

• Large majorities in every age group believe most women have to work these days to support their families (79 to 87 percent).

Younger people are far more likely than older generations to say they:

• Disagree with the idea that women should run the home and men should run the country. Fully 88 to 91 percent of people under age 50 disagree with the statement, but this proportion falls to only 58 percent among people aged 70 or older;

• Do not believe the best arrangement is for the wife to be the homemaker and the husband the breadwinner (81 percent of people under age 30 disagree, dropping to 24 percent among people aged 70 or older);

• Don't agree that women are less suited emotionally for politics than are men (71 to 81 percent of people under age 70 disagree compared with only 55 percent of those aged 70 or older);

• Do not believe it is a bad idea for the man to be Mr. Mom while his wife goes off to work (63 percent of people under age 30, declining to only 32 of those aged 70 or older);

• Would vote for a women for president (91 to 94 percent of people under age 60). This proportion drops to 83 percent among people in their 60s and 75 percent among those aged 70 or older;

• Disagree with the idea that a woman should support her husband's career rather than pursue her own (80 to 87 percent of people under age 50 compared with 66 to 76 of those aged 50 to 69 and 40 percent of those aged 70 or older);

- Approve of married women working even if their husbands can support them (80 to 86 percent of people under age 60 compared with 75 percent of people in their 60s and 64 percent of those aged 70 or older);

- Believe a working mother can have as good a relationship with her children as a mother who does not work. From 72 to 79 percent of people under age 50 agree compared with 62 to 66 percent of people aged 50 to 69 and 48 percent of those aged 70 or older;

- Do not feel preschool children are likely to suffer if their mothers work (68 percent of people under age 30, dropping to 31 percent of those aged 70 or older).

Younger couples are more likely than older ones to say household chores are shared by the man and woman. They are done usually or always by the woman, say older couples.

- While only half of people under age 30 say laundry is usually or always the woman's job, a solid three-quarters of people aged 50 or older say it is.

- The proportion saying the man handles household repairs is lowest among people under age 30 (59 percent) and highest among those aged 50 or older (70 to 73 percent).

- Well over half (57 to 62 percent) of people aged 40 or older say the woman usually or always plans the dinner, but among people under age 30, half say the task is shared and only one-third say it is the woman's job.

- Over half of people under age 30 say caring for sick family members is shared. People aged 30 to 59 are about as likely to share nursing responsibility as to leave it up to the woman. Couples aged 60 or older, however, are more likely to say it is the woman's job.

- Grocery shopping is a shared responsibility for most people under age 30 (52 percent). Couples in their 40s are most likely to say this task usually or always falls to the woman (53 percent).

Traditional Roles Preferred by the Less-Educated

People with lower levels of education (who are also likely to be older) are more likely to believe in traditional sex roles.

- Similar percentages of people with a high school diploma or college degree say they would vote for a woman for president (90 to 96 percent), but people who did not complete high school are less likely to say this (82 percent).

- People who did not complete high school are also the exception on whether a working mother's relationship with her children can be as good as that of a non-working mother. Only 59 percent of those without a high school diploma agree, compared to 71 to 77 percent of people with at least a high school diploma.

- More education increases the likelihood that people will approve of married women working even if their husbands can support them (from a low of 67 percent among those who did not complete high school to a high of 91 percent among people with graduate degrees).

- The more educated are more likely to disagree that preschool children suffer if their mothers work (only 47 percent of people without a high school diploma disagree, versus 64 percent of those with graduate degrees).

College graduates are more likely than people with less education to:

- Disagree with the idea that men are better suited emotionally for politics (82 to 88 percent of college graduates compared with 74 percent of high school graduates and 61 percent of people who did not complete high school);

- Reject the idea that the best arrangement is for the woman to care for the home and the man to make the money (75 to 83 percent of people with college degrees compared with 63 percent of high school graduates and only 42 percent of people who did not complete high school);

- Say they do not believe women should stick to running their homes and leave running the country up to men (92 percent of college graduates compared with 84 percent of people with high school diplomas and 62 percent of those who did not complete high school);

- Reject the premise that a husband's career is more important than his wife's (85 to 88 percent of college graduates compared with 77 percent of high school graduates and 55 percent of people who did not complete high school);

- Disagree that it is not good for the man to be "Mr. Mom" while his wife earns the family's income (66 to 69 percent of people with college degrees compared with 53 percent of high school graduates and 41 percent of those without high school diplomas).

There is surprising agreement by education about who does the household chores. Similar percentages of people say:

- The woman handles the laundry (60 to 68 percent);

- The woman is most likely to be responsible for dinner planning (48 to 56 percent);

- The woman shops for groceries (44 to 50 percent) or it is a shared responsibility (38 to 43 percent).

But there are some differences.

- Those with less education are less likely to say the man and woman share responsibility for nursing sick family members (34 percent of people who did not complete high school compared with 46 to 50 percent of others).

- Couples with at least a high school diploma are more likely to say the man handles the repairs (67 to 76 percent compared with 56 percent of people who did not complete high school).

Should Men Run the Country?

Should women stick to running the home and leave running the country up to men? A majority of Americans (83 percent) say no. This majority is much larger than in 1974 (62 percent).

Men and women are about equally likely to disagree with this traditional division of labor (84 percent of women and 81 percent of men), as was the case in 1974.

Blacks and whites are also more or less in agreement (78 percent of blacks and 83 percent of whites). In 1974, however, whites were much more likely than blacks to disagree that women should leave running the country up to men (52 percent of blacks compared with 64 percent of whites).

Baby boomers and Generations Xers (people under age 50) think differently than older generations. While 88 to 91 percent of the younger generations disagree with the idea that women should stay at home and men should run the country, this is true for only 81 percent of those in their 50s, 77 percent of those in their 60s, and 58 percent of people aged 70 or older. Each age group was more likely to disagree with this statement in 1994 than it was in 1974. There has also been some change of opinion within generations. In 1974, for example, 62 percent of people in their 40s disagreed with the notion that women should leave running the country up to men. By 1994, 77 percent of this group (now in their 60s) disagreed.

Only 62 percent of people who did not finish high school disagree with the idea that women should run the home and men should run the country. In contrast, fully 84 percent of people who completed high school and 92 percent of those with college degrees disagree.

Should Men Run the Country? 1994

"Do you agree or disagree with this statement?
Women should take care of running their homes
and leave running the country up to men."

(percent responding by sex, race, age, and education, 1994)

	agree	disagree
Total	14%	83%
Women	13	84
Men	14	81
Black	18	78
White	13	83
Aged 18 to 29	8	91
Aged 30 to 39	7	89
Aged 40 to 49	10	88
Aged 50 to 59	12	81
Aged 60 to 69	23	77
Aged 70 or older	33	58
Not a high school graduate	30	62
High school graduate	13	84
Bachelor's degree	7	92
Graduate degree	5	92

Note: Percents may not add to 100 percent because "not sure" and no answer are not included.
Source: General Social Survey, National Opinion Research Center, University of Chicago

Should Men Run the Country? 1974 to 1994

*"Do you agree or disagree with this statement?
Women should take care of running their homes
and leave running the country up to men."*

(percent responding by sex, race, age, and education, 1974-94)

	agree			disagree		
	1994	**1985**	**1974**	**1994**	**1985**	**1974**
Total	14%	25%	34%	83%	72%	62%
Women	13	26	34	84	71	63
Men	14	24	35	81	73	61
Black	18	33	42	78	61	52
White	13	24	33	83	73	64
Aged 18 to 29	8	14	21	91	83	76
Aged 30 to 39	7	19	28	89	81	71
Aged 40 to 49	10	19	32	88	79	62
Aged 50 to 59	12	27	42	81	69	54
Aged 60 to 69	23	42	44	77	56	52
Aged 70 or older	33	47	60	58	49	37
Not a high school graduate	30	50	56	62	47	41
High school graduate	13	20	26	84	77	70
Bachelor's degree	7	11	10	92	88	89
Graduate degree	5	6	10	92	94	88

Note: Percents may not add to 100 percent because "not sure" and no answer are not included.
Source: General Social Survey, National Opinion Research Center, University of Chicago

Are Men Better Suited for Politics?

Three-quarters of Americans do not agree that men are better suited emotionally for politics than are women. But in 1974, the nation was about evenly divided on this question.

Women and men are about equally likely to disagree with the notion that men are better suited for politics than are women (76 percent of women and 72 percent of men). The sexes were in agreement on this issue in 1974 as well. Likewise, blacks and whites roughly agree (70 percent of blacks and 75 percent of whites), as they did in 1974.

Younger adults are far more likely to disagree with this statement than are the oldest Americans. Only 55 percent of people aged 70 or older disagree that men are better suited for politics. This compares with 78 to 81 percent of people under age 50. Fully one-third of people aged 70 or older agree with the statement. The opinion gap by age was smaller in 1994 than it was in 1974.

A difference of opinion also exists by education. Only 61 percent of people who did not complete high school disagree with the idea that men are better suited for politics. This rises to 74 percent among people with high school diplomas and to at least 82 percent among those with college degrees. Although opinions have changed within each educational group, the gap was wider in 1994 than it was in 1974.

Are Men Better Suited for Politics? 1994

"Most men are better suited emotionally for politics than are most women—do you agree or disagree?"

(percent responding by sex, race, age, and education, 1994)

	agree	disagree	not sure
Total	20%	74%	6%
Women	19	76	4
Men	20	72	7
Black	22	70	7
White	19	75	5
Aged 18 to 29	17	79	4
Aged 30 to 39	13	81	6
Aged 40 to 49	18	78	4
Aged 50 to 59	20	75	6
Aged 60 to 69	25	71	4
Aged 70 or older	33	55	11
Not a high school graduate	27	61	12
High school graduate	20	74	5
Bachelor's degree	14	82	4
Graduate degree	10	88	1

Note: Percents may not add to 100 because no answer is not included.
Source: General Social Survey, National Opinion Research Center, University of Chicago

Are Men Better Suited for Politics? 1974 to 1994

"Most men are better suited emotionally for politics than are most women—do you agree or disagree?"

(percent responding by sex, race, age, and education, 1974-94)

	agree			disagree		
	1994	1985	1974	1994	1985	1974
Total	20%	37%	44%	74%	59%	49%
Women	19	36	44	76	59	51
Men	20	37	43	72	59	47
Black	22	35	40	70	57	51
White	19	37	44	75	59	49
Aged 18 to 29	17	25	31	79	69	62
Aged 30 to 39	13	34	38	81	63	53
Aged 40 to 49	18	29	46	78	68	47
Aged 50 to 59	20	40	46	75	58	47
Aged 60 to 69	25	52	55	71	43	40
Aged 70 or older	33	53	61	55	41	30
Not a high school graduate	27	50	53	61	46	41
High school graduate	20	35	39	74	60	53
Bachelor's degree	14	27	34	82	71	58
Graduate degree	10	28	35	88	75	60

Note: Percents may not add to 100 because "not sure" and no answer are not included.
Source: General Social Survey, National Opinion Research Center, University of Chicago

Woman Presidential Candidate

Nearly nine out of ten Americans say they would vote for a woman presidential candidate if their party nominated one and she was qualified for the job. Women and men agree on this (90 percent of women and 88 percent of men) as do blacks and whites (90 percent of blacks and 89 percent of whites).

There is also solid agreement among people under age 60, 91 to 94 percent of whom say they would vote for a woman presidential candidate. But older Americans are not quite as willing to accept a woman president. Only 83 percent of people in their 60s and 75 percent of those aged 70 or older would vote for a woman for president. The opinions of the oldest Americans have not changed much over the past 20 years. In 1974, 81 percent of people in their 40s said they would vote for a woman presidential candidate, almost identical to the 83 percent of this group (now in their 60s) who said they would do so in 1994.

There was less disagreement among people by education in 1994 than in 1974. Between 90 and 96 percent of people with at least a high school diploma say they would vote for a woman for president, compared with 82 percent of people who did not complete high school. This 14 percentage point gap between the most- and least-educated is smaller than the 22 percentage point gap in 1974.

Woman Presidential Candidate, 1994

"If your party nominated a woman for president, would you vote for her if she were qualified for the job?"

(percent responding by sex, race, age, and education, 1994)

	yes	*no*
Total	89%	8%
Women	90	8
Men	88	8
Black	90	7
White	89	8
Aged 18 to 29	93	4
Aged 30 to 39	94	4
Aged 40 to 49	93	6
Aged 50 to 59	91	7
Aged 60 to 69	83	14
Aged 70 or older	75	19
Not a high school graduate	82	13
High school graduate	90	8
Bachelor's degree	92	6
Graduate degree	96	3

Note: Percents may not add to 100 because "don't know" and no answer are not included.
Source: General Social Survey, National Opinion Research Center, University of Chicago

Woman Presidential Candidate, 1974 to 1994

"If your party nominated a woman for president, would you vote for her if she were qualified for the job?"

(percent responding by sex, race, age, and education, 1974-94)

	yes			no		
	1994	*1985*	*1974*	*1994*	*1985*	*1974*
Total	89%	80%	78%	8%	17%	19%
Women	90	77	77	8	20	19
Men	88	82	78	8	14	19
Black	90	81	76	7	11	21
White	89	80	78	8	17	19
Aged 18 to 29	93	86	89	4	11	9
Aged 30 to 39	94	86	82	4	12	13
Aged 40 to 49	93	87	81	6	11	15
Aged 50 to 59	91	79	72	7	16	26
Aged 60 to 69	83	71	63	14	27	34
Aged 70 or older	75	59	63	19	35	32
Not a high school graduate	82	66	68	13	29	28
High school graduate	90	83	82	8	15	15
Bachelor's degree	92	87	84	6	9	15
Graduate degree	96	91	90	3	6	8

Note: Percents may not add to 100 because "don't know" and no answer are not included.
Source: General Social Survey, National Opinion Research Center, University of Chicago

Is a Husband's Career More Important?

In the past, even if a married woman worked, her career was assumed to be secondary to that of her husband—the primary breadwinner. In 1977, a majority of Americans (55 percent) agreed that it was more important for a wife to help her husband's career rather than have one herself. But in 1994, fully three-quarters of Americans disagreed with this statement.

On this issue there is no argument between men and women or between blacks and whites. Interestingly, in 1977 women were more likely than men to feel a husband's career was more important.

A substantial percentage of older people are still likely to hold this view. Among people under age 40, 85 to 87 percent say they do not agree that a husband's career is more important. Smaller percentages of people in their 40s and 50s disagree (76 to 80). But only two-thirds of people in their 60s, and just 40 percent of those aged 70 or older disagree. In 1977, a majority of those aged 40 or older felt a husband's career was more important, while most of those under age 40 did not.

A bare majority (55 percent) of people who did not complete high school say they disagree that a husband's career takes priority over a wife's. Three-quarters of people with a high school diploma and 85 to 88 percent of those with college degrees do not believe a husband's career is more important.

Is a Husband's Career More Important? 1994

"It is more important for a wife to help her husband's career than to have one herself—do you agree or disagree?"

(percent responding by sex, race, age, and education, 1994)

	strongly agree	agree	disagree	strongly disagree	agree, total	disagree, total
Total	3%	18%	54%	22%	21%	76%
Women	3	17	50	26	20	76
Men	2	19	58	16	21	74
Black	4	19	51	21	23	72
White	3	18	53	22	21	75
Aged 18 to 29	2	11	55	30	13	85
Aged 30 to 39	2	9	55	32	11	87
Aged 40 to 49	3	13	56	24	16	80
Aged 50 to 59	2	17	58	18	19	76
Aged 60 to 69	5	25	58	8	30	66
Aged 70 or older	6	45	37	3	51	40
Not a high school graduate	6	31	45	10	37	55
High school graduate	3	17	56	21	20	77
Bachelor's degree	1	10	55	30	11	85
Graduate degree	1	10	52	36	11	88

Note: Percents may not add to 100 because "don't know" and no answer are not included.
Source: General Social Survey, National Opinion Research Center, University of Chicago

Is a Husband's Career More Important? 1977 to 1994

"It is more important for a wife to help her husband's career than to have one herself—do you agree or disagree?"

(percent responding by sex, race, age, and education, 1977-94)

	agree/strongly agree			disagree/strongly disagree		
	1994	**1985**	**1977**	**1994**	**1985**	**1977**
Total	21%	36%	55%	76%	60%	41%
Women	20	36	59	76	60	38
Men	21	36	50	74	60	45
Black	23	30	52	72	64	44
White	21	36	55	75	59	41
Aged 18 to 29	13	18	35	85	79	63
Aged 30 to 39	11	22	43	87	75	53
Aged 40 to 49	16	23	57	80	72	37
Aged 50 to 59	19	50	65	76	44	32
Aged 60 to 69	30	58	76	66	36	21
Aged 70 or older	51	69	80	40	26	17
Not a high school graduate	37	57	66	55	36	30
High school graduate	20	32	54	77	65	43
Bachelor's degree	11	24	33	85	71	65
Graduate degree	11	13	30	88	85	64

Note: Percents may not add to 100 because "don't know" and no answer are not included.
Source: General Social Survey, National Opinion Research Center, University of Chicago

Should Women Work if They Don't Have To?

A solid majority (79 percent) of Americans say it is fine for a married woman to work even if her husband makes enough to support the family. This proportion is somewhat higher than in 1974 when only 68 percent felt this way.

Similar percentages of women and men say they approve of women working regardless of their husband's income (80 percent of women and 79 percent of men). Women were slightly more likely than men to approve in 1974 (70 versus 64 percent).

Black and white Americans were in agreement on this issue in 1994 (80 percent of whites and 77 percent of blacks). In 1974 there was a small gap because blacks were less likely to approve.

People of all ages in 1994 were more likely to approve of women working even if they did not need the money than they were in 1974. In both years, younger people were more likely than their elders to find this acceptable. Eighty-six percent of people under age 30 approved in 1994, compared with only 64 percent of those aged 70 or older. This gap is far smaller than it was in 1974, however, when just 41 percent of people aged 70 or older agreed, versus 83 percent of those under age 30.

The more education people have the more likely they are to approve of women working even if they don't need the money. In 1994, only 67 percent of people who did not complete college said this was acceptable, compared with 91 percent of those with graduate degrees.

Should Women Work if They Don't Have To? 1994

"Do you approve or disapprove of a married woman
earning money in business or industry if she has
a husband capable of supporting her?"

(percent responding by sex, race, age, and education, 1994)

	approve	disapprove
Total	79%	18%
Women	80	18
Men	79	19
Black	77	20
White	80	18
Aged 18 to 29	86	13
Aged 30 to 39	82	16
Aged 40 to 49	82	17
Aged 50 to 59	80	17
Aged 60 to 69	75	24
Aged 70 or older	64	30
Not a high school graduate	67	31
High school graduate	79	18
Bachelor's degree	84	15
Graduate degree	91	6

Note: Percents may not add to 100 because "don't know" and no answer are not included.
Source: General Social Survey, National Opinion Research Center, University of Chicago

Should Women Work if They Don't Have To? 1974 to 1994

"Do you approve or disapprove of a married woman earning money in business or industry if she has a husband capable of supporting her?

(percent responding by sex, race, age, and education, 1974-94)

	approve			disapprove		
	1994	*1985*	*1974*	*1994*	*1985*	*1974*
Total	79%	84%	68%	18%	14%	30%
Women	80	83	70	18	14	27
Men	79	84	64	19	13	34
Black	77	81	61	20	16	35
White	80	84	68	18	13	30
Aged 18 to 29	86	88	83	13	10	17
Aged 30 to 39	82	86	75	16	12	23
Aged 40 to 49	82	87	72	17	12	27
Aged 50 to 59	80	82	60	17	14	35
Aged 60 to 69	75	80	51	24	16	44
Aged 70 or older	64	73	41	30	21	55
Not a high school graduate	67	72	51	31	22	47
High school graduate	79	86	74	18	12	23
Bachelor's degree	84	92	89	15	7	9
Graduate degree	91	92	77	6	8	19

Note: Percents may not add to 100 because "don't know" and no answer are not included.
Source: General Social Survey, National Opinion Research Center, University of Chicago

Women Work to Support Families

Much of the debate over whether women should work ignores the reality that many women have to work to support their families. A majority of Americans know this to be true (83 percent). On this issue there is little disagreement no matter how the population is sliced up.

Men are about as likely as women to agree that most women work these days because their family needs the money (86 percent of women and 80 percent of men). Blacks and whites also agree (85 percent of blacks and 83 percent of whites).

Regardless of whether they think it is good for women to work or not, the generations are remarkably united in their belief that work is a necessity for most women (79 to 87 percent).

By education, most people also agree that women have to work. Surprisingly, those with bachelor's degrees are least likely to think so. While 83 to 87 percent of other educational segments believe women have to work, a smaller 76 percent of those with bachelor's degrees agree.

Women Work to Support Families, 1994

"Most women have to work these days to support
their families—do you agree or disagree?"

(percent responding by sex, race, age, and education, 1994)

	strongly agree	agree	neither	disagree	strongly disagree	agree, total	disagree, total
Total	28%	55%	8%	5%	2%	83%	7%
Women	35	51	8	4	2	86	6
Men	18	62	9	7	1	80	8
Black	42	43	5	4	2	85	6
White	26	57	9	5	1	83	6
Aged 18 to 29	30	54	8	5	0	84	5
Aged 30 to 39	34	53	6	5	2	87	7
Aged 40 to 49	24	59	8	6	3	83	9
Aged 50 to 59	28	54	11	4	1	82	5
Aged 60 to 69	23	57	10	7	0	80	7
Aged 70 or older	22	57	10	6	1	79	7
Not a high school graduate	32	51	8	5	1	83	6
High school graduate	29	56	8	5	1	85	6
Bachelor's degree	20	56	10	10	3	76	13
Graduate degree	27	60	8	3	0	87	3

Note: Percents may not add to 100 because "can't choose" and no answer are not included.
Source: General Social Survey, National Opinion Research Center, University of Chicago

Female Homemakers and Male Breadwinners

Once upon a time, life was divided into two spheres: his and hers. The woman's domain was the home while the man's was everything else. Most Americans once felt this was the best arrangement. In 1977, fully 65 percent supported separate spheres for men and women. By 1994, a 63 percent majority did not.

Women are slightly more likely than men to disagree that "it is better if the man is the achiever outside the home and the woman takes care of the home and family" (65 percent of women versus 59 percent of men). The gap between the sexes is about the same as it was in 1977, although in that year a majority of both sexes agreed with the statement.

Blacks and whites also agree on this issue. Sixty-four percent of blacks and whites say they do not think traditional sex roles are best.

The generations could hardly disagree more. Fully 81 percent of Generation Xers (under age 30) disagree with traditional sex roles, as do 71 to 74 percent of baby boomers (aged 30 to 49). In contrast, only a small majority of people in their 50s and 60s disagree with the idea that men should be breadwinners and women homemakers (53 to 57 percent). Among people aged 70 or older, only 24 percent disagree. While there was wide disagreement among the generations in 1977 as well, the gap was even wider in 1994.

There is also disagreement by education. Those with less education (many of whom are older) are more likely to believe traditional sex roles are better. A majority (56 percent) of people who did not complete high school say traditional sex roles are best. This proportion drops with education to just 12 percent of those with graduate degrees.

Female Homemakers and Male Breadwinners, 1994

"It is much better for everyone involved if the man is the achiever outside the home and the woman takes care of the home and family—do you agree or disagree?"

(percent responding by sex, race, age, and education, 1994)

	strongly agree	agree	disagree	strongly disagree	agree, total	disagree, total
Total	7%	27%	45%	18%	34%	63%
Women	7	25	44	21	32	65
Men	7	30	47	12	37	59
Black	6	26	49	15	32	64
White	7	27	45	19	34	64
Aged 18 to 29	3	15	52	29	18	81
Aged 30 to 39	4	20	52	22	24	74
Aged 40 to 49	6	20	51	20	26	71
Aged 50 to 59	7	32	41	16	39	57
Aged 60 to 69	8	37	46	7	45	53
Aged 70 or older	16	55	21	3	71	24
Not a high school graduate	13	43	32	10	56	42
High school graduate	7	27	47	16	34	63
Bachelor's degree	4	19	52	23	23	75
Graduate degree	1	11	50	33	12	83

Note: Percents may not add to 100 because "don't know" and no answer are not included.
Source: General Social Survey, National Opinion Research Center, University of Chicago

Female Homemakers and Male Breadwinners, 1977 to 1994

"It is much better for everyone involved if the man is the achiever outside the home and the woman takes care of the home and family—do you agree or disagree?"

(percent responding by sex, race, age, and education, 1977-94)

	agree/strongly agree			disagree/strongly disagree		
	1994	1985	1977	1994	1985	1977
Total	34%	47%	65%	63%	50%	34%
Women	32	45	62	65	53	36
Men	37	50	68	59	46	30
Black	32	50	61	64	45	37
White	34	47	65	64	50	33
Aged 18 to 29	18	30	45	81	69	54
Aged 30 to 39	24	32	51	74	65	47
Aged 40 to 49	26	41	67	71	59	30
Aged 50 to 59	39	64	79	57	29	21
Aged 60 to 69	45	66	84	53	32	15
Aged 70 or older	71	75	88	24	23	11
Not a high school graduate	56	67	79	42	28	19
High school graduate	34	45	61	63	54	38
Bachelor's degree	23	29	45	75	67	53
Graduate degree	12	30	45	83	71	54

Note: Percents may not add to 100 because "don't know" and no answer are not included.
Source: General Social Survey, National Opinion Research Center, University of Chicago

Is "Mr. Mom" a Bad Idea?

Traditional sex roles are changing, but is it wrong if the man stays home to care for the kids while the woman goes off to work every day? Slightly over half (55 percent) of Americans do not think this is a bad idea.

Women are slightly more likely than men to say this is not wrong (57 percent of women compared with 50 percent of men). Whites are slightly more likely than blacks to say it's not a bad idea (56 percent of whites compared with 48 percent of blacks).

But the old and young are miles apart. Well over half (59 to 63 percent) of people under age 50 say it's not a bad thing. But fewer than half of people aged 50 to 69, and only one-third of those aged 70 or older agree.

Most of the college-educated do not think Mr. Mom is a bad idea (66 to 69 percent), but only 53 percent of those with no more than a high school diploma and 41 percent of those who did not complete high school agree. Some of the differences by education may be due to age, however, since those with less education are more likely to be older.

Is Mr. Mom a Bad Idea? 1994

"It is not good if the man stays at home and cares
for the children and the woman goes to work—
do you agree or disagree?"

(percent responding by sex, race, age, and education, 1994)

	strongly agree	agree	neither	disagree	strongly disagree	agree, total	disagree, total
Total	7%	16%	20%	39%	16%	23%	55%
Women	7	15	19	39	18	22	57
Men	7	17	22	38	12	24	50
Black	8	14	24	31	17	22	48
White	7	16	20	40	16	23	56
Aged 18 to 29	5	11	19	40	23	16	63
Aged 30 to 39	5	9	20	40	23	14	63
Aged 40 to 49	4	15	19	43	16	19	59
Aged 50 to 59	10	15	24	37	12	25	49
Aged 60 to 69	6	26	23	37	4	32	41
Aged 70 or older	14	31	18	29	3	45	32
Not a high school graduate	13	24	15	33	8	37	41
High school graduate	8	16	21	38	15	24	53
Bachelor's degree	4	14	17	46	20	18	66
Graduate degree	0	8	22	40	29	8	69

Note: Percents may not add to 100 because "can't choose" and no answer are not included.
Source: General Social Survey, National Opinion Research Center, University of Chicago

Are Working Mothers as Good?

A solid majority of Americans (69 percent) believe a working mother can establish as warm and secure a relationship with her children as a mother who does not work. This was not the case in 1977, however. Nearly two decades ago, when mothers of young children were pouring into the labor force for the first time, many worried that children would be neglected. At that time, half of Americans believed that a working mother's relationship with her children would not be as good as that of a non-working mother. Only 48 percent felt it would be just as good.

Women are more likely than men to believe working mothers can have just as good a relationship with her children as nonworking mothers (75 percent of women compared with 60 percent of men). While both men and women are more likely to feel this way than they were in 1977, the gap between the sexes was about as large in 1994 as it was in 1977.

Blacks are more likely than whites to feel a working mother can be as close to her children (74 percent of blacks compared with 67 percent of whites). Blacks were also more likely to believe this in 1977.

A wide generation gap exists on this question, as it did in 1977. While 72 to 79 percent of people under age 50 believe a working mother can have as good a relationship with her children as one who does not work, only 62 to 66 percent of people aged 50 to 69, and just 48 percent of those aged 70 or older, agree.

In 1977, the college-educated were much more likely than those with less education to believe working mothers could have just as good a relationship with their children. By 1994, the gap had closed considerably. Still, only 59 percent of those without a high school diploma say working mothers can have as warm a relationship with their children as nonworking mothers.

Is a Working Mother as Good? 1994

"A working mother can establish just as warm and secure
a relationship with her children as a mother who
does not work—do you agree or disagree?"

(percent responding by sex, race, age, and education, 1994)

	strongly agree	agree	disagree	strongly disagree	agree, total	disagree, total
Total	23%	46%	25%	5%	69%	30%
Women	30	45	19	5	75	24
Men	14	46	33	5	60	38
Black	28	46	22	4	74	26
White	22	45	26	5	67	31
Aged 18 to 29	26	53	19	1	79	20
Aged 30 to 39	28	46	22	3	74	25
Aged 40 to 49	27	45	22	4	72	26
Aged 50 to 59	21	45	28	5	66	33
Aged 60 to 69	18	44	27	10	62	37
Aged 70 or older	10	38	38	11	48	49
Not a high school graduate	16	43	32	7	59	39
High school graduate	22	47	25	5	69	30
Bachelor's degree	27	45	24	5	72	29
Graduate degree	36	41	18	2	77	20

Note: Percents may not add to 100 because "don't know" and no answer are not included.
Source: General Social Survey, National Opinion Research Center, University of Chicago

Is a Working Mother as Good? 1977 to 1994

"A working mother can establish just as warm and secure a relationship with her children as a mother who does not work—do you agree or disagree?"

(percent responding by sex, race, age, and education, selected years, 1977-94)

	agree/strongly agree			disagree/strongly disagree		
	1994	1985	1977	1994	1985	1977
Total	69%	59%	48%	30%	40%	50%
Women	75	66	54	24	33	44
Men	60	50	41	38	49	57
Black	74	56	56	26	38	44
White	67	59	47	31	41	51
Aged 18 to 29	79	65	60	20	34	38
Aged 30 to 39	74	68	60	25	31	38
Aged 40 to 49	72	69	45	26	31	54
Aged 50 to 59	66	46	43	33	52	57
Aged 60 to 69	62	48	32	37	50	66
Aged 70 or older	48	44	30	49	55	68
Not a high school graduate	59	44	37	39	55	61
High school graduate	69	62	52	30	37	47
Bachelor's degree	72	67	61	29	33	39
Graduate degree	77	75	64	20	25	31

Note: Percents may not add to 100 because "don't know" and no answer are not included.
Source: General Social Survey, National Opinion Research Center, University of Chicago

Do Young Children Suffer if Mother Works?

Over half of Americans (56 percent) disagree that preschool children suffer if their mothers work. While this is a small majority, the figure is sharply higher than in 1977, when only 32 percent disagreed.

Women are much more likely than men to disagree that preschoolers suffer when their mothers work (63 percent of women versus 48 percent of men). The gap in the opinions of men and women was slightly wider in 1994 than it was in 1977, although both men and women are less likely to think preschoolers suffer than they once did.

Blacks are slightly more likely than whites to disagree (62 percent versus 56 percent). This is a change from 1977, when blacks were 16 percentage points more likely than whites to disagree that preschoolers suffer when their mothers work.

The generations were more divided in 1994 than they were in 1977. The percentage of people who do not think preschoolers suffer if their mothers work falls sharply with age. Sixty-eight percent of people under age 30 disagree compared with only 31 percent of those aged 70 or older.

By education, there was as much disagreement on this issue in 1994 as in 1977. Only 47 percent of people who did not complete high school disagree that preschoolers suffer if their mothers work. This compares with 56 to 58 percent of people with a high school diploma or bachelor's degree and 64 percent of those with graduate degrees.

Do Young Children Suffer if Mother Works? 1994

"A preschool child is likely to suffer if his or her mother works—do you agree or disagree?"

(percent responding by sex, race, age, and education, 1994)

	strongly agree	agree	disagree	strongly disagree	agree, total	disagree, total
Total	7%	34%	45%	11%	41%	56%
Women	6	30	49	14	36	63
Men	9	40	41	7	49	48
Black	8	29	49	13	37	62
White	7	35	45	11	42	56
Aged 18 to 29	4	26	56	13	30	68
Aged 30 to 39	4	31	48	15	34	63
Aged 40 to 49	7	31	46	13	38	59
Aged 50 to 59	9	34	45	11	43	56
Aged 60 to 69	10	40	45	5	50	50
Aged 70 or older	15	50	28	3	65	31
Not a high school graduate	11	40	41	6	51	47
High school graduate	8	33	47	11	41	58
Bachelor's degree	7	36	42	14	43	56
Graduate degree	2	31	50	14	33	64

Note: Percents may not add to 100 because "don't know" and no answer are not included.
Source: General Social Survey, National Opinion Research Center, University of Chicago

Do Young Children Suffer if Mother Works? 1977 to 1994

"A preschool child is likely to suffer if his or her mother works—do you agree or disagree?"

(percent responding by sex, race, age, and education, 1977-94)

	agree/strongly agree			disagree/strongly disagree		
	1994	1985	1977	1994	1985	1977
Total	41%	53%	66%	56%	45%	32%
Women	36	46	61	63	52	37
Men	49	62	72	48	36	26
Black	37	48	52	62	48	46
White	42	53	68	56	44	30
Aged 18 to 29	30	40	55	68	58	44
Aged 30 to 39	34	44	55	63	54	43
Aged 40 to 49	38	50	69	59	48	29
Aged 50 to 59	43	65	73	56	33	25
Aged 60 to 69	50	71	82	50	27	16
Aged 70 or older	65	64	78	31	34	19
Not a high school graduate	51	61	73	47	34	24
High school graduate	41	52	64	58	47	35
Bachelor's degree	43	47	60	56	51	40
Graduate degree	33	51	55	64	49	39

Note: Percents may not add to 100 because "don't know" and no answer are not included.
Source: General Social Survey, National Opinion Research Center, University of Chicago

Who Does the Household Chores?

Attitudes about the roles of men and women have changed a lot in the past two decades. Within the household, however, the burden still falls on women. A majority of couples say the woman always or usually does the laundry (65 percent) and plans dinner (52 percent). A plurality say the woman always or usually shops for groceries (47 percent). Caring for sick family members is as likely to be handled by the woman (47 percent) as it is to be shared by both (45 percent). Of the five household chores examined by the General Social Survey, only one is done always or usually by men—household repairs.

Men and women think they do more. One-quarter of women say household repairs are handled equally by the man and the woman. Only 15 percent of men agree. While one-third of men say they always do the household repairs, only 14 percent of women agree. Forty-two percent of men, but only 34 percent of women, say they share dinner planning. Caring for the sick is a shared task according to 49 percent of men, but only 42 percent of women agree.

Black couples are considerably more likely than whites to say household chores are shared by the man and woman. Grocery shopping is a shared responsibility in a majority of black households (59 percent), but in only 40 percent of white households. Nearly half of whites, but only 32 percent of blacks, say the woman usually or always does the shopping. Only 55 percent of blacks say the woman always does the laundry, while 38 percent say the man and woman share this responsibility. In contrast, 68 percent of whites say the woman usually handles the laundry, while only 22 percent say they both do. Forty-nine percent of blacks, but only 37 percent of whites, say dinner planning is shared by the man and the woman. Blacks are about 10 percentage points more likely than whites to say household repairs are shared, while whites are about 10 points more likely to say the man usually does them.

By age, there are distinct differences in the percentages who adhere to traditional sex roles. Women usually do the laundry in a majority of households, but the majority is slim among people under age 30 (51 percent), rising to a peak of 74 to 77 percent among households headed by couples aged 50 or older. The man is usually responsible for repairs according to 59 percent of people under age 30, rising to 70 to 73 percent among people aged 50 or older. Only one-third of people under age 30 say the woman usually plans dinner, compared with 62 percent of those aged 70 or older. Only 36 percent of couples under age 30, but 52 percent of those aged 70 or older, say the woman usually nurses the sick. Grocery shopping is the only chore with little difference by age. Those least likely to say the woman usually shops for food are people under age 30 (37 percent). Most likely to say so are people in their 40s (53 percent). The oldest age group falls in between (48 percent).

There is not much difference in who does the household chores by education. Majorities or pluralities say the woman usually or always does the laundry (60 to 68 percent), plans dinner (48 to 56 percent), and shops for groceries (44 to 50 percent). Less-educated couples are more likely to share responsibility for household repairs, however (25 percent do so compared with 13 percent of those with at least a high school diploma).

Who Does the Laundry? 1994

"In your household, who does the laundry?"

(percent responding by sex, race, age, and education, 1994)

	woman always	woman usually	about equal or both together	man usually	man always	usually/ always woman	usually/ always man
Total	31%	34%	24%	3%	1%	65%	4%
Women	37	31	24	2	1	68	3
Men	24	39	24	4	2	63	6
Black	32	23	38	3	0	55	3
White	32	36	22	3	2	68	5
Aged 18 to 29	20	31	35	6	2	51	8
Aged 30 to 39	23	39	30	3	1	62	4
Aged 40 to 49	29	35	26	4	2	64	6
Aged 50 to 59	38	36	18	3	2	74	5
Aged 60 to 69	48	29	14	1	1	77	2
Aged 70 or older	46	29	13	2	2	75	4
Not a high school graduate	41	24	22	3	1	65	4
High school graduate	35	33	24	3	2	68	5
Bachelor's degree	24	41	24	5	1	65	6
Graduate degree	22	38	25	6	3	60	9

Note: Percentages are based on respondents who were married or living as married. Percents may not add to 100 because a third person, "can't choose," and no answer are not included.
Source: General Social Survey, National Opinion Research Center, University of Chicago

Who Plans Dinner? 1994

"In your household, who decides what to have for dinner?"

(percent responding by sex, race, age, and education, 1994)

	woman always	woman usually	about equal or both together	man usually	man always	usually/ always woman	usually/ always man
Total	18%	34%	38%	5%	1%	52%	6%
Women	24	35	34	3	0	59	3
Men	12	34	42	6	2	46	8
Black	20	20	49	7	0	40	7
White	18	35	37	4	1	53	5
Aged 18 to 29	11	22	51	7	2	34	9
Aged 30 to 39	17	32	43	6	1	49	7
Aged 40 to 49	20	39	33	4	1	59	5
Aged 50 to 59	23	35	37	2	1	58	3
Aged 60 to 69	20	37	29	5	0	57	5
Aged 70 or older	21	41	31	2	1	62	3
Not a high school graduate	21	27	38	5	0	48	5
High school graduate	21	32	39	4	2	53	6
Bachelor's degree	15	40	35	7	0	55	7
Graduate degree	10	46	35	6	0	56	6

Note: Percentages are based on respondents who were married or living as married. Percents may not add to 100 because a third person, "can't choose," and no answer are not included.
Source: General Social Survey, National Opinion Research Center, University of Chicago

Who Does the Grocery Shopping? 1994

"In your household, who shops for groceries?"

(percent responding by sex, race, age, and education, 1994)

	woman always	woman usually	about equal or both together	man usually	man always	usually/ always woman	usually/ always man
Total	16%	31%	42%	5%	2%	47%	7%
Women	22	28	42	4	1	50	5
Men	10	34	43	5	3	44	8
Black	18	14	59	5	0	32	5
White	16	33	40	5	1	49	6
Aged 18 to 29	15	22	52	4	3	37	7
Aged 30 to 39	16	31	44	5	1	47	6
Aged 40 to 49	16	37	37	5	1	53	6
Aged 50 to 59	22	27	42	4	1	49	5
Aged 60 to 69	16	29	43	4	1	45	5
Aged 70 or older	14	34	37	6	3	48	9
Not a high school graduate	24	20	41	5	1	44	5
High school graduate	18	30	43	4	2	48	6
Bachelor's degree	13	33	42	6	1	46	7
Graduate degree	6	44	38	9	0	50	9

Note: Percentages are based on respondents who were married or living as married. Percents may not add to 100 because a third person, "can't choose," and no answer are not included.
Source: General Social Survey, National Opinion Research Center, University of Chicago

Who Cares for Sick Family Members? 1994

"In your household, who cares for sick family members?"

(percent responding by sex, race, age, and education, 1994)

	woman always	woman usually	about equal or both together	man usually	man always	usually/ always woman	usually/ always man
Total	15%	32%	45%	1%	1%	47%	2%
Women	21	31	42	1	0	52	1
Men	7	33	49	2	2	40	4
Black	22	19	49	1	0	41	1
White	13	33	44	1	1	46	2
Aged 18 to 29	13	23	54	1	2	36	3
Aged 30 to 39	13	34	47	1	0	47	1
Aged 40 to 49	13	35	44	1	1	48	2
Aged 50 to 59	17	29	47	1	1	46	2
Aged 60 to 69	20	26	40	2	0	46	2
Aged 70 or older	16	36	36	2	2	52	4
Not a high school graduate	20	29	34	2	2	49	4
High school graduate	16	31	46	1	1	47	2
Bachelor's degree	10	34	50	1	0	44	1
Graduate degree	6	38	50	1	0	44	1

Note: Percentages are based on respondents who were married or living as married. Percents may not add to 100 because a third person, "can't choose," and no answer are not included.
Source: General Social Survey, National Opinion Research Center, University of Chicago

Who Makes the Repairs? 1994

"In your household, who makes small repairs around the house?"

(percent responding by sex, race, age, and education, 1994)

	woman always	woman usually	about equal or both together	man usually	man always	usually/ always woman	usually/ always man
Total	2%	3%	21%	45%	22%	5%	67%
Women	3	5	25	46	14	8	60
Men	1	1	15	43	33	2	76
Black	3	1	28	39	19	4	58
White	2	3	19	46	23	5	69
Aged 18 to 29	2	4	28	39	20	6	59
Aged 30 to 39	2	3	23	48	19	5	67
Aged 40 to 49	2	4	23	45	21	6	66
Aged 50 to 59	3	2	17	50	23	5	73
Aged 60 to 69	2	2	16	48	22	4	70
Aged 70 or older	3	5	12	37	35	8	72
Not a high school graduate	4	3	25	31	25	7	56
High school graduate	2	3	19	49	22	5	71
Bachelor's degree	2	6	17	43	24	8	67
Graduate degree	0	1	13	51	25	1	76

Note: Percentages are based on respondents who were married or living as married. Percents may not add to 100 because a third person, "can't choose," and no answer are not included.
Source: General Social Survey, National Opinion Research Center, University of Chicago

8

Personal Outlook

Most Americans are happy with their own lives, but they have their doubts about other people. Their assessment of the fairness, trustworthiness, and helpfulness of others has gotten more negative over the last 20 years.

A solid majority of Americans:

- Rate their health as excellent or good (78 percent);

- Say they get great satisfaction from their friendships (69 percent).

But smaller majorities say:

- They are pretty happy (59 percent). Only 29 percent say they are very happy, down from 38 percent in 1974;

- They get a great or very great deal of satisfaction from their hobbies and other activities outside of work (57 percent);

- Most people try to be fair (53 percent). This is down from the 62 percent who had faith in the motives of others in 1975.

On some personal issues, Americans are decidedly pessimistic and anti-social.

- Most are not joiners. Out of ten different types of organizations, only one has a sizable percentage of Americans as members: church-affiliated groups (33 percent). Only 19 percent of Americans are members of professional or academic societies and 16 percent are members of school service clubs.

- Most say you can't be too careful in dealing with people (61 percent). Only one-third say most people can be trusted, down from 39 percent in 1975.

On five of the issues, Americans divide into two camps. They are split on whether:

- Life is exciting (47 percent) or pretty routine (48). Only 4 percent of adults feel their lives are dull;

- People are generally helpful (46 percent) or just looking out for themselves (47 percent). This is a big change from 1975 when 56 percent said most people try to be helpful and only 37 percent felt people were generally selfish;

- Humans evolved from earlier species of animals. Forty-three percent say this definitely or probably true, while 46 percent say it is definitely or probably not true;

- There is some scientific truth to astrology. Forty-seven percent say it is definitely or probably true, while 43 percent say it is definitely or probably not true;

- They get a great or very great deal of satisfaction from the place in which they live (48 percent).

Women Are Fond of Friends and Star Signs

Men and women have a similar outlook on most of the issues considered here. About the same percentages of men and women say:

- They are pretty happy (59 percent of women and 58 percent of men) or very happy (28 percent of women and 30 percent of men);

- They get a great or very great deal of satisfaction from their hobbies and other non-work activities (57 percent of men and women);

- Most people try to be fair rather than take advantage of others (53 percent of both men and women);

- Life is exciting (45 percent of women and 49 percent of men) or routine (50 percent of women and 46 percent of men);

- Their health is good or excellent (48 percent of both women and men).

Women are more likely than men to say:

- They get a great or very great deal of satisfaction from the place in which they live in (50 percent of women compared with 43 percent of men);

- Most people try to be helpful (50 percent of women compared with 42 percent of men);

- You can't be too careful in dealing with people (65 percent of women compared with 57 percent of men);

- They don't believe in evolution (49 percent of women compared with 41 percent of men).

There are also small differences in the percentages of men and women who are members of various types of organizations.

- Women are more likely than men to be members of a church group (36 percent versus 30 percent) or school group (19 percent versus 13 percent).

- Men are more likely to be members of a fraternal group (14 percent of men, 7 percent of women) or veterans group (13 percent of men, 4 percent of women).

Women are more likely than men to value friends.

- About three-quarters of women, compared with 63 percent of men, say they get a great or very great deal of satisfaction from their friendships.

- About half of women (53 percent), but only 40 percent of men, believe there is definitely or probably some scientific basis for astrology.

Blacks and Whites Differ in Their Opinions of Others

Blacks and whites have markedly different outlooks on almost all of the issues considered here. They are in agreement on only one:

- Similar percentages say they get a great or very great deal of satisfaction from their hobbies (60 percent of blacks and 57 percent of whites).

On a few issues, there are only small differences between blacks and whites.

- Blacks are more likely to say there is definitely or probably some scientific truth to astrology (54 percent of blacks compared with 46 percent of whites).

- Blacks are only slightly less likely than whites to rate their health as good or excellent (71 percent of blacks compared with 80 percent of whites).

- Whites are more likely to say they get a great or very great deal of satisfaction from friendships (70 percent of whites compared with 61 percent of blacks).

- Whites are more likely to be members of professional or academic societies (21 percent) than are blacks (10 percent). Whites are also more likely to belong to fraternal groups (11 percent of whites, 3 percent of blacks). Blacks are slightly more likely to be members of youth groups (16 percent compared with 9 percent of whites).

- Whites more likely than blacks to believe in evolution (45 percent of whites compared with 33 percent of blacks).

- Blacks and whites are about equally likely to say they are pretty happy. But blacks are more likely to say they are not too happy (23 percent of blacks compared with 10 percent of whites), while whites are more likely to say they are very happy (31 percent versus 17 percent).

- Blacks are less likely than whites to say life is exciting (36 percent of blacks compared with 49 percent of whites), but they are not much more likely to think life is dull. Instead, they say it is pretty routine (56 percent of blacks compared with 46 percent of whites).

There are large differences between blacks and whites on the remaining issues. Blacks are far more likely than whites to say:

- You can't be too careful in dealing with people (82 percent of blacks compared with 58 percent of whites);

- Other people would take advantage of you if they got a chance (61 percent of blacks compared with 35 percent of whites).

Blacks are less likely than whites to say:

- Most people try to be helpful instead of just looking out for themselves (only 30 percent of blacks compared with 50 percent of whites);

- They get a great or very great deal of satisfaction from the place in which they live (30 percent of blacks compared with 50 percent of whites).

Life Is Less Exciting for Older Americans

Age clearly plays a role in determining attitudes on some of the issues considered here. But on about half of the questions, there is no clear dividing line between younger and older respondents.

- There is little variation by age in the percentage of people who believe there is definitely or probably some scientific truth in astrology. Those least likely to believe in astrology are people in their 40s (42 percent). Those most likely to believe in it are people in their 60s (51 percent).

- People under age 30 are most likely to say you can't be too careful in dealing with others (69 percent). Those aged 40 to 49 are least likely to feel this way (56 percent). The other age groups fall in between.

- Those least likely to say they get a great or very great deal of satisfaction from their friendships are people in their 40s (63 percent). People in their 50s and 60s are most likely to say this (77 percent).

- Those most likely to get a great or very great deal of satisfaction from their hobbies are people aged 30 to 59 (60 to 64 percent). The oldest and youngest adults are most likely to say they get only some satisfaction (21 percent).

- The oldest Americans are much more likely to say they get a great or very great deal of satisfaction from the place in which they live (only 33 percent of people under age 30 compared with 62 percent of those aged 70 or older).

Differences between the attitudes of younger and older Americans are more apparent on the remaining issues.

- Older people are slightly more likely to say they are very happy. Only 25 to 28 percent of people under age 50 say they are very happy, compared with 30 to 34 percent of people aged 50 or older.

- The younger the person, the more likely he or she is to believe that most people try to take advantage of others given the chance. Over half of people under age 30 say most people try to take advantage, compared with only 29 percent of people aged 70 or older.

- Excitement falls off after age 60. Among people under age 60, 46 to 53 percent say life is exciting; only 39 percent of people in their 60s and 35 percent of those aged 70 or older agree.

- Not surprisingly, the percentage of people rating their health as excellent or good declines with age. Only 68 percent of people in their 60s and 58 percent of those aged 70 or older say they are in excellent or good health.

- Opinions on whether others are selfish or helpful differ substantially by age. Those most likely to believe people are looking out for themselves are the young (61 percent of people under age 30 and 53 percent of people in their 30s). Only 35 to 42 percent of the other age groups agree.

- Belief in evolution divides at age 60. While 45 to 48 percent of those under age 60 say evolution is definitely or probably true, only 25 to 31 percent of those aged 60 or older agree.

- Fraternal groups have little appeal to people under age 50. While 20 to 24 percent of those aged 50 or older are members of fraternal groups, this compares with 0 to 5 percent of younger people. The well-educated boomer generation (aged 30 to 49) is more likely than other age groups to belong to professional or academic societies. Membership in church groups is lowest among the young (under age 40).

Life Is Better for the Well-Educated

Education makes a bigger difference in attitudes about personal issues than does sex, race, or age. On almost all of the issues, the highly-educated have a strikingly different outlook than those with less education. Only three issues show little difference of opinion by education.

- There is not much variation by education in the percentage of people who say they get a great or very great deal of satisfaction from friendships (67 to 72 percent).

- People with bachelor's degrees are most likely to say they get a great or very great deal of satisfaction from hobbies (67 percent compared with 52 to 56 percent of others).

- There are small differences by education in the percentages who say they get a great or very great deal of satisfaction from the place they live. Most likely to say this are those with graduate degrees (58 percent), compared with 45 to 50 percent of people with less education.

On the remaining issues, the differences in attitude by education are enormous. The more education people have, the more likely they are to say:

- They are very happy (from 24 percent of people who did not complete high school to 38 percent of people with graduate degrees). People without a high school diploma are most likely to say they are not too happy (19 percent), a proportion that drops to 4 percent among people with graduate degrees;

- Their health is excellent (only 17 percent of people who did not complete high school compared with 50 percent of people with graduate degrees). This is partly due to the fact that the least-educated are older, with health problems associated with aging;

- Life is exciting (62 to 66 percent of people with college degrees versus only 43 percent of those with high school diplomas and 31 percent of people who did not complete high school). Twelve percent of people who did not complete high school, but only 1 to 4 percent of others, say life is dull;

- Most people try to be fair rather than take advantage of others. Fully 71 percent of people with graduate degrees say this, compared with 66 percent of those with bachelor's degrees, 51 percent of high school graduates, and just 37 percent of people who did not complete high school;

- Most people can be trusted. Only 20 percent of people without a high school diploma say this, compared with 31 percent of high school graduates, 46 percent of those with bachelor's degrees, and 56 percent of people with graduate degrees;

- Most people try to be helpful instead of just looking out for themselves. While about one-half to two-thirds of people with college degrees hold this opinion, only 37 to 45 percent of people with less education agree;

- Darwin was definitely or probably right. While only 31 to 38 percent of people with a high school diploma or less think evolution is definitely or probably true, 58 percent of people with a bachelor's degree and 70 percent of those with graduate degrees think Darwin was right;

- Astrology has no scientific merit (well over half of those with at least a bachelor's degree say this, versus just 27 to 39 percent of people without college degrees).

Personal Happiness

Americans are neither dancing in the streets nor wallowing in despair. A majority (59 percent) say they are pretty happy. Only 29 percent say they are very happy, down from 38 percent in 1974.

Men and women are equally likely to say they are very happy, pretty happy, or not too happy. The proportion of women saying they are very happy has dropped substantially since 1974, however, from 41 to 28 percent. For men, the drop has been less, from 34 percent in 1974 to 30 percent in 1994.

Among all demographic segments, blacks are most likely to say they are not too happy. About one-quarter say this, compared with 10 percent of whites. Only 17 percent of blacks versus 31 percent of whites say they are very happy.

Older people are slightly more likely than younger ones to say they are very happy. From 25 to 28 percent of people under age 50 say they are very happy, compared with 30 to 34 percent of those aged 50 or older. The gap was much wider in 1974, when only 29 percent of people under age 30 and 45 percent of people in their 60s said they were very happy.

Educated people are more likely to be very happy. The proportion rises from only 24 percent of people who did not complete high school to 38 percent of those with graduate degrees. In 1974, the percentage of people saying they were very happy did not vary much by education. Since then, the percentage of people saying they are very happy has dropped substantially among those without a bachelor's degree.

Personal Happiness, 1994

"Taken all together, how would you say things are these days—would you say that you are very happy, pretty happy, or not too happy?"

(percent responding by sex, race, age, and education, 1994)

	very happy	pretty happy	not too happy
Total	29%	59%	12%
Women	28	59	13
Men	30	58	11
Black	17	60	23
White	31	58	10
Aged 18 to 29	25	63	12
Aged 30 to 39	28	60	12
Aged 40 to 49	28	59	13
Aged 50 to 59	32	57	11
Aged 60 to 69	34	54	11
Aged 70 or older	30	56	14
Not a high school graduate	24	57	19
High school graduate	27	60	12
Bachelor's degree	34	56	9
Graduate degree	38	57	4

Note: Numbers may not add to 100 because "don't know" and no answer are not included.
Source: General Social Survey, National Opinion Research Center, University of Chicago

Personal Happiness, 1974 to 1994

"Taken all together, how would you say things are these days—would you say that you are very happy, pretty happy, or not too happy?"

(percent responding by sex, race, age, and education, 1974-94)

	very happy			pretty happy			not too happy		
	1994	1984	1974	1994	1984	1974	1994	1984	1974
Total	29%	34%	38%	59%	51%	49%	12%	13%	13%
Women	28	36	41	59	50	46	13	12	12
Men	30	31	34	58	53	52	11	14	14
Black	17	24	27	60	53	46	23	22	25
White	31	35	39	58	52	49	10	11	11
Aged 18 to 29	25	29	29	63	58	56	12	12	15
Aged 30 to 39	28	29	38	60	56	49	12	13	13
Aged 40 to 49	28	37	38	59	49	48	13	13	14
Aged 50 to 59	32	35	41	57	48	45	11	15	14
Aged 60 to 69	34	43	45	54	41	44	11	12	11
Aged 70 or older	30	43	43	56	45	45	14	12	11
Not a high school graduate	24	33	34	57	47	49	19	20	17
High school grad.	27	32	40	60	54	49	12	11	12
Bachelor's degree	34	42	39	56	50	52	9	5	9
Graduate degree	38	48	38	57	44	53	4	8	8

Note: Numbers may not add to 100 because "don't know" and no answer are not included.
Source: General Social Survey, National Opinion Research Center, University of Chicago

Is Life Exciting?

Americans can be divided about equally between those who find life exciting and those who find it pretty routine. Almost no one says life is dull, however.

About the same proportions of men and women find life exciting, but this was not true in 1974. In that year, women were somewhat less likely than men to say life is exciting.

Whites are considerably more likely than blacks to say life is exciting (49 percent of whites compared with 36 percent of blacks). This was also true in 1974, but in 1984 the proportion was about the same. The percentage of blacks finding life exciting was higher in 1984 than ten years before or after.

People in their post-retirement years have more time to do what they want, but this doesn't translate into more excitement. Only 35 percent of people aged 70 or older and 39 percent of those in their 60s say life is exciting, compared with 46 to 53 percent of people under age 60. People in their 50s in 1994 were far more likely than those who were in their 50s in 1974 to say life is exciting (36 percent in 1974 compared with 51 percent in 1994).

The well-educated are more likely than those with less education to say life is exciting (62 to 66 percent of people with a bachelor's degree or more compared with 42 percent of high school graduates and 31 percent of people who did not complete high school). This was also true in 1974. The largest percentage of people who say life is dull is found among people without a high school diploma (12 percent).

Is Life Exciting? 1994

"In general, do you find life exciting,
pretty routine, or dull?"

(percent responding by sex, race, age, and education, 1994)

	exciting	pretty routine	dull
Total	47%	48%	4%
Women	45	50	5
Men	49	46	4
Black	36	56	7
White	49	46	4
Aged 18 to 29	53	43	4
Aged 30 to 39	50	47	3
Aged 40 to 49	46	51	3
Aged 50 to 59	51	44	4
Aged 60 to 69	39	56	4
Aged 70 or older	35	52	9
Not a high school graduate	31	54	12
High school graduate	43	53	4
Bachelor's degree	66	32	1
Graduate degree	62	36	2

Note: Numbers may not add to 100 because "no opinion" and no answer are not included.
Source: General Social Survey, National Opinion Research Center, University of Chicago

Is Life Exciting? 1974 to 1994

"In general, do you find life exciting, pretty routine, or dull?"

(percent responding by sex, race, age, and education, 1974-94)

	exciting			pretty routine			dull		
	1994	1984	1974	1994	1984	1974	1994	1984	1974
Total	47%	46%	42%	48%	48%	50%	4%	5%	5%
Women	45	44	38	50	50	54	5	5	5
Men	49	50	47	46	45	46	4	5	4
Black	36	45	35	56	46	54	7	8	7
White	49	47	43	46	48	50	4	5	4
Aged 18 to 29	53	54	50	43	43	45	4	3	4
Aged 30 to 39	50	48	42	47	47	51	3	4	2
Aged 40 to 49	46	46	42	51	51	49	3	2	5
Aged 50 to 59	51	46	36	44	47	58	4	6	4
Aged 60 to 69	39	42	39	56	48	52	4	9	6
Aged 70 or older	35	31	40	52	57	48	9	10	10
Not a high school graduate	31	34	32	54	53	56	12	12	8
High school grad.	43	46	44	53	51	51	4	3	3
Bachelor's degree	66	66	59	32	31	37	1	2	2
Graduate degree	62	62	63	36	38	32	2	0	3

Note: Percents may not add to 100 because "no opinion" and no answer are not included.
Source: General Social Survey, National Opinion Research Center, University of Chicago

Health Status

A large majority of Americans (78 percent) rate their health as excellent or good. Since 1974, the percentage who say their health is excellent or good has increased, despite the continuing aging of the population.

Women and men rate their health similarly. But women were considerably more likely in 1994 to rate their health as good than they were in 1974. For men, there has not been much change over the past 20 years.

Similar percentages of blacks and whites rate their health as good, but whites are more likely to say their health is excellent (33 percent of whites versus 22 percent of blacks). The proportion of blacks who rate their health as excellent or good has increased significantly since 1974, from 57 to 71 percent.

As one would expect, the percentage of people rating their health as excellent declines with age. While about 40 percent of people under age 30 say their health is excellent, only half as many people aged 70 or older say the same. Overall, at least 85 percent of people under age 40 say their health is good or excellent, as do slightly more than three-quarters of those aged 40 to 59. Only 68 percent of people in their 60s and 58 percent of those aged 70 or older rate their health as excellent or good. Those most likely to rate their health as poor are people aged 70 or older (13 percent).

Younger Americans were about as likely in 1994 as in 1974 to say their health was excellent or good, but people aged 50 or older are much more likely to say so. Among people in their 50s, 76 percent said their health was excellent or good in 1994, up from 63 percent in 1974.

While 43 to 50 percent of people with at least a bachelor's degree say they are in excellent health, only 30 percent of people who have a high school diploma and 17 percent of those with less education agree. Many less-educated Americans are older people with age-related health problems.

Health Status, 1994

"Would you say your own health, in general, is excellent, good, fair, or poor?"

(percent responding by sex, race, age, and education, 1994)

	excellent	good	fair	poor
Total	31%	47%	17%	5%
Women	30	48	17	4
Men	33	45	17	5
Black	22	49	20	9
White	33	47	17	4
Aged 18 to 29	39	48	12	1
Aged 30 to 39	35	50	13	2
Aged 40 to 49	32	47	19	3
Aged 50 to 59	28	48	18	6
Aged 60 to 69	25	43	23	9
Aged 70 or older	20	38	27	13
Not a high school graduate	17	42	32	9
High school graduate	30	50	16	5
Bachelor's degree	43	43	13	2
Graduate degree	50	42	5	3

Note: Numbers may not add to 100 because no answer is not included.
Source: General Social Survey, National Opinion Research Center, University of Chicago

Health Status, 1974 to 1994

"Would you say your own health, in general, is excellent, good, fair, or poor?"

(percent responding by sex, race, age, and education, 1974-94)

	excellent			good			fair			poor		
	1994	1984	1974	1994	1984	1974	1994	1984	1974	1994	1984	1974
Total	31%	30%	33%	47%	47%	40%	17%	18%	21%	5%	5%	6%
Women	30	28	30	48	47	39	17	19	24	4	5	7
Men	33	32	36	45	47	41	17	16	18	5	4	6
Black	22	24	15	49	45	42	20	21	30	9	8	12
White	33	31	35	47	47	39	17	17	20	4	4	5
Aged 18 to 29	39	34	44	48	51	44	12	14	11	1	1	1
Aged 30 to 39	35	32	39	50	54	43	13	12	16	2	1	2
Aged 40 to 49	32	34	36	47	46	38	19	15	23	3	4	3
Aged 50 to 59	28	31	27	48	43	36	18	19	28	6	7	10
Aged 60 to 69	25	25	18	43	41	40	23	25	27	9	9	15
Aged 70 or older	20	11	17	38	40	31	27	31	36	13	16	15
Not a high school graduate	17	17	19	42	39	37	32	31	31	9	13	12
High school graduate	30	30	38	50	53	42	16	15	17	5	2	3
Bachelor's degree	43	47	48	43	44	42	13	7	9	2	2	1
Graduate degree	50	48	41	42	44	40	5	7	16	3	0	3

Note: Numbers may not add to 100 because no answer is not included.
Source: General Social Survey, National Opinion Research Center, University of Chicago

Trustworthiness of Others

Americans do not trust others like they used to. Only 34 percent now say most people can be trusted, while 61 percent say you just can't be too careful. Women are less trusting than men, with 65 percent saying you can't be too careful compared with 57 percent of men. Blacks are far more wary than whites. Fully 82 percent of blacks say you can't be too careful, compared with 58 percent of whites.

By age, people in their 40s are slightly more trusting (40 percent), while those under age 30 are slightly less trusting (27 percent) than other age groups. All age groups except those aged 70 or older were considerably less likely in 1994 than in 1975 to trust others.

The more educated people are, the more trusting they become. The proportion saying most people can be trusted rises sharply from a low of 20 percent among people who did not complete high school to a high of 56 percent among those with graduate degrees.

Trustworthiness of Others, 1994

"Generally speaking, would you say that most
people can be trusted or that you can't be
too careful in dealing with people?"

(percent responding by sex, race, age, and education, 1994)

	you can't be too careful	most people can be trusted
Total	61%	34%
Women	65	31
Men	57	38
Black	82	14
White	58	38
Aged 18 to 29	69	27
Aged 30 to 39	63	32
Aged 40 to 49	56	40
Aged 50 to 59	60	36
Aged 60 to 69	62	34
Aged 70 or older	57	34
Not a high school graduate	75	20
High school graduate	65	31
Bachelor's degree	48	46
Graduate degree	35	56

Note: Numbers may not add to 100 because "other/depends," "don't know," and no answer are not included. "Depends" was not included because it was a volunteered response.
Source: General Social Survey, National Opinion Research Center, University of Chicago

Trustworthiness of Others, 1975 to 1994

"Generally speaking, would you say that most people can be trusted or that you can't be too careful in dealing with people?"

(percent responding by sex, race, age, and education, 1975-94)

	you can't be too careful			most people can be trusted		
	1994	*1984*	*1975*	*1994*	*1984*	*1975*
Total	61%	49%	56%	34%	48%	39%
Women	65	50	60	31	47	35
Men	57	47	51	38	49	44
Black	82	77	79	14	21	17
White	58	45	53	38	52	42
Aged 18 to 29	69	59	59	27	38	37
Aged 30 to 39	63	47	56	32	49	38
Aged 40 to 49	56	39	46	40	59	49
Aged 50 to 59	60	47	53	36	50	45
Aged 60 to 69	62	48	62	34	49	31
Aged 70 or older	57	46	58	34	48	34
Not a high school graduate	75	65	70	20	34	24
High school graduate	65	48	53	31	48	43
Bachelor's degree	48	33	32	46	62	62
Graduate degree	35	17	26	56	79	64

Note: Numbers may not add to 100 because "other/depends," "don't know," and no answer are not included. "Depends" was not included because it was a volunteered response.
Source: General Social Survey, National Opinion Research Center, University of Chicago

Fairness of People

Only 53 percent of Americans believe most people try to be fair rather than take advantage of others, down from 62 percent in 1975.

Men and women are equally likely to say most people try to be fair (53 percent). But in 1975, women were more likely to think so than men (64 versus 58 percent).

Blacks are much less likely than whites to believe most people are fair. Only 28 percent of blacks, compared with 58 percent of whites, say most people don't try to take advantage of others.

Young people have always been less trusting than their elders, but the gap was wider in 1994 than it was in 1974. In that year 59 percent of people under age 30 believed most people try to be fair, but this dropped to 41 percent by 1994. In contrast, 61 percent of people aged 70 or older feel most people are fair, a drop of only 7 percentage points since 1975.

Well-educated people are far more likely than those with less education to have faith in the motives of others. While 66 to 71 percent of people with at least a bachelor's degree say most people try to be fair, only 51 percent of people with high school diplomas and 37 percent of those who did not complete high school agree.

Fairness of People, 1994

"Do you think most people would try to take advantage of you if they got a chance, or would they try to be fair?"

(percent responding by sex, race, age, and education, 1994)

	would take advantage	would try to be fair
Total	39%	53%
Women	39	53
Men	39	53
Black	61	28
White	35	58
Aged 18 to 29	52	41
Aged 30 to 39	42	51
Aged 40 to 49	36	57
Aged 50 to 59	36	56
Aged 60 to 69	33	56
Aged 70 or older	29	61
Not a high school graduate	54	37
High school graduate	42	51
Bachelor's degree	27	66
Graduate degree	17	71

Note: Numbers may not add to 100 because "other/depends," "don't know," and no answer are not included. "Depends" was not included because it was a volunteered response.
Source: General Social Survey, National Opinion Research Center, University of Chicago

Fairness of People, 1975 to 1994

"Do you think most people would try to take advantage of you if they got a chance, or would they try to be fair?"

(percent responding by sex, race, age, and education, 1975-94)

	would take advantage			try to be fair		
	1994	1984	1975	1994	1984	1975
Total	39%	34%	31%	53%	62%	62%
Women	39	33	28	53	63	64
Men	39	37	33	53	60	58
Black	61	51	55	28	43	35
White	35	32	28	58	65	65
Aged 18 to 29	52	45	35	41	52	59
Aged 30 to 39	42	37	30	51	59	59
Aged 40 to 49	36	30	27	57	68	69
Aged 50 to 59	36	28	29	56	71	62
Aged 60 to 69	33	28	34	56	68	56
Aged 70 or older	29	24	23	61	69	68
Not a high school graduate	54	44	39	37	53	51
High school graduate	42	35	29	51	61	65
Bachelor's degree	27	24	14	66	73	77
Graduate degree	17	8	16	71	90	74

Note: Numbers may not add to 100 because "other/depends," "don't know," and no answer are not included. "Depends" was not included because it was a volunteered response.
Source: General Social Survey, National Opinion Research Center, University of Chicago

Helpfulness of Others

Americans are almost evenly divided on whether other people are selfish or want to be helpful. Only 46 percent believe that most of the time people try to be helpful. The percentage who have faith in their fellow humans has fluctuated somewhat over the years, but it was a full 10 percentage points lower in 1994 than it was in 1975.

Women are slightly more likely than men to believe people really want to help, but both men and women were less inclined to hold this opinion in 1994 than they were in 1975.

Blacks are far less likely than whites to believe most people try to be helpful. Only 30 percent of blacks compared with 50 percent of whites believe other people try to be helpful most of the time. Blacks and whites were both less likely to see others as helpful in 1994 than they were in 1974.

Cynicism is greatest among younger people. While 51 to 57 percent of people aged 40 or older believe most people try to be helpful, only 40 percent of those in their 30s and 32 percent of people under age 30 agree. In 1974, there was more agreement by age.

The more education people have, the higher their opinion of others. Only 37 percent of those who did not complete high school think other people usually try to be helpful, versus 66 percent of people with graduate degrees.

Helpfulness of Others, 1994

"Would you say that most of the time people try to be helpful, or that they are mostly just looking out for themselves?"

(percent responding by sex, race, age, and education, 1994)

	just look out for themselves	try to be helpful
Total	47%	46%
Women	44	50
Men	50	42
Black	65	30
White	43	50
Aged 18 to 29	61	32
Aged 30 to 39	53	40
Aged 40 to 49	42	51
Aged 50 to 59	38	56
Aged 60 to 69	34	57
Aged 70 or older	40	52
Not a high school graduate	57	37
High school graduate	49	45
Bachelor's degree	40	53
Graduate degree	21	66

Note: Numbers may not add to 100 because "other/depends," "don't know," and no answer are not included. "Depends" was not included because it was a volunteered response.
Source: General Social Survey, National Opinion Research Center, University of Chicago

Helpfulness of Others, 1975 to 1994

"Would you say that most of the time people try to be helpful, or that they are mostly just looking out for themselves?"

(percent responding by sex, race, age, and education, 1975-94)

	just looking out for themselves			try to be helpful		
	1994	1984	1975	1994	1984	1975
Total	47%	44%	37%	46%	52%	56%
Women	44	42	33	50	54	60
Men	50	48	42	42	49	52
Black	65	66	47	30	27	41
White	43	40	35	50	56	58
Aged 18 to 29	61	53	41	32	44	53
Aged 30 to 39	53	42	38	40	52	54
Aged 40 to 49	42	41	29	51	56	64
Aged 50 to 59	38	44	36	56	53	57
Aged 60 to 69	34	42	37	57	55	56
Aged 70 or older	40	34	36	52	61	55
Not a high school graduate	57	58	45	37	39	47
High school graduate	49	42	35	45	53	59
Bachelor's degree	40	33	22	53	63	70
Graduate degree	21	22	24	66	74	66

Note: Numbers may not add to 100 because "other/depends," "don't know," and no answer are not included. "Depends" was not included because it was a volunteered response.
Source: General Social Survey, National Opinion Research Center, University of Chicago

Belief in Astrology

Nearly half (47 percent) of Americans think it is definitely or probably true that astrology has some scientific truth. But an almost equal percentage (43) think astrology probably or definitely does not have any scientific basis.

Women are stronger believers than men. Over half (55 percent) think the study of star signs has some factual basis, compared with only 40 percent of men. Blacks are slightly more likely than whites to believe in astrology.

By age, those most skeptical of astrology are people in their 40s (only 42 percent think there is some truth to it). This group is also the most highly educated. The largest percentage of believers is found among people in their 60s (51 percent).

The best-educated Americans are least likely to believe in astrology. Only 31 to 35 percent of people with college degrees believe there is some scientific foundation for astrology, compared with 52 to 53 percent of people with less education.

Belief in Astrology, 1994

"Astrology—the study of star signs—has some scientific truth. How true do you think this is?"

(percent responding by sex, race, age, and education, 1994)

	definitely true	probably true	probably not true	definitely not true	can't choose	true, total	not true, total
Total	9%	38%	24%	19%	7%	47%	43%
Women	9	44	23	15	8	53	38
Men	8	32	25	24	7	40	49
Black	9	45	17	15	11	54	32
White	9	37	24	20	7	46	24
Aged 18 to 29	10	40	25	17	8	50	42
Aged 30 to 39	9	39	26	21	4	48	47
Aged 40 to 49	7	35	25	26	4	42	51
Aged 50 to 59	9	40	22	19	6	49	41
Aged 60 to 69	8	43	22	13	11	51	35
Aged 70 or older	9	36	18	13	18	45	31
Not a high school graduate	11	42	17	10	16	53	27
High school graduate	9	43	23	16	6	52	39
Bachelor's degree	6	29	26	31	5	35	57
Graduate degree	4	27	27	37	5	31	64

Note: Numbers may not add to 100 because "can't choose" and no answer are not included.
Source: General Social Survey, National Opinion Research Center, University of Chicago

Belief in Evolution

Americans are divided in their opinions about evolution. While 46 percent say it is probably or definitely not true that humans developed from earlier species of animals, 43 percent think it is true.

Men are more likely than women and whites are more likely than blacks to believe in evolution. By age, the dividing line is found at age 60. While 46 to 48 percent of people under age 60 think the theory of evolution is correct, only 25 percent of those aged 60 to 69 and 31 percent of people aged 70 or older agree.

While there is an opinion gap by age, the differences by education are best described as a canyon. Fewer than one-third of people who did not complete high school and 38 percent of those who attained only a high school diploma believe in evolution. By comparison, 58 percent of people with bachelor's degrees are believers, as are 70 percent of people with graduate degrees.

Belief in Evolution, 1994

"Human beings developed from earlier species of
animals. How true do you think this is?"

(percent responding by sex, race, age, and education, 1994)

	definitely true	probably true	probably not true	definitely not true	can't choose	true, total	not true, total
Total	14%	29%	16%	30%	8%	43%	46%
Women	11	28	18	31	9	39	49
Men	17	31	14	27	7	48	41
Black	7	26	21	33	9	33	54
White	15	30	15	30	8	45	45
Aged 18 to 29	19	29	19	27	6	48	46
Aged 30 to 39	13	32	17	28	6	45	45
Aged 40 to 49	17	30	16	27	6	47	43
Aged 50 to 59	13	35	13	30	7	48	43
Aged 60 to 69	10	15	15	40	15	25	55
Aged 70 or older	5	26	15	33	15	31	48
Not a high school graduate	7	24	22	29	13	31	51
High school graduate	9	29	16	35	8	38	51
Bachelor's degree	25	33	11	22	5	58	33
Graduate degree	39	31	10	10	8	70	20

Note: Numbers may not add to 100 because "can't choose" and no answer are not included.
Source: General Social Survey, National Opinion Research Center, University of Chicago

Satisfaction With Friendships

Most Americans (69 percent) get great or very great satisfaction from their friendships. This proportion has not changed much since 1974.

Conventional wisdom says women are closer to their friends than men, and the statistics support this notion. Only 63 percent of men compared with 74 percent of women get a lot of satisfaction from their friendships. In 1974 the percentages were about the same, but men are now less likely to say they get a lot of satisfaction from friendships.

Blacks are less likely than whites to say they get a lot of satisfaction from friendships, and this was also true in 1974.

By age, there is little variation in the proportion who are satisfied with their friendships, indicating that friends provide about the same degree of satisfaction at each stage of life.

By education, people are about equally likely to say they get great or very great satisfaction from friendships.

Satisfaction With Friendships, 1994

"How much satisfaction do you get from your friendships?"

(percent responding by sex, race, age, and education, 1994)

	a very great deal	a great deal	quite a bit	a fair amount	some	a little	none	very/ great	quite/ fair	little/ none
Total	31%	38%	17%	9%	3%	1%	1%	69%	26%	5%
Women	38	36	14	9	2	0	1	74	23	3
Men	22	41	21	10	4	1	0	63	31	5
Black	29	32	10	16	8	0	5	61	26	13
White	31	39	18	8	3	1	0	70	26	4
Aged 18 to 29	31	38	16	9	3	0	3	69	25	6
Aged 30 to 39	27	42	20	7	4	0	2	69	27	6
Aged 40 to 49	33	30	19	14	4	0	0	63	33	4
Aged 50 to 59	37	40	10	6	5	2	0	77	16	7
Aged 60 to 69	31	46	13	11	0	0	0	77	24	0
Aged 70 or older	31	35	21	9	1	3	0	66	30	4
Not a high school graduate	29	43	5	11	5	2	4	72	16	11
High school graduate	27	40	20	9	4	0	0	67	29	4
Bachelor's degree	41	29	18	10	3	0	0	70	28	3
Graduate degree	40	27	22	11	0	0	0	67	33	0

Note: Numbers may not add to 100 because "don't know" and no answer are not included.
Source: General Social Survey, National Opinion Research Center, University of Chicago

Satisfaction With Friendships, 1974 to 1994

"How much satisfaction do you get
from your friendships."

(percent responding by sex, race, age, and education, 1974-94)

	very great/great deal			quite a bit/fair amount			some/a little/none		
	1994	*1984*	*1974*	*1994*	*1984*	*1974*	*1994*	*1984*	*1974*
Total	69%	74%	72%	26%	21%	22%	5%	4%	5%
Women	74	76	73	23	19	22	3	4	5
Men	63	71	71	31	25	23	5	4	6
Black	61	59	62	26	29	27	13	11	12
White	70	76	74	26	20	22	6	3	5
Aged 18 to 29	69	72	68	25	22	27	6	6	5
Aged 30 to 39	69	74	70	27	21	23	5	5	7
Aged 40 to 49	63	73	69	33	24	23	4	1	7
Aged 50 to 59	77	80	77	16	19	19	7	1	4
Aged 60 to 69	77	76	75	24	21	22	0	2	4
Aged 70 or older	66	74	81	30	19	14	4	5	5
Not a high school graduate	72	66	72	16	27	23	11	6	6
High school grad.	67	76	73	29	19	22	4	4	5
Bachelor's degree	70	78	69	28	22	25	3	1	6
Graduate degree	67	86	77	33	14	22	0	0	1

Note: Numbers may not add to 100 because "don't know" and no answer are not included.
Source: General Social Survey, National Opinion Research Center, University of Chicago

Satisfaction With Hobbies

Over half of Americans (57 percent) are lucky enough to have hobbies and other activities outside work that give them great or very great satisfaction. This is similar to the percentage who responded this way in 1974.

Men and women are about equally likely to say they get a lot of satisfaction from their hobbies. Similar proportions of blacks and whites also say they get a lot of satisfaction from their hobbies. But in 1974 and 1984, whites were more likely than blacks to say their hobbies were very satisfying. The proportion of blacks saying their non-work activities are very satisfying rose from a low of 45 percent in 1984 to 60 percent in 1994.

Satisfaction with activities outside work is greatest among people aged 30 to 59 (60 to 64 percent). Only 50 to 55 percent of people in their 20s and 60s agree. Among those aged 70 or older, just 47 percent say they get great or very great satisfaction from their hobbies. In 1974, the differences by age were smaller.

By education, the largest proportion saying they get a lot of satisfaction from their hobbies is among people with bachelor's degrees. In 1974, people with graduate degrees were most satisfied with their hobbies.

Satisfaction With Hobbies, 1994

"How much satisfaction do you get from your non-working activities—hobbies and so on."

(percent responding by sex, race, age, and education, 1994)

	a very great deal	a great deal	quite a bit	a fair amount	some	a little	none	very/ great	quite/ fair	some/ little/ none
Total	23%	34%	18%	11%	7%	3%	4%	57%	29%	14%
Women	23	34	18	10	7	4	5	57	28	16
Men	22	35	19	13	6	2	3	57	32	11
Black	22	38	14	8	5	3	6	60	22	14
White	23	34	19	12	7	3	4	57	31	14
Aged 18 to 29	18	32	15	14	8	9	4	50	29	21
Aged 30 to 39	23	37	15	12	10	1	3	60	27	14
Aged 40 to 49	27	36	20	8	4	0	4	63	28	8
Aged 50 to 59	24	40	13	18	2	0	3	64	31	5
Aged 60 to 69	26	29	29	7	2	4	4	55	36	10
Aged 70 or older	17	30	23	10	10	4	7	47	33	21
Not a high school graduate	20	32	15	14	6	3	9	52	29	18
High school graduate	21	34	18	11	7	4	4	55	29	15
Bachelor's degree	28	39	20	9	3	0	3	67	29	6
Graduate degree	29	27	20	13	9	2	0	56	33	11

Note: Numbers may not add to 100 because "don't know" and no answer are not included.
Source: General Social Survey, National Opinion Research Center, University of Chicago

Satisfaction With Hobbies, 1974 to 1994

"How much satisfaction do you get from your non-working activities—hobbies and so on."

(percent responding by sex, race, age, and education, 1974-94)

	very great/great deal			quite a bit/fair amount			some/a little/none		
	1994	1984	1974	1994	1984	1974	1994	1984	1974
Total	57%	61%	55%	29%	29%	29%	14%	10%	16%
Women	57	59	54	28	28	30	16	11	16
Men	57	62	56	32	29	29	11	8	15
Black	60	45	47	22	30	28	14	23	24
White	57	63	56	31	28	30	14	8	14
Aged 18 to 29	50	63	53	29	26	32	21	11	15
Aged 30 to 39	60	54	54	27	36	29	14	9	16
Aged 40 to 49	63	60	51	28	31	34	8	7	16
Aged 50 to 59	64	58	59	31	33	26	5	9	15
Aged 60 to 69	55	67	60	36	21	23	10	11	16
Aged 70 or older	47	64	54	33	20	30	21	13	15
Not a high school graduate	52	54	51	29	28	26	18	16	23
High school grad.	55	61	56	29	30	31	15	9	13
Bachelor's degree	67	71	53	29	25	37	6	3	10
Graduate degree	56	66	66	33	30	25	11	4	10

Note: Numbers may not add to 100 because "don't know" and no answer are not included.
Source: General Social Survey, National Opinion Research Center, University of Chicago

Satisfaction With Where They Live

Americans are not entirely enamored with the city or place in which they live, but neither are they wholly dissatisfied. A plurality (48 percent) say they get a great or very great deal of satisfaction from the place they live. Another 40 percent say they get quite a bit or a fair amount of satisfaction. These proportions are about the same as in 1974.

Women are slightly more likely than men to get a lot of satisfaction from the place in which they live. Between blacks and whites, however, there is a wide gap. Only 30 percent of blacks compared with 50 percent of whites say they get a lot of satisfaction from the place in which they live. In 1974, the gap was smaller (37 percent of blacks and 48 percent of whites).

Young people are less likely than their elders to be satisfied with the place in which they live. Only 33 percent of people under age 30 say they get a great or very great deal of satisfaction from the area in which they live. In general, satisfaction with place of residence rises with age, peaking at 62 percent among people aged 70 or older. Mobility rates, not coincidentally, go in the opposite direction, with younger adults far more likely to move in a given year than older people.

There is some variation by education, but not in any particular direction. People with graduate degrees are most likely to be satisfied with their area of residence (58 percent), while those who went no further than high school are least likely (45 percent) to be satisfied.

Satisfaction With Where You Live, 1994

"How much satisfaction do you get from the city or place you live in?"

(percent responding by sex, race, age, and education, 1994)

	a very great deal	a great deal	quite a bit	a fair amount	some	a little	none	very/great	quite/fair	some/little/none
Total	16%	32%	21%	19%	7%	3%	3%	48%	40%	13%
Women	17	33	19	18	6	3	4	50	37	13
Men	14	29	22	21	7	4	3	43	43	15
Black	11	19	22	25	14	5	2	30	47	21
White	17	33	20	19	6	3	3	50	39	12
Aged 18 to 29	9	24	19	27	11	1	10	33	46	22
Aged 30 to 39	16	33	20	19	4	6	2	49	39	12
Aged 40 to 49	11	29	26	19	8	4	3	40	45	15
Aged 50 to 59	19	38	18	13	10	0	2	57	31	12
Aged 60 to 69	15	35	24	20	6	2	0	50	44	8
Aged 70 or older	28	34	16	17	1	3	1	62	33	5
Not a high school graduate	19	31	11	19	12	2	5	50	30	19
High school graduate	15	30	22	21	7	3	3	45	43	13
Bachelor's degree	14	34	18	25	5	4	1	48	43	10
Graduate degree	16	42	31	4	0	4	2	58	35	6

Note: Numbers may not add to 100 because "don't know" and no answer not included.
Source: General Social Survey, National Opinion Research Center, University of Chicago

Satisfaction With Where You Live, 1974 to 1994

"How much satisfaction do you get from
the city or place you live in?"

(percent responding by sex, race, age, and education, 1974-94)

	very great/great deal			quite a bit/fair amount			some/a little/none		
	1994	*1984*	*1974*	*1994*	*1984*	*1974*	*1994*	*1984*	*1974*
Total	48%	52%	47%	40%	35%	40%	13%	12%	13%
Women	50	52	48	37	35	40	13	12	12
Men	43	51	45	43	36	41	15	13	14
Black	30	40	37	47	41	42	21	19	21
White	50	54	48	39	35	40	12	11	12
Aged 18 to 29	33	39	29	46	42	50	22	19	21
Aged 30 to 39	49	43	43	39	43	42	12	14	15
Aged 40 to 49	40	53	48	45	35	41	15	12	11
Aged 50 to 59	57	63	58	31	31	33	12	5	8
Aged 60 to 69	50	68	55	44	24	37	8	6	9
Aged 70 or older	62	72	66	33	21	28	5	6	7
Not a high school graduate	50	52	50	30	32	37	19	14	12
High school grad.	45	50	46	43	37	41	13	12	13
Bachelor's degree	48	53	37	43	38	46	10	9	17
Graduate degree	58	60	49	35	30	40	6	10	11

Note: Numbers may not add to 100 because "don't know" and no answer are not included.
Source: General Social Survey, National Opinion Research Center, University of Chicago

Memberships in Organizations

Few Americans have time to join school, church, or service groups, judging from the percentages who say they are members of one or more groups. Americans are most likely to be members of church-affiliated groups (33 percent), professional groups (19 percent), or school service groups (16 percent). For each of the remaining ten groups examined here, 10 percent or fewer Americans are members.

Americans were about as likely to be members of at least one of these groups in 1994 as in 1974, except for church-affiliated groups. Church-group membership fell from 42 percent of adults in 1974 to 33 percent in 1994.

Men are more likely than women to be members of fraternal or veterans' groups. Women are more likely to be found in church or school groups.

Similar percentages of blacks and whites are members of the various organizations. But blacks are more likely to join youth or church groups, while whites are more likely to include professional societies and fraternal groups in their extracurricular activities.

Group memberships are linked to lifestyle. People in the parenting age groups are most likely to be members of youth or school groups. Adults under age 50 are more likely to be members of professional or academic societies than older people. Fraternal groups show the greatest generational difference: while 20 to 24 percent of people aged 50 or older are members of fraternal groups, the figure ranges from 0 to 5 percent among people under age 50.

The more educated people are, the more likely they are to be a member of a group, particularly professional societies.

Membership in Organizations, 1994

"Here is a list of various organizations. Could you tell me whether or not you are a member of each type?"

(percent saying they are members by sex, race, age, and education, 1994)

	church-affiliated groups	professional or academic societies	school service groups	fraternal groups	service clubs	literary, art, discussion/study groups	youth groups	veterans' groups	hobby or garden clubs	school fraternities or sororities
Total	33%	19%	16%	10%	10%	10%	10%	8%	9%	6%
Women	36	17	19	7	10	12	11	4	10	5
Men	30	20	13	14	10	7	10	13	8	6
Black	38	10	16	3	8	8	16	5	8	6
White	33	21	16	11	11	10	9	9	10	6
Aged 18 to 29	23	16	18	0	8	10	14	5	8	5
Aged 30 to 39	28	23	22	4	8	6	12	2	7	5
Aged 40 to 49	39	28	25	5	15	14	14	9	15	4
Aged 50 to 59	40	19	10	22	10	11	6	6	5	10
Aged 60 to 69	40	11	6	24	11	13	7	16	13	6
Aged 70 or older	39	7	4	20	10	9	3	17	9	6
Not a high school graduate	31	2	9	9	4	3	6	11	3	2
High school graduate	28	9	13	10	9	8	11	9	10	2
Bachelor's degree	45	38	20	10	11	13	9	5	13	16
Graduate degree	38	80	36	18	22	27	16	7	16	13

Source: General Social Survey, National Opinion Research Center, University of Chicago

Membership in Organizations, 1974 to 1994

"Here is a list of various organizations. Could you tell me whether or not you are a member of each type?"

(percent saying they are members by sex, race, age, and education, 1974-94)

	church-affiliated groups			professional or academic societies			school service groups			fraternal groups		
	1994	1984	1974	1994	1984	1974	1994	1984	1974	1994	1984	1974
Total	33%	33%	42%	19%	15%	13%	16%	12%	18%	10%	9%	14%
Women	36	39	46	17	13	11	19	15	23	7	6	9
Men	30	25	37	20	18	15	13	8	11	14	14	19
Black	38	41	50	10	7	5	16	14	17	3	6	8
White	33	33	41	21	17	14	16	12	18	11	10	14
Aged 18 to 29	23	23	28	16	16	15	18	12	12	0	3	6
Aged 30 to 39	28	29	40	23	20	12	22	19	31	4	7	12
Aged 40 to 49	39	36	47	28	16	19	25	14	30	5	11	14
Aged 50 to 59	40	46	46	19	16	11	10	12	15	22	16	18
Aged 60 to 69	40	37	55	11	14	10	6	7	7	24	17	18
Aged 70 or older	39	45	49	7	4	9	4	4	4	20	10	23
Not a high school graduate	31	28	37	2	2	1	9	7	7	9	6	9
High school graduate	28	32	44	9	9	9	13	12	19	10	9	14
Bachelor's degree	45	44	41	38	47	40	20	20	29	10	16	21
Graduate degree	38	44	58	80	73	81	36	29	47	18	13	26

(continued)

(continued from previous page)

	service clubs			literary, art, discussion/study groups			youth groups		
	1994	1984	1974	1994	1984	1974	1994	1984	1974
Total	10%	10%	9%	10%	9%	9%	10%	9%	10%
Women	10	11	8	12	10	11	11	10	10
Men	10	10	10	7	6	7	10	8	10
Black	8	8	7	8	7	5	16	11	10
White	11	11	9	10	9	10	9	9	10
Aged 18 to 29	8	9	5	10	9	10	14	12	10
Aged 30 to 39	8	13	10	6	9	10	12	12	16
Aged 40 to 49	15	8	12	14	11	11	14	11	18
Aged 50 to 59	10	12	11	11	9	8	6	9	8
Aged 60 to 69	11	10	13	13	8	10	7	3	5
Aged 70 or older	10	10	5	9	7	7	3	4	1
Not a high school graduate	4	4	4	3	3	3	6	4	5
High school graduate	9	8	9	8	8	9	11	11	13
Bachelor's degree	11	25	14	13	17	20	9	15	14
Graduate degree	22	29	33	27	25	37	16	14	18

(continued)

(continued from previous page)

	veterans' groups			hobby or garden clubs			school fraternities/sororities		
	1994	1984	1974	1994	1984	1974	1994	1984	1974
Total	8%	7%	9%	9%	9%	10%	6%	6%	5%
Women	4	3	4	10	10	12	5	6	4
Men	13	12	14	8	7	7	6	5	5
Black	5	4	4	8	6	6	6	5	6
White	9	7	10	10	9	10	6	6	5
Aged 18 to 29	5	2	4	8	11	10	5	7	6
Aged 30 to 39	2	4	6	7	7	11	5	6	6
Aged 40 to 49	9	5	13	15	10	8	4	6	6
Aged 50 to 59	6	15	18	5	10	8	10	8	4
Aged 60 to 69	16	17	7	13	8	13	6	4	2
Aged 70 or older	17	6	9	9	7	7	6	2	3
Not a high school graduate	11	7	8	3	5	6	2	1	1
High school graduate	9	7	9	10	9	10	2	3	3
Bachelor's degree	5	5	7	13	17	19	16	22	17
Graduate degree	7	9	12	16	13	10	13	23	21

Source: General Social Survey, National Opinion Research Center, University of Chicago

9

Sex and Morality

After decades of dramatic change in sexual mores, most Americans still agree about many sexual issues—perhaps none more so than the immorality of adultery. But they are ambivalent about some issues, including pornography. Large majorities of Americans say:

• Married people should only have sex with each other. Fully 78 percent say extramarital sex is always wrong;

• Homosexual sex is always wrong (63 percent). But the percentage of people who say homosexual sex is not wrong at all was much higher in 1994 (22 percent), than in 1974 (12 percent).

Smaller majorities believe that:

• It should be illegal to distribute pornography to people under age 18 (59 percent), versus making it illegal regardless of age (37 percent) or having no laws regarding pornography (3 percent);

• Pornography provides information about sex (59 percent);

• Pornography leads to a breakdown of morals (57 percent);

• Pornography "provides an outlet for bottled-up impulses" (57 percent).

Americans have changed their minds about one issue since 1974.

- A plurality (42 percent) say premarital sex is not wrong at all. One-quarter say it is always wrong. In 1974, Americans were more divided, with 32 percent saying it was always wrong and 30 percent saying it was not wrong at all.

Americans are divided on whether or not:

- People choose to be gay (41 percent) or homosexuality is something people cannot change (44 percent);

- It is all right for a couple to live together without intending to get married (41 percent say this is OK, while 41 percent say it is not);

- Couples planning to marry should try living together first (33 percent agree, 42 percent disagree, and 23 percent say they neither agree nor disagree);

- Pornography leads people to commit rape (48 percent say yes, while 42 percent say no).

Men and Women Disagree on Many Issues

On over half of the sex and morality issues examined here, the opinions of men and women are far apart. But on some issues, there is only slight disagreement. For example, similar percentages of women and men say:

- Pornography provides "an outlet for bottled-up impulses" (56 percent of women and 58 percent of men);

- Pornography provides information about sex (57 percent of women and 61 percent of men);

- Sexual relations between adults of the same sex is always wrong (61 percent of women and 65 percent of men);

- Extramarital sex is always wrong (80 percent of women and 74 percent of men).

Women are more likely than men to say:

- Being gay is something people cannot change (48 percent of women compared with 39 percent of men);

- It is a not a good idea for couples to live together if they don't plan on marrying (44 percent of women compared with 35 percent of men);

- Pornography leads to a breakdown of morals (64 percent of women compared with 49 percent of men);

- Pornography leads people to commit rape (55 percent of women compared with 40 percent of men);

- Distributing pornography to people of any age should be illegal (45 percent of women compared with 26 percent of men). Men are more likely to say it should simply be kept out of the hands of minors (68 percent of men compared with 52 percent of women);

- It is not a good idea for couples to live together before marrying (47 percent of women compared with 34 percent of men).

Men are more likely than women to say:

- Sex before marriage is not wrong at all (49 percent of men compared with 37 percent of women).

Whites More Likely to Favor Ban on Pornography

Blacks and whites differ, sometimes strongly, in their attitudes about sexual mores. They are in agreement on only 4 of the 11 issues examined here. The same percentages of blacks and whites say:

- Premarital sex is not wrong (42 percent) or always wrong (26 and 25 percent, respectively);

- They don't believe it is a good idea for a couple intending to marry to live together first (42 percent of blacks and 41 percent of whites);

- Pornography leads to rape (45 percent of blacks and 48 percent of whites);

- Pornography provides "an outlet for bottled-up impulses" (57 percent of both races).

Blacks are more likely than whites to say:

- Homosexual sex is always wrong (70 percent of blacks compared with 62 percent of whites);

- Pornography provides information about sex (70 percent of blacks compared with 57 percent of whites);

- People choose to be gay (54 percent of blacks compared with 40 percent of whites).

Whites are more likely than blacks to say:

- It is all right for couples to live together even if they don't see marriage in their future (42 percent of whites compared with 36 percent of blacks);

- Distribution of pornography should be completely illegal (38 percent of whites compared with 29 percent of blacks). Blacks are more likely than whites to say laws should prevent distribution only to people under age 18 (65 percent versus 58 percent);

- Pornography leads to a breakdown of morals (58 percent of whites compared with 48 percent of blacks);

- Extramarital sex is always wrong (79 percent of whites compared with 68 percent of blacks).

A Generation Gap in Sexual Mores

Younger generations have different sexual mores than their elders. Baby boomers—who partook of the "free-love" era—still disagree with their parents on most issues of sexual morality. In fact, agreement between the generations is found on only 3 of the 11 issues examined here.

- People of different ages roughly agree that pornography can be educational (53 to 62 percent).

- They also more or less agree that pornography provides "an outlet for bottled-up impulses" (53 to 62 percent).

- People aged 30 to 59 are slightly less likely to feel adultery is always wrong than are people younger or older (about three-quarters of people aged 30 to 59 compared with 81 to 82 percent of those younger or older).

Strong generational differences can be seen in responses to some of the questions. Younger adults are more likely than their elders to say:

- Being gay is something people choose (45 to 49 percent of those under age 40 compared with 34 to 41 percent of older people);

- Younger people are less likely to say pornography leads people to commit rape (half of people in their 50s and two-thirds of those aged 60 or older believe this is true, compared with 40 to 44 percent of people under age 50);

- Pornography leads to a breakdown of morals. Those least likely to agree are people under age 40 (48 to 49 percent), while those most in agreement are aged 60 or older (74 percent);

- There's nothing wrong with premarital sex (over half of people under age 40 compared with fewer than 30 percent of those aged 60 or older);

- There is nothing wrong with living together without intending to marry (from 56 to 58 percent of people under age 40 to only 9 percent of those aged 70 or older);

- A "trial marriage" is a good idea. While 46 to 48 percent of people under age 40 think it's a good idea for couples to live together before marrying, the agreement declines with age to just 8 percent of people aged 70 or older.

Older people are more likely to believe that:

- Homosexual sex is always wrong (from 54 percent of people under age 30 to 76 percent of those aged 70 or older). One-third of people under age 30 say it is not wrong at all, a proportion that falls with age;

- Pornography should be made illegal (64 percent among those aged 70 or older compared with 25 percent of people under age 40).

Less-Educated Americans Hold Stricter Views

Younger Americans are better educated than their elders, which accounts for some of the differences in opinion by education. On most of the issues examined here, people with different levels of education have different points of view. There are only a few areas of agreement, such as:

- At all educational levels, a majority believe extramarital sex is always wrong. More than three out of four people with a bachelor's degree or less education hold this opinion, while people with graduate degrees are somewhat more ambivalent (66 percent say it is always wrong);

- Majorities say pornography can provide information about sex (56 to 60 percent);

- Except for those with advanced degrees, pluralities say it is not a good idea for a couple to live together before marriage;

- Better-educated people are only slightly more likely to believe pornography provides "an outlet for bottled-up impulses" (55 to 56 percent of people with a high school diploma or less compared with 59 to 62 percent of those with college degrees).

The less education they have, the more likely Americans are to believe:

- It is not all right for a couple to live together without intending to marry. Forty-eight percent of people who did not complete high school disapprove of cohabitation. This drops to 33 percent among people with graduate degrees;

- Premarital sex is wrong. While only 35 percent of people without high school diplomas say premarital sex is OK, from 42 to 49 percent of people with more education think it's OK;

- Pornography leads to a breakdown of morals. A large majority of people who did not complete high school believe this to be true (63 percent), compared with only 49 percent of those with advanced degrees;

- There should be laws against the distribution of pornography to people of any age. While nearly half of people without high school diplomas take this position, only 37 percent of those with high school diplomas, 30 percent of people with bachelor's degrees, and 29 percent of those with graduate degrees agree;

- Pornography leads people to commit rape (58 percent of people who did not complete high school believe this to be true, but only 35 percent of those with graduate degrees);

- Being homosexual is a choice people make. Among people without a college degree, 44 to 46 percent hold this view. But only 37 percent of people with bachelor's degrees and 16 percent of those with advanced degrees say this is true;

- Homosexual sex is always wrong. Fully 77 percent of people who did not complete high school believe it is always wrong, with only 12 percent saying it is never wrong. Among college graduates, only 39 to 49 percent say it is always wrong, while 33 to 34 percent say it is never wrong.

Premarital Sex

Since the "sexual revolution" of the 1960s, Americans' attitudes about sex have changed. Today, a 42 percent plurality say there is nothing wrong with sex before marriage. Only one-quarter believe premarital sex is always wrong. In 1974, Americans were much more divided, with 32 percent saying premarital sex was always wrong and 30 percent saying it was not wrong.

Men and women don't entirely agree on this issue. Both sexes were more likely in 1994 than in 1974 to think premarital sex is OK, but women have remained less accepting than men. While nearly half of men think it's not wrong, only 37 percent of women agree.

Blacks and whites are now in agreement on this issue, but that was not the case in 1974. In that year, blacks were considerably more likely than whites to say there was nothing wrong with sex before marriage.

Age is a strong predictor of attitudes about premarital sex. Over half of people under age 40 say there is nothing wrong with sex before marriage, but fewer than 30 percent of those aged 60 or older agree. In 1994, almost all age groups were less likely to believe premarital sex was wrong than in 1974.

One-third of people who did not complete high school say sex before marriage is always wrong. The proportion who believe it is always wrong falls with education, to just 15 percent of those with graduate degrees. The belief that premarital sex is not at all wrong has increased sharply at all educational levels, except at the bachelor's degree level where it has remained at just over 40 percent for the past two decades.

Premarital Sex, 1994

"If a man and woman have sexual relations before marriage, do you think it is always wrong, almost always wrong, wrong only sometimes, or not wrong at all?"

(percent responding by sex, race, age, and education, 1994)

	always wrong	almost always wrong	wrong only sometimes	not wrong at all
Total	25%	10%	20%	42%
Women	30	10	20	37
Men	18	9	20	49
Black	26	10	17	42
White	25	10	21	42
Aged 18 to 29	17	8	21	52
Aged 30 to 39	16	6	22	55
Aged 40 to 49	24	9	20	45
Aged 50 to 59	26	12	20	35
Aged 60 to 69	35	15	20	28
Aged 70 or older	47	14	13	20
Not a high school graduate	34	11	15	35
High school graduate	26	10	19	43
Bachelor's degree	21	9	26	42
Graduate degree	15	10	25	49

Note: Percents may not add to 100 because "don't know" and no answer are not included.
Source: General Social Survey, National Opinion Research Center, University of Chicago

Premarital Sex, 1974 to 1994

"If a man and woman have sexual relations before marriage, do you think it is always wrong, almost always wrong, wrong only sometimes, or not wrong at all?"

(percent saying it is always wrong or not wrong at all, by sex, race, age, and education, 1974-94)

	always wrong			not wrong at all		
	1994	*1985*	*1974*	*1994*	*1985*	*1974*
Total	25%	28%	32%	42%	42%	30%
Women	30	33	35	37	37	25
Men	18	21	28	49	48	35
Black	26	19	29	42	59	46
White	25	28	32	42	40	28
Aged 18 to 29	17	14	11	52	56	50
Aged 30 to 39	16	17	27	55	56	35
Aged 40 to 49	24	30	32	45	45	25
Aged 50 to 59	26	34	43	35	30	18
Aged 60 to 69	35	36	46	28	28	17
Aged 70 or older	47	50	58	20	18	11
Not a high school graduate	34	38	43	35	33	23
High school graduate	26	26	27	43	44	32
Bachelor's degree	21	20	19	42	47	41
Graduate degree	15	14	18	49	48	30

Note: Percents may not add to 100 because "don't know" and no answer are not included.
Source: General Social Survey, National Opinion Research Center, University of Chicago

Extramarital Sex

The sexual mores of Americans are much more liberal than they were a couple of decades ago. But on one issue, Americans are just as strict as ever. Extramarital sexual activity (i.e., adultery) was as likely to be condemned in 1994 as it was in 1974. Fully 78 percent of adults say extramarital sex is always wrong. Only 2 percent believe it is not wrong.

Women are somewhat more likely than men to say extramarital sex is always wrong (80 percent of women compared with 74 percent of men). Both men and women were more likely to condemn it in 1994 than they were in 1974.

Whites are more likely than blacks to say extramarital sex is always wrong (79 percent of whites compared with 68 percent of blacks). Both races were slightly more likely to condemn extramarital sex in 1994 than they were in 1974.

People aged 30 to 59 are slightly less likely to feel adultery is always wrong than are people younger or older. Only 74 to 75 percent of people aged 30 to 59 believe it is always wrong, compared with 81 to 82 percent of those younger or older. Opinions by age have shifted since 1974. In that year, the older the person, the more likely he or she was to say adultery was always wrong. Today, baby boomers are the most ambivalent age group, while the youngest adults are just as likely as the oldest to condemn extramarital sex.

With the exception of people with graduate degrees, people of different educational backgrounds are equally likely to say extramarital sex is always wrong (75 to 79 percent of people with a bachelor's degree or less compared with 66 percent of those with graduate degrees).

Extramarital Sex, 1994

"What is your opinion about a married person having sexual relations with someone other than the marriage partner—is it always wrong, almost always wrong, wrong only sometimes, or not wrong at all?"

(percent responding by sex, race, age, and education, 1994)

	always wrong	almost always wrong	wrong only sometimes	not wrong at all
Total	78%	12%	7%	2%
Women	80	11	6	2
Men	74	14	7	3
Black	68	15	9	5
White	79	12	6	2
Aged 18 to 29	82	10	5	3
Aged 30 to 39	75	13	8	2
Aged 40 to 49	74	14	8	2
Aged 50 to 59	75	15	6	3
Aged 60 to 69	82	11	3	2
Aged 70 or older	81	9	6	2
Not a high school graduate	79	9	7	4
High school graduate	79	12	5	2
Bachelor's degree	75	16	7	1
Graduate degree	66	17	15	2

Note: Percents may not add to 100 because "don't know" and no answer are not included.
Source: General Social Survey, National Opinion Research Center, University of Chicago

Extramarital Sex, 1974 to 1994

"What is your opinion about a married person having
sexual relations with someone other than the marriage
partner — is it always wrong, almost always wrong,
wrong only sometimes, or not wrong at all?"

(percent saying it is always wrong or not wrong at all, by sex, race, age, and education, 1974-94)

	always wrong			not wrong at all		
	1994	*1985*	*1974*	*1994*	*1985*	*1974*
Total	78%	74%	73%	2%	3%	2%
Women	80	76	77	2	2	2
Men	74	71	68	3	4	3
Black	68	69	61	5	5	6
White	79	75	74	2	3	2
Aged 18 to 29	82	69	59	3	2	5
Aged 30 to 39	75	67	69	2	4	3
Aged 40 to 49	74	67	74	2	5	2
Aged 50 to 59	75	82	81	3	3	0
Aged 60 to 69	82	81	81	2	2	1
Aged 70 or older	81	87	91	2	2	1
Not a high school graduate	79	84	82	4	3	2
High school graduate	79	75	71	2	3	3
Bachelor's degree	75	62	56	1	2	4
Graduate degree	66	48	56	2	1	1

Source: General Social Survey, National Opinion Research Center, University of Chicago

Homosexual Sex

A majority (63 percent) of Americans say that sex between two adults of the same sex is always wrong. But a growing minority say it is not wrong. In 1974 only 12 percent of adults said homosexual sex was not wrong at all, a share that rose to 22 percent by 1994.

Similar percentages of men and women say homosexual sex is always wrong (61 percent of women and 65 percent of men). But both men and women were considerably more likely in 1994 than in 1974 to say it is not wrong (rising from just 12 and 13 percent of men and women, respectively, to over 20 percent).

Blacks are slightly more likely than whites to say homosexual sex is always wrong (70 percent of blacks compared with 62 percent of whites). Although black opinions have not changed much since 1974, whites are far more likely to say it is not wrong (rising from 12 to 23 percent).

Strong differences of opinion exist between people of different ages. Among people under age 30, a small majority (54 percent) say homosexual sex is always wrong. The proportion who believe it is always wrong rises sharply with age. Among people aged 30 to 49, 60 to 61 percent believe homosexual sex is always wrong, as do 66 percent of people in their 50s. Among people in their 60s, 71 percent believe it is always wrong, as do fully 76 percent of those aged 70 or older. A similar pattern was evident in 1974 as well.

The percentage who believe homosexual sex is always wrong declines with education. A large majority (77 percent) of people without a college degree feel it is always wrong, but the share drops to only 39 percent among people with graduate degrees. Likewise, the percentage of people who say it is not wrong at all rises with education, from just 12 percent of those without a high school diploma to 34 percent of those with graduate degrees.

Homosexual Sex, 1994

"What about sexual relations between two adults of the same sex—do you think it is always wrong, almost always wrong, wrong only sometimes, or not wrong at all?"

(percent responding by sex, race, age, and education, 1994)

	always wrong	almost always wrong	wrong only sometimes	not wrong at all
Total	63%	4%	6%	22%
Women	61	3	6	24
Men	65	4	6	20
Black	70	4	2	17
White	62	4	6	23
Aged 18 to 29	54	4	6	32
Aged 30 to 39	60	4	5	26
Aged 40 to 49	61	4	8	22
Aged 50 to 59	66	5	6	18
Aged 60 to 69	71	2	4	17
Aged 70 or older	76	3	4	8
Not a high school graduate	77	3	3	12
High school graduate	66	4	5	20
Bachelor's degree	49	4	8	33
Graduate degree	39	6	14	34

Note: Percents may not add to 100 because "don't know" and no answer are not included.
Source: General Social Survey, National Opinion Research Center, University of Chicago,

Homosexual Sex, 1974 to 1994

"What about sexual relations between two adults of the same sex—do you think it is always wrong, almost always wrong, wrong only sometimes, or not wrong at all?"

(percent saying it is always wrong or not wrong at all, by sex, race, age, and education, 1974-94)

	always wrong			not wrong at all		
	1994	*1985*	*1974*	*1994*	*1985*	*1974*
Total	63%	73%	67%	22%	13%	12%
Women	61	73	66	24	13	13
Men	65	73	69	20	13	12
Black	70	81	70	17	9	15
White	62	72	67	23	14	12
Aged 18 to 29	54	67	51	32	17	22
Aged 30 to 39	60	64	66	26	21	12
Aged 40 to 49	61	66	66	22	16	15
Aged 50 to 59	66	82	79	18	7	7
Aged 60 to 69	71	83	76	17	9	6
Aged 70 or older	76	87	84	8	3	3
Not a high school graduate	77	86	79	12	7	8
High school graduate	66	75	65	20	13	12
Bachelor's degree	49	53	45	33	22	25
Graduate degree	39	40	44	34	27	19

Source: General Social Survey, National Opinion Research Center, University of Chicago

Do People Choose to Be Gay?

It's a question science hasn't yet answered, so perhaps it is not surprising that Americans are divided in their opinions about whether homosexuality is a choice. Forty-one percent of adults believe it is a choice people make, while 44 percent think it is something people cannot change. Fourteen percent say they just don't know.

Women are more likely than men to say homosexuality is something people cannot change (48 percent of women compared with 39 percent of men). Blacks are far more likely than whites to say people choose to be gay (54 percent of blacks compared with 40 percent of whites).

People under age 40 are considerably more likely than their elders to say being gay is a choice. People in their 40s are more likely than other age groups to think homosexuality is predetermined, with over half saying it is something people can't change. The oldest Americans are the most undecided, with nearly one-quarter saying they don't know.

People without a college degree are more likely than those with more education to view being gay as a lifestyle choice (46 percent). In contrast, fully 66 percent of people with graduate degrees say it is something people can't change.

Do People Choose to Be Gay? 1994

"Do you think being homosexual is something people choose to be, or do you think it is something they cannot change?"

(percent responding by sex, race, age, and education, 1994)

	something people choose to be	something they can't change	don't know
Total	41%	44%	14%
Women	38	48	14
Men	46	39	13
Black	54	36	10
White	40	45	14
Aged 18 to 29	49	36	14
Aged 30 to 39	45	43	11
Aged 40 to 49	34	54	10
Aged 50 to 59	41	48	11
Aged 60 to 69	38	46	16
Aged 70 or older	35	38	23
Not a high school graduate	46	40	14
High school graduate	44	43	12
Bachelor's degree	37	47	14
Graduate degree	16	66	16

Note: Percents may not add to 100 because no answer is not included.
Source: General Social Survey, National Opinion Research Center, University of Chicago

Living Together

Since the 1960s, the number of couples living together without being married has increased sharply. But Americans are not yet ready to fully embrace this custom. Equal percentages agree or disagree on the morality of couples living together without intending to get married (41 percent).

Women and men are somewhat divided on this issue. Forty-six percent of men, but only 38 percent of women, think there's nothing wrong with cohabitation. Women are more likely than men to say it is wrong.

Whites are more likely than blacks to agree that there is nothing wrong with cohabitation (42 percent of whites compared with 36 percent of blacks). But the races are equally likely to disagree.

Those who were young adults during the 1970s or later are more accepting of cohabitation than older people. A majority of people under age 40 agree that cohabitation is OK. Among people in their 40s, 43 percent think it's OK. But only one-third of people in their 50s, 18 percent of those in their 60s, and just 9 percent of those aged 70 or older agree.

People with more education are more likely to agree that cohabitation is acceptable. Only 34 percent of people without a high school degree approve of cohabitation, a share that rises to 49 percent among those with graduate degrees.

Living Together, 1994

"It is all right for a couple to live together without intending to get married—do you agree or disagree?"

(percent responding by sex, race, age, and education, 1994)

	strongly agree	agree	neither	disagree	strongly disagree	agree, total	disagree, total
Total	10%	31%	16%	25%	16%	41%	41%
Women	10	28	16	26	18	38	44
Men	10	36	17	22	13	46	35
Black	10	26	18	27	13	36	40
White	10	32	16	24	16	42	40
Aged 18 to 29	16	40	14	16	11	56	27
Aged 30 to 39	15	43	15	15	10	58	25
Aged 40 to 49	7	36	19	23	14	43	37
Aged 50 to 59	7	25	16	32	18	32	50
Aged 60 to 69	6	12	21	37	21	18	58
Aged 70 or older	1	8	13	42	31	9	73
Not a high school graduate	7	27	13	29	19	34	48
High school graduate	10	31	16	26	14	41	40
Bachelor's degree	8	30	17	21	21	38	42
Graduate degree	12	37	17	19	14	49	33

Note: Percents may not add to 100 because "can't choose" and no answer are not included.
Source: General Social Survey, National Opinion Research Center, University of Chicago

"Trial" Marriage Is a Good Idea

With divorce rates at an all-time high, you might think Americans would support cohabitation as a sort of "trial" marriage before tying the knot. But Americans are far from convinced that this is a good idea. A plurality of 42 percent say they don't think cohabitation before marriage is a good idea, while only 33 percent say it is. A quarter neither agree nor disagree that couples should live together before marriage.

Men and women are in opposite camps on this issue. Only 26 percent of women think living together before marriage is a good idea. But 41 percent of men think it is a good idea.

Blacks and whites are in rough agreement on this issue, as are people of different educational backgrounds. The real differences show up among different age groups. While 46 to 48 percent of people under age 40 support the idea of a "trial marriage," the percentage who agree falls with age. Fully 71 percent of people aged 70 or older disapprove of this practice.

"Trial" Marriage Is a Good Idea, 1994

"It is a good idea for a couple who intend to get married to live together first—do you agree or disagree?"

(percent responding by sex, race, age, and education, 1994)

	strongly agree	agree	neither	disagree	strongly disagree	agree, total	disagree, total
Total	10%	23%	23%	27%	15%	33%	42%
Women	8	18	24	30	17	26	47
Men	12	29	22	22	12	41	34
Black	10	21	19	29	13	31	42
White	10	23	24	26	15	33	41
Aged 18 to 29	18	30	26	14	10	48	24
Aged 30 to 39	15	31	23	19	8	46	27
Aged 40 to 49	8	24	26	22	17	32	39
Aged 50 to 59	4	21	22	36	16	25	52
Aged 60 to 69	4	12	22	39	19	16	58
Aged 70 or older	2	6	15	45	26	8	71
Not a high school graduate	10	25	19	25	15	35	40
High school graduate	9	24	23	27	14	33	41
Bachelor's degree	6	19	27	25	20	25	45
Graduate degree	12	22	26	25	13	34	38

Note: Percents may not add to 100 because "can't choose" and no answer are not included.
Source: General Social Survey, National Opinion Research Center, University of Chicago

Pornography Laws

A small majority of Americans (59 percent) believe the best legal approach to pornography is simply to keep it out of the hands of minors. Another 37 percent would make distribution to people of any age illegal. While the proportion who would make pornography wholly illegal has not changed much over the years, there has been a significant shift away from support for no laws to laws against distribution to minors.

Women are far more likely than men to support making the distribution of pornography completely illegal (45 percent of women compared with 26 percent of men). More than two out of three men think it only should be illegal to distribute pornography to minors, versus 52 percent of women.

There is a big difference in attitudes by age, which may indicate the future trend on this issue. People under age 50 overwhelmingly support laws against the distribution of pornography to people under age 18, while few in this age group support making pornography completely illegal. Among people aged 60 or older, most support making pornography completely illegal. All age groups were less likely in 1994 than in 1975 to favor no legal restrictions on pornography.

By education, those with the least schooling are more supportive of laws making all pornography illegal. Nearly half of people who did not complete high school would make all distribution of pornography illegal, a proportion that drops to only 29 to 30 percent among people with college degrees.

Pornography Laws, 1994

"Which of these statements comes closest to your feelings about pornography laws? 1) There should be laws against the distribution of pornography whatever the age; 2) There should be laws against the distribution of pornography to persons under 18; 3) There should be no laws forbidding the distribution of pornography."

(percent responding by sex, race, age, and education, 1994)

	illegal for all ages	illegal under age 18	not illegal
Total	37%	59%	3%
Women	45	52	2
Men	26	68	5
Black	29	65	4
White	38	58	3
Aged 18 to 29	24	73	2
Aged 30 to 39	23	73	3
Aged 40 to 49	34	62	2
Aged 50 to 59	41	53	4
Aged 60 to 69	57	38	4
Aged 70 or older	64	30	2
Not a high school graduate	48	45	6
High school graduate	37	60	2
Bachelor's degree	30	67	3
Graduate degree	29	66	2

Note: Percents may not add to 100 because "don't know" and no answer are not included.
Source: General Social Survey, National Opinion Research Center, University of Chicago

Pornography Laws, 1975 to 1994

"Which of these statements comes closest to your feelings about pornography laws? 1) There should be laws against the distribution of pornography whatever the age; 2) There should be laws against the distribution of pornography to persons under 18; 3) There should be no laws forbidding the distribution of pornography."

(percent responding by sex, race, age, and education, 1975-94)

	illegal for all ages			illegal under age 18			not illegal		
	1994	1984	1975	1994	1984	1975	1994	1984	1975
Total	37%	40%	40%	59%	54%	48%	3%	4%	11%
Women	45	48	46	52	47	44	2	3	9
Men	26	30	34	68	63	52	5	7	12
Black	29	37	25	65	52	56	4	5	17
White	38	41	42	58	54	47	3	4	10
Aged 18 to 29	24	22	22	73	72	66	2	5	11
Aged 30 to 39	23	29	32	73	65	56	3	5	10
Aged 40 to 49	34	40	42	62	56	45	2	2	11
Aged 50 to 59	41	57	47	53	35	40	4	6	13
Aged 60 to 69	57	62	60	38	31	29	4	4	10
Aged 70 or older	64	65	66	30	28	24	2	1	8
Not a high school graduate	48	51	48	45	42	40	6	5	11
High school grad.	37	40	39	60	56	51	2	4	9
Bachelor's degree	30	29	29	67	66	56	3	4	15
Graduate degree	29	23	28	66	68	48	2	8	22

Note: Percents may not add to 100 because "don't know" and no answer are not included.
Source: General Social Survey, National Opinion Research Center, University of Chicago

Pornography as Education

Advertisements in the back pages of mainstream magazines offer sexually explicit videos designed to help couples learn new ways to enhance their sex lives. Is this education or thinly disguised pornography? A slim majority (59 percent) of Americans say they believe such sexual materials provide information about sex, a proportion that has not changed much since 1975.

There is no real difference of opinion between men and women on this issue, as was the case in 1975. Blacks and whites differ strongly, however, with 70 percent of blacks compared with 57 percent of whites saying pornography is educational. A similar gap was found in the 1975 survey.

Opinions by age do not show much of a generation gap. This is in contrast to 1975, when people under age 40 were considerably more likely than their elders to view sexual materials as a source of information.

By education, people are about equally likely to say pornography is a source of information about sex. In 1975, people with bachelor's degrees were slightly more likely than others to believe this.

Pornography as Education, 1994

"Do you think sexual materials* provide information about sex?"

(percent responding by sex, race, age, and education, 1994)

	yes	no	don't know
Total	59%	36%	5%
Women	57	36	7
Men	61	35	3
Black	70	23	6
White	57	38	5
Aged 18 to 29	59	39	3
Aged 30 to 39	62	35	3
Aged 40 to 49	58	39	2
Aged 50 to 59	62	33	5
Aged 60 to 69	53	38	9
Aged 70 or older	56	30	14
Not a high school graduate	60	29	10
High school graduate	58	37	4
Bachelor's degree	58	38	3
Graduate degree	56	41	2

* *Defined for respondents as pornography—books, movies, magazines, and photographs that show or describe sexual activities.*
Note: Percents may not add to 100 because no answer is not included.
Source: General Social Survey, National Opinion Research Center, University of Chicago

Pornography as Education, 1975 to 1994

"Do you think sexual materials* provide information about sex?"

(percent responding by sex, race, age, and education, 1975-94)

	yes			no		
	1994	1984	1975	1994	1984	1975
Total	59%	57%	62%	36%	37%	29%
Women	57	55	61	36	37	29
Men	61	60	64	35	37	30
Black	70	63	72	23	28	17
White	57	57	61	38	38	31
Aged 18 to 29	59	64	71	39	32	25
Aged 30 to 39	62	58	67	35	39	28
Aged 40 to 49	58	52	59	39	43	32
Aged 50 to 59	62	61	57	33	36	34
Aged 60 to 69	53	51	54	38	42	31
Aged 70 or older	56	49	54	30	36	26
Not a high school graduate	60	59	61	29	31	27
High school graduate	58	57	61	37	39	30
Bachelor's degree	58	56	69	38	41	29
Graduate degree	56	55	64	41	44	34

* *Defined for respondents as pornography—books, movies, magazines, and photographs that show or describe sexual activities.*
Note: Percents may not add to 100 because "don't know" and no answer are not included.
Source: General Social Survey, National Opinion Research Center, University of Chicago

Pornography and Morals

A small majority of Americans (57 percent) believe that pornography leads to a breakdown of morals. This is slightly higher than the percentage who felt this way in 1975, but among some demographic groups the increase has been much greater.

Women are far more likely than men to believe pornography leads to a breakdown of morals (64 percent of women compared with 49 percent of men). While men and women also differed in their opinions in 1975, the difference was far larger in 1994.

Both blacks and whites were slightly more likely to believe pornography leads to a breakdown in morals in 1994 than in 1974, but there is still a gap in opinions. While 58 percent of whites believe pornography leads to moral decay, only 48 percent of blacks agree.

In 1974, there were large differences of opinion on this issue by age. The generation gap was smaller in 1994. About half of people under age 40 feel pornography leads to a breakdown of morals, with the percentage rising in each successive age group and peaking at 74 percent among people aged 60 or older. In 1975, only 32 percent of people under age 30 believed pornography led to a breakdown in morals. But among 40-to-49-year-olds in 1994 (who were under age 30 in 1975), a 53 percent majority held that opinion.

People without high school diplomas are most likely to say pornography leads to moral decay (63 percent). The proportion falls to only 49 percent among people with graduate degrees. But opinions in the most-educated segment are far different than they were in 1975, when only 24 percent believed pornography led to a breakdown of morals.

Pornography and Morals, 1994

"Do you think sexual materials* lead to a breakdown of morals?"

(percent responding by sex, race, age, and education, 1994)

	yes	no	don't know
Total	57%	36%	7%
Women	64	28	8
Men	49	45	5
Black	48	40	10
White	58	36	6
Aged 18 to 29	48	44	8
Aged 30 to 39	49	45	6
Aged 40 to 49	53	42	5
Aged 50 to 59	62	28	10
Aged 60 to 69	74	22	4
Aged 70 or older	74	17	10
Not a high school graduate	63	27	9
High school graduate	58	35	6
Bachelor's degree	54	40	6
Graduate degree	49	44	6

* Defined for respondents as pornography—books, movies, magazines, and photographs that show or describe sexual activities.
Note: Percents may not add to 100 because no answer is not included.
Source: General Social Survey, National Opinion Research Center, University of Chicago

Pornography and Morals, 1975 to 1994

"Do you think sexual materials* lead to a breakdown of morals?"

(percent responding by sex, race, age, and education, 1975-94)

	yes			no		
	1994	1984	1975	1994	1984	1975
Total	57%	61%	51%	36%	33%	40%
Women	64	67	54	28	25	36
Men	49	52	49	45	45	44
Black	48	56	42	40	33	49
White	58	62	53	36	33	38
Aged 18 to 29	48	52	32	44	43	62
Aged 30 to 39	49	54	50	45	42	43
Aged 40 to 49	53	60	51	42	35	39
Aged 50 to 59	62	70	59	28	24	32
Aged 60 to 69	74	74	68	22	19	19
Aged 70 or older	74	77	72	17	12	11
Not a high school graduate	63	66	59	27	25	29
High school graduate	58	63	52	35	32	40
Bachelor's degree	54	53	37	40	43	57
Graduate degree	49	46	24	44	52	68

* Defined for respondents as pornography—books, movies, magazines, and photographs that show or describe sexual activities.
Note: Percents may not add to 100 because "don't know" and no answer are not included.
Source: General Social Survey, National Opinion Research Center, University of Chicago

Pornography Leads to Rape

Americans are divided on whether or not there is a connection between pornography and rape. While 48 percent believe there is, 42 percent do not think so. Ten percent say they don't know. These opinions are not much different from what they were in 1975.

Women and men disagree on this issue, with fully 55 percent of women compared with only 40 of men saying that pornography leads to rape. While women's opinions have not changed much since 1975, men in 1994 were less likely to think pornography leads to rape than they were in 1975.

Blacks and whites are about equally likely to think pornography leads to rape, with both races about evenly divided on the issue. This was also the case in 1975.

Younger people are less likely than their elders to link pornography with rape. Only 40 percent of people under age 40 say pornography leads to rape. But among those aged 60 or older, two out of three believe pornography leads to rape. Opinions by age have not changed much in the past two decades.

By education, there are large differences in opinion on this issue. Those with the least education are most likely to think pornography leads to rape (58 percent). Only 35 percent of people with graduate degrees think this is true. The pattern was similar in 1975, but in that year the gap was much larger.

Pornography Leads to Rape, 1994

"Do you think sexual materials* lead people to commit rape?"

(percent responding by sex, race, age, and education, 1994)

	yes	no	don't know
Total	48%	42%	10%
Women	55	33	11
Men	40	51	9
Black	45	41	12
White	48	42	10
Aged 18 to 29	40	51	9
Aged 30 to 39	40	50	9
Aged 40 to 49	44	46	9
Aged 50 to 59	50	35	13
Aged 60 to 69	66	24	10
Aged 70 or older	65	22	13
Not a high school graduate	58	30	11
High school graduate	49	41	9
Bachelor's degree	40	49	11
Graduate degree	35	52	12

* Defined for respondents as pornography—books, movies, magazines, and photographs that show or describe sexual activities.
Note: Percents may not add to 100 because no answer is not included.
Source: General Social Survey, National Opinion Research Center, University of Chicago

Pornography Leads to Rape, 1975 to 1994

"Do you think sexual materials* lead people to commit rape?"

(percent responding by sex, race, age, and education, 1975-94)

	yes			no		
	1994	1984	1975	1994	1984	1975
Total	48%	55%	52%	42%	37%	38%
Women	55	61	57	33	30	31
Men	40	46	46	51	48	46
Black	45	55	47	41	34	41
White	48	55	52	42	37	37
Aged 18 to 29	40	45	38	51	47	54
Aged 30 to 39	40	46	48	50	47	43
Aged 40 to 49	44	55	46	46	37	41
Aged 50 to 59	50	65	59	35	26	31
Aged 60 to 69	66	65	70	24	26	18
Aged 70 or older	65	74	69	22	15	16
Not a high school graduate	58	68	64	30	24	26
High school graduate	49	54	50	41	38	39
Bachelor's degree	40	40	34	49	51	54
Graduate degree	35	38	30	52	51	68

* Defined for respondents as pornography—books, movies, magazines, and photographs that show or describe sexual activities.
Note: Percents may not add to 100 because "don't know" and no answer are not included.
Source: General Social Survey, National Opinion Research Center, University of Chicago

Pornography as an Outlet for Impulses

It has been suggested that pornography provides an outlet for pent-up impulses that might otherwise be expressed in a less acceptable manner. Only a slim majority of Americans buy the idea (57 percent), an opinion that is essentially unchanged from 1975.

The opinions of women and men on this issue have not changed much since 1975, with 56 percent of women and 58 percent of men saying it provides an outlet. Blacks and whites are also in agreement, with 57 percent of both races saying it is an outlet.

This issue sparks only small disagreements by age. From 60 to 62 percent of people in their 30s and 40s say pornography is an outlet for impulses, versus 53 to 56 percent of people of other ages.

The proportion who agree that pornography is an outlet rises from 55 percent of people without high school diplomas to 62 percent of those with graduate degrees. The differences were bigger by education in 1975, when the percentages saying pornography provides an outlet ranged from 54 to 55 percent among people with a high school diploma or less to 70 percent among those with advanced degrees.

Pornography as an Outlet for Impulses, 1994

"Do you think sexual materials* provide an outlet for bottled-up impulses?"

(percent responding by sex, race, age, and education, 1994)

	yes	no	don't know
Total	57%	30%	13%
Women	56	27	16
Men	58	32	9
Black	57	30	12
White	57	30	13
Aged 18 to 29	53	32	16
Aged 30 to 39	60	30	10
Aged 40 to 49	62	30	8
Aged 50 to 59	55	27	17
Aged 60 to 69	53	32	15
Aged 70 or older	56	25	19
Not a high school graduate	55	26	19
High school graduate	56	30	14
Bachelor's degree	59	34	7
Graduate degree	62	27	10

* Defined for respondents as pornography—books, movies, magazines, and photographs that show or describe sexual activities.
Note: Percents may not add to 100 because no answer is not included.
Source: General Social Survey, National Opinion Research Center, University of Chicago

Pornography as an Outlet for Impulses, 1975 to 1994

"Do you think sexual materials* provide an outlet for bottled-up impulses?"

(percent responding by sex, race, age, and education, 1975-94)

	yes			no		
	1994	1984	1975	1994	1984	1975
Total	57%	60%	56%	30%	27%	28%
Women	56	59	57	27	26	26
Men	58	62	56	32	29	30
Black	57	54	50	30	29	29
White	57	61	57	30	27	28
Aged 18 to 29	53	62	61	32	28	28
Aged 30 to 39	60	61	53	30	28	35
Aged 40 to 49	62	59	57	30	28	27
Aged 50 to 59	55	60	53	27	28	31
Aged 60 to 69	53	54	57	32	30	21
Aged 70 or older	56	62	50	25	18	19
Not a high school graduate	55	60	54	26	23	25
High school graduate	56	59	55	30	30	31
Bachelor's degree	59	66	66	34	25	26
Graduate degree	62	66	70	27	26	16

* Defined for respondents as pornography—books, movies, magazines, and photographs that show or describe sexual activities.
Note: Percents may not add to 100 because "don't know" and no answer are not included.
Source: General Social Survey, National Opinion Research Center, University of Chicago

Index

Make your demographic research more efficient with the

AMERICAN CONSUMER SERIES

The Official Guide to
American Attitudes

Find out who thinks what about the issues that shape our lives—marriage and family, sex, work and money, religion, the environment, race and immigration, personal outlook, and the public arena. The nationally representative data are broken out by the variables that are most important to you—age, sex, race (black and white), and education. It's a must-have book that gives you a complete picture of what your customers want out of life. (ISBN 1-885070-02-0; April 1996) **$89.95**

The Official Guide to
Racial & Ethnic Diversity

An in-depth guide to the most important trend in the U.S.—the growing diversity of our population. You get the latest data on Asians, blacks, Hispanics, Native Americans, and whites—their education, health, households and living arrangements, housing, income and poverty, labor force participation, population, spending and wealth. You also get demographics on the largest ethnic groups among Asians and Hispanics, such as Chinese Americans and Mexican Americans. (ISBN 1-885070-03-9; April 1996)   **$89.95**

The Official Guide to
the Generations

Here is *the* sourcebook for researchers who want to improve their accuracy in targeting adult consumers— Generation X, born 1965-76; the Baby Boom, born 1946-64; the Swing Generation, born 1933-45; and the World War II Generation, born before 1933. You get detailed numbers on the current and projected size of each generation, plus complete information on their demographics and spending patterns.
(ISBN 0-9628092-8-4; May 1995)   **$69.95**

The Official Guide to
the American Marketplace, 2nd ed.

The consumer researcher's bible, written by Cheryl Russell, a nationally recognized trend spotter. You get an in-depth look at the trends that define who we are as consumers—our education, health, incomes, occupations, living arrangements, racial and ethnic makeup, spending patterns, and wealth, all accompanied by the author's insightful analysis. *The Wall Street Journal* said this book "should be on your bookshelf."
(ISBN 0-9628092-4-1; Jan. 1995)   **$79.95**

The Official Guide to
Household Spending, 3rd ed.

(formerly Consumer Power: How Americans Spend Their Money)

This classic guide has helped thousands of businesses find out what consumers do with their money. Widely praised when the first edition appeared in 1991, it gives you specific answers to the most important questions you can ask about consumers...who buys? what do they buy? how much do they spend? You get spending data on almost 1,000 products, broken out by scores of demographic variables. (ISBN 1-885070-01-2; Oct. 1995)
$89.95

The Official Guide to
American Incomes

This remarkable guide, which was selected as a Best Reference Source by *Library Journal*, is a must for anyone seriously interested in the ultimate key to what consumers buy—their incomes. A storehouse of information, it gives you income trends, household and personal income, discretionary income, household income projections, spending and wealth data, and poverty trends. (ISBN 0-9628092-2-5; July 1993)   **$69.95**